ROUTLEDGE LIBRARY EDITIONS:
THE MEDIEVAL WORLD

Volume 32

MEDIEVAL TEXTS AND IMAGES

MEDIEVAL TEXTS AND IMAGES
Studies of Manuscripts from the Middle Ages

Edited by
MARGARET M. MANION AND BERNARD J. MUIR

First published in 1991 by Harwood Academic Publishers GmbH

This edition first published in 2020
by Routledge
2 Park Square, Milton Park, Abingdon, Oxon OX14 4RN

and by Routledge
52 Vanderbilt Avenue, New York, NY 10017

Routledge is an imprint of the Taylor & Francis Group, an informa business

© 1991 Harwood Academic Publishers GmbH

All rights reserved. No part of this book may be reprinted or reproduced or utilised in any form or by any electronic, mechanical, or other means, now known or hereafter invented, including photocopying and recording, or in any information storage or retrieval system, without permission in writing from the publishers.

Trademark notice: Product or corporate names may be trademarks or registered trademarks, and are used only for identification and explanation without intent to infringe.

British Library Cataloguing in Publication Data
A catalogue record for this book is available from the British Library

ISBN: 978-0-367-22090-7 (Set)
ISBN: 978-0-429-27322-3 (Set) (ebk)
ISBN: 978-0-367-18741-5 (Volume 32) (hbk)
ISBN: 978-0-429-19797-0 (Volume 32) (ebk)

Publisher's Note
The publisher has gone to great lengths to ensure the quality of this reprint but points out that some imperfections in the original copies may be apparent.

Disclaimer
The publisher has made every effort to trace copyright holders and would welcome correspondence from those they have been unable to trace.

Medieval Texts and Images
Studies of Manuscripts from the Middle Ages

Edited by

Margaret M. Manion
Department of Fine Arts, The University of Melbourne

and

Bernard J. Muir
Department of English, The University of Melbourne

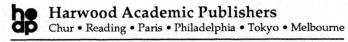

Copyright © 1991 by Harwood Academic Publishers GmbH, Poststrasse 22, 7000 Chur, Switzerland. All rights reserved.

Published in conjunction with Craftsman House BVI Ltd, Tortola, BVI, c/o Craftsman House, P.O. Box 480, Roseville, New South Wales 2069, Australia.

First Published 1991
Second Printing 1992
Third Printing 1993

Harwood Academic Publishers

Private Bag 8
Camberwell, Victoria 3124
Australia

3-14-9, Okubo
Shinjuku-ku, Tokyo 169
Japan

58, rue Lhomond
75005 Paris
France

Emmaplein 5
1075 AW Amsterdam
Netherlands

Glinkastrasse 13–15
O-1086 Berlin
Germany

820 Town Center Drive
Langhorne, Pennsylvania 19047
United States of America

Post Office Box 90
Reading, Berkshire RG1 8JL
Great Britain

Library of Congress Cataloging-in-Publication Data

Medieval texts and images: studies of manuscripts from the Middle Ages/edited by Margaret M. Manion and Bernard J. Muir.
    p. cm.
    Includes bibliographical references and indexes.
    ISBN 3-7186-5133-5. —ISBN 9768097175 (Craftsman House)
    1. Manuscripts, Medieval. 2. Illumination of books and manuscripts, Medieval. 3. Literature, Medieval—Criticism, Textual. 4. Literature, Medieval—Illustrations. 5. Art and literature.
I. Manion, Margaret M. II. Muir, Bernard James.
Z6.M43 1991
002—dc20

          91-8868
          CIP

ISBN (Harwood Academic Publishers): 3-7186-5133-5
ISBN (Craftsman House): 976-8097-17-5

No part of this book may be reproduced or utilized in any form or by any means, electronic or mechanical, including photocopying and recording, or by any information storage or retrieval system, without permission in writing from the publishers. Printed in Singapore by Kyodo Printing Co (S'pore) Pte Ltd.

Contents

Introduction	vii
Acknowledgements	xiii
Abbreviations	xiv
List of Plates	xv
List of Figures	xvii

I   Pictures for Aristocrats: the Manuscripts of the *Légende dorée*
Hilary Maddocks   1

II   Liturgy and Image: the Advent Miniature in the *Salisbury Breviary*
Judith Pearce   25

III   The Significance of Text Scrolls : Towards a Descriptive Terminology
Alison R. Flett   43

IV   The Rolin Master's Hand in London BL MS Additional 25695
Peter Rolfe Monks   57

V   Renaissance Books and Raphael's *Disputa:* Contextualizing the Image
Cecilia O'Brien   71

VI   An Unusual Pentecost Cycle in a Fourteenth Century Missal
Veronica Condon   91

VII   A Minimally-intrusive Presence : Portraits in Illustrations for Prayers to the Virgin
Joan Naughton   111

VIII	Reading Medieval Images : Two Miniatures in a Fifteenth Century Missal *Vera F. Vines*	127
IX	Editing the *Exeter Book:* A Progress Report *Bernard J. Muir*	149
X	Art and Devotion: The Prayer-books of Jean de Berry *Margaret M. Manion*	177
XI	Et Verbum Caro Factum Est: The Prayer-book of Michelino da Besozzo *Katherine McDonald*	201
General Index		211
Index of Manuscripts Cited		221
Index of Biblical References		224

Introduction

This collection of essays has its genesis in the authors' shared interests in manuscripts broadly called Medieval, since they belong to the tradition of book production before the age of printing, although there is some overlap with the Renaissance period.

Hilary Maddocks' examination of some of the characteristics of the illumination of the *Légende dorée* and its relationship to the aristocratic patrons who commissioned these manuscripts stems from her recently completed doctoral dissertation on this topic.[1] Through the generosity of two scholars in medieval English, Vida Russell (formerly of Adelaide University) and Richard Hamer (Oxford), she was able to take as the starting point for her research their identification and categorization of thirty-two extant copies of the *Légende*, all but four of which are illuminated.[2]

Judith Pearce and Peter Rolfe Monks also develop aspects of their doctoral research. They are concerned with the tradition of French illumination as it developed in Paris in the so-called Bedford Master's workshop in the 1420s and was continued by The Master of Jean Rolin II c. 1435–1465. This Master's work is in turn linked with that of Maître François around whose name has been grouped a large number of manuscripts produced in Paris and the Loire Valley c. 1465–1490s. The Maître François "school" has long been of interest to Melbourne-based scholars since the National Gallery of Victoria possesses a fine example of his hand in *The Wharncliffe Hours*.[3] Monks provided in his dissertation an analysis of the Rolin Master's mature style as displayed in the illustration of Jean Gerson's treatise *L'Horloge de Sapience*, Brussels Bibl. Royale ms IV.111.[4] In his present article he concentrates on an earlier phase of the artist's style in the Book of Hours, British Library MS Additional 25695. Pearce's dissertation sets the illustration of the *Salisbury Breviary* within a liturgical and iconographical context of mixed French and English influence.[5] Her study of the Advent Miniature explores the complex visual and textual traditions behind an image which is of considerable importance in the book since it introduces the Liturgical Year.

Veronica Condon and Vera Vines are also concerned with the illustration of liturgical texts. Veronica Condon discusses an apparently unique cycle of

---

[1] "The Illuminated Manuscripts of the *Légende dorée*: Jean de Vignay's translation of Jacobus de Voragine's *Legenda aurea*", diss., Melbourne University, 1989.

[2] Russell and Hamer are preparing an English edition of the *Golden Legend* which is dependent on the French translation.

[3] See M. Manion, *The Wharncliffe Hours* (London: 1981).

[4] "A Study of the Art Work of the Rolin Master in the *Horloge de Sapience*, Brussels, Bibliothèque Royale ms IV.111, and of his other known surviving Works", diss., Melbourne University, 1986.

[5] "Text and Image in the Salisbury Breviary (BN ms lat. 17294): the decorative cycle and its Paris precursors", diss., Australian National University, 1987. This complements the more stylistically oriented study of Catherine Reynolds, "The Salisbury Breviary (BN ms lat. 17294) and some related manuscripts", diss., Courtauld Institute of Art, University of London, 1986.

viii MEDIEVAL TEXTS AND IMAGES

illustrations for the season of Pentecost in a fourteenth century French Missal for Franciscan Use, Oxford, Bodleian MS Douce 313. This is a continuation of a series of studies she has published on this exceptional manuscript.[6] Vera Vines drew attention to the fully illustrated two-volume Missal executed for Charles de Neufchâtel, Archbishop of Besançon c.1464, in the catalogue of *Medieval and Renaissance Manuscripts in New Zealand Collections* (1989). Here she examines two miniatures from the Missal distinguished by their unusual iconography, and demonstrates how the knowledge of iconographic conventions, popular legend and liturgical and ecclesiastical ceremonial, as well as of the specific interests of the patron, can assist the reading of medieval narrative imagery.

Alison Flett also uses medieval material now located in New Zealand as the basis for her theoretical investigation into the role of the written scroll within the painted composition. She compares its various compositional and thematic functions in the depiction of a Crucifixion from a fifteenth century Book of Hours (Dunedin, Public Library, Reed Fragment 45) with examples in two other Crucifixion miniatures from a Flemish Book of Hours (Canberra, National Library of Australia, Clifford Collection MS 1097/9).

Two other contributors focus attention on the role of illumination in a devotional context. Joan Naughton demonstrates how artists manipulated the relationship between text, devotional image and patron portraits in a group of illustrations for prayers to the Virgin so that the user of these fifteenth century Books of Hours might be affectively attuned to the spirit of the Marian devotion. Both miniature and border decoration in the fifteenth century Italian prayer-book of Michelino da Besozzo are studied by Katherine McDonald with special reference to the way in which they reflect and amplify the intensely emotional and personal tone of the prayers—prayers that are based on the *libelli precum* tradition and were composed for meditation.

Cecilia O'Brien indicates the continuing influence of written and liturgical traditions on monumental Renaissance art in her challenging reading of Raphael's *Disputa*. She argues that textual and visual liturgical references, together with *topoi* developed for library decoration, are used in the fresco to allude to the function of the room and to Julius II's own personal ambitions.

The essay by Bernard J. Muir stands out from the others presented here in that it deals with a manuscript from a much earlier period. Commonly known as the *Exeter Book*, this contains the earliest surviving English anthology of Christian vernacular poetry, comprising approximately 130 poems representing a number of genres otherwise unknown from early England. Many of the poetic texts are inspired by the liturgy or can be related to the English "Monastic Revival" of the tenth century. Muir's work on a new edition of this important manuscript is being supported by a substantial grant from the Australian Research Council, and a comprehensive bibliography of the manuscript and its texts is scheduled to be published in 1991. There are a number of drypoint designs and figures in the margins of the manuscript (some of which are reproduced here) that may be of interest to art

---

[6] See V. Condon, "The Mystery of the Provenance of a Fourteenth Century Missal," *Scriptorium* XXXV (1981): 295-303; *MS Douce 313, A Fourteenth Century Missal in the Bodleian Library, Oxford* (Melbourne: 1984); and "The Franciscan Confrères in the Illustration of a Fourteenth Century Missal (MS Douce 313)," *Bodleian Library Record* (1988): 18-29.

INTRODUCTION

historians. Their style and the tradition which inspired them has never been properly studied and there is little with which to compare them; but now that they are being published here, someone with specialist training in the area may be able to throw light upon their ancestry and affiliations.

As part of her research for a joint project with Vera Vines and Cecilia O'Brien, called "Art, Worship and the Book in Medieval Culture", supported by the Australian Research Council, Margaret M. Manion is studying the various Prayer-books—Books of Hours, Psalters etc.—which were commissioned for members of the French royal family in the fourteenth and early fifteenth centuries, with a view to defining the ways in which these often sumptuously illuminated manuscripts enshrine family customs and traditions and reveal the nature of the interaction between patron, clerical adviser and artist-illuminator. In the article published here, she concentrates on certain aspects of the prayer-books of Jean de Berry, especially the illumination of prayers for use at Mass.

Margaret M. Manion and Bernard J. Muir

Acknowledgements

Illustrations are reproduced from the collections of the following institutions with their permission:

Auckland, Public Library; Baltimore, Walters Gallery; Berlin, Dahlem Staatliche Museum; Brussels, Bibliothèque Royale; Cambridge, Fitzwilliam Museum; Canberra, National Library; Chantilly, Musée Condé; Châteauroux, Bibliothèque Municipale; Dunedin, Public Library; Exeter, Cathedral Library; Geneva, Bibliothèque Publique et Universitaire; London, British Library; Lyons, Bibliothèque de la Ville; Manchester, John Rylands University Library; Melbourne, National Gallery of Victoria; New York, The Metropolitan Museum of Art, The Cloisters Collection; New York, Pierpont Morgan Library; Oxford, Bodleian Library; Paris, Bibliothèque de l'Arsenal; Bibliothèque Mazarine; Bibliothèque Nationale; Musée Jacquemart-André; Rome, *Fratelli Alinari*; Turin, Museo Civico; Vatican City, Biblioteca Vaticana; Vienna, Österreichisches Nationalbibliothek.

This volume has been produced with the assistance of grants from:

The Committee of Research and Graduate Studies, The University of Melbourne; The Committee of Research and Graduate Studies, The Faculty of Arts, The University of Melbourne; and The E.B. Myer Charity Fund.

The articles by Manion, Muir, O'Brien and Vines are the result of research supported by the Australian Research Grants Council.

The Helen Schutt Trust has also generously supported this research.

We should like to express our appreciation to Mary Werther of Harwood Academic Publishers and Gordon and Breach Publishers for her care, advice and interest in the production of this book.

Abbreviations

Add.	Additional (BL collection)	mins.	miniatures (in *Tables* only)
Ars.	Bibliothèque de l'Arsenal (Paris)	MS(S) / ms(s)	manuscript(s) / manuscrit(s)
		Mun.	Municipale
Bibl.	Bibliothèque / Bibliothek	Mus.	Museum
BL	British Library (London)	n.	note
		Nouv. Acq.	Nouvelle Acquisition
BN	Bibliothèque Nationale (Paris)	no(s).	number(s)
		Öst.	Österreichisches Nationalbibliothek (Vienna)
c.	circa		
chap(s).	chapter(s)		
cod.	codex	Pl(s).	Plate(s)
CUL	Cambridge, University Library	Plut.	Plutarch (Laurenziana)
		p(p).	page(s)
diss.	dissertation	Pub.	Publique
f. / fols.	folio / folios	r	(superscript) recto
Fitz.	Fitzwilliam (Cambridge)	Roy.	Royale
		sig.	sigla (in *Tables* only)
fr.	français (BN collection)	s.n.	series nova (in MS references)
gr.	grec (BN collection)		
Harl.	Harleian (BL collection)	Staatsbibl.	Bayerische Staatsbibliothek (Munich)
ital.	italien (BN collection)		
lat.	latin (BN collection)	Univ.	University / Universitaire
Laur.	Laurenziana (Florence)	v	(superscript) verso
Maz.	Mazarine (Paris)	Vat.	Vaticana (Biblioteca Apostolica)
med.	medieval (in *Tables* only)		

List of Plates

Plate 1   The Trinity. Breviary, Châteauroux, Bibliothèque Municipale ms 2, f. 106.

Plate 2   The Coronation of the Virgin. *Légende dorée*, Geneva, Universitaire ms fr. 57, f. 1.

Plate 3   St. Catherine presents the patron to the Virgin and Child. *Hours of Isabella Stuart*, Cambridge, Fitzwilliam Museum MS 62, f. 20.

Plate 4   The Purification of the Virgin. Prayer-book, New York, Pierpont Morgan Lib. MS M. 944, f. 8; 170×120 mm.

Plate 5   Meeting of the Magi. Missal, Besançon, Auckland, Public Library MSS G. 138–139, vol. 1, f. 22.

Plate 6   The Crucifixion. Book of Hours, London, British Library MS Additional 25695, f. 121.

Plate 7   Christmas Mass. *Très Riches Heures*, Chantilly, Musée Condé, f. 157ᵛ.

Plate 8   Raphael, *Disputa*, Stanza della Segnatura, Vatican, c. 1508–09.

Plate 1 The Trinity. Châteauroux, Bibliothèque Municipale ms 2, f. 106; 280×195 mm.

Plate 2 The Coronation of the Virgin. *Légende dorée*, Geneva, Universitaire ms fr. 57, f. 1; 365×265 mm.

Plate 3 St. Catherine presents the patron to the Virgin and Child. *Hours of Isabella Stuart.* Cambridge, Fitzwilliam Museum MS 62, f. 20; 248×178 mm.

Plate 4 The Purification of the Virgin. Prayer-book, New York, Pierpont Morgan Library MS M. 944, f. 8; 170×120 mm.

Plate 5 Meeting of the Magi. Missal, Besançon, Auckland, Public Library MSS G. 138-139, vol. 1, f. 22; 305×225 mm.

Plate 6 The Crucifixion. Book of Hours, London, British Library MS Additional 25695, f. 121; 190×135 mm.

Plate 7 Christmas Mass. *Très Riches Heures*, Chantilly, Musée Condé, f. 157ᵛ; 290×210 mm.

Plate 8 Raphael, *Disputa*, Stanza della Segnatura, Vatican, c. 1508-09.

List of Figures

1   The Coronation of the Virgin. *Légende dorée*, Paris, Bibliothèque Mazarine ms 1729, f. 1.

2   The Martyrdom of St. Valentine and St. Juliana with a tethered demon. *Légende dorée*, Paris, BN ms fr. 242, f. 59^v.

3   St. Christopher. *Légende dorée*, Brussels, Bibliothèque Royale ms fr. 9282–5, f. 161.

4   St. Christopher. *Légende dorée*, Paris, Bibliothèque Nationale ms fr. 245, f. 5^v.

5   The Martyrdom of St. Andrew. *Légende dorée*, Paris, Bibliothèque de l'Arsenal ms 3682, f. 8^v.

6   The Martyrdom of St. Andrew. *Fleurs des histoires*, Brussels, Bibliothèque Royale ms 9232, f. 9.

7   The Crucifixion. *Légende dorée*, Brussels, Bibliothèque Royale ms 9282, f. 82.

8   St. Cecilia converts her husband Valerian. *Légende dorée*, Paris, Bibliothèque Nationale ms 245, f. 179^v.

9   The Torture and Martyrdom of St. Euphemia. *Légende dorée*, New York, Pierpont Morgan Library MS M. 675, f. 90.

10 St. Germain of Auxerre is instructed by St. Amator; St. Germain becomes Bishop of Auxerre. *Légende dorée*, New York, Pierpont Morgan Library MS M. 674, f. 357^v.

11 Advent. *Salisbury Breviary*, Paris, Bibliothèque Nationale ms lat. 17294, f. 7.

12 The Annunciation and *Procès du Paradis*. *The Wharncliffe Hours*, Melbourne, National Gallery of Victoria MS Felton 1 (1072–3) 1920, f. 15.

13 The Trinity. Breviary, Paris, Bibliothèque Nationale ms lat. 1052, f. 154.

14 The Trinity. Breviary, Manchester, John Rylands University Library MS 136, f. 90.

15 Advent. Breviary, Paris, Bibliothèque Nationale ms lat. 10483, f. 213.

16 Easter. *Salisbury Breviary*, Paris, Bibliothèque Nationale ms lat. 17294, f. 228^v.

17 Trinity-Baptism of Christ. *Salisbury Breviary*, Paris, Bibliothèque Nationale ms lat. 17294, f. 278^v.

18 The Trinity. *Bedford Hours*, London, British Library MS Add. 18850, f. 113^v.

19 Pentecost. *Salisbury Breviary*, Paris, Bibliothèque Nationale ms lat. 17294, f. 270^v.

20 The Crucifixion. Book of Hours, Dunedin, Public Library, Reed Fragment 45.

21 The Crucifixion. Book of Hours, Canberra, National Library, Clifford Collection MS 1097/9, f. 46.

22 The Crucifixion. Book of Hours, Canberra, National Library, Clifford Collection MS 1097/9, f. 68^v.

xviii MEDIEVAL TEXTS AND IMAGES

23   The Annunciation. Book of Hours, London, British Library MS Additional 25695, f. 29.

24   David and Nathan. Book of Hours, London, British Library MS Additional 25695, f. 153.

25   The Coronation of the Virgin. Book of Hours, London, British Library MS Additional 25695, f. 147.

26   Wrapping a Corpse. Book of Hours, London, British Library MS Additional 25695, f. 165.

27   The Annunciation. Book of Hours, Baltimore, Walters Art Gallery MS Walters 251, f. 26.

28   The Crucifixion. Missal, Lyons, Bibliothèque de la Ville ms 517, f. 183^v.

29   Christ offered the Sop. *Horloge de Sapience*, Brussels, Bibliothèque Royale ms IV. 111, f. 80.

30   Temptations of the Flesh and The Repentant in his Cell. *Horloge de Sapience*, Brussels, Bibliothèque Royale ms IV. 111, f. 18.

31   The Disciple Offering his Heart to Sapientia; Sapientia with Faith, Hope and Charity and The Disciple Shutting out Sapientia. *Horloge de Sapience*, Brussels, Bibliothèque Royale ms IV. 111, f. 49^v.

32   Christ in Judgment. *Missal of Matthias Corvinus*, Brussels, Bibliothèque Royale ms 9008, f. 206.

33   Common of the Saints. *Breviary of Matthias Corvinus*, Vatican Urb. ms lat. 112, f. 555^v.

34   Common of the Saints. *Breviary of Matthias Corvinus*, Vatican Urb. ms lat. 112, f. 556.

35   Collect for the Vigil of Pentecost. Oxford, Bodleian Library MS Douce 313, f. clxxvii^a.

36   Introit for Pentecost Monday. Oxford, Bodleian Library MS Douce 313, f. clxxxi.

37   Introit for Pentecost Tuesday. Oxford, Bodleian Library MS Douce 313, f. clxxxii^{va}.

38   Lesson for the Vigil of Pentecost. Oxford, Bodleian Library MS Douce 313, f. clxxviii^{vb}.

39   Lesson for the Feast of Pentecost. Oxford, Bodleian Library MS Douce 313, f. clxxx^a (bottom).

40   Lesson for Pentecost Saturday. Oxford, Bodleian Library MS Douce 313, f. clxxxvii^{vb}.

41   Epistle for Pentecost Saturday. Oxford, Bodleian Library MS Douce 313, f. cxc^b.

42   Gospel for Pentecost Wednesday. Oxford, Bodleian Library MS Douce 313, f. clxxxiv^{vb}.

43   Gospel for Pentecost Tuesday. Oxford, Bodleian Library MS Douce 313, f. clxxxvi^{vb}.

44   Amadée de Saluces and saints with the Virgin and Child. *Saluces Hours*, London, British Library MS Additional 27697, f. 19.

45   The Boucicaut patrons and vision of the Virgin and Child. *Boucicaut Hours*, Paris, Musée Jacquemart-André ms 2, f. 26^v.

46   The Assumption of the Virgin; and The Faithful at worship. *Belles Heures*, New York, Metropolitan Museum of Art, The Cloisters, f. 88.

FIGURES   xix

47 Jean de Berry at prayer. *Belles Heures*, New York, Metropolitan Museum of Art, The Cloisters, f. 91.

48 Virgo lactans; Joanna of Castile and St. John the Evangelist. *Hours of Joanna of Castile*, London, British Library MS Additional 18852, fols. 287^v–288.

49 The Holy Family and angels with the patron at prayer. Book of Hours, Vienna, Österreichisches Nationalbibliothek, cod. 1954, f. 63.

50 The Virgin and Child with the patron at prayer. Book of Hours, Oxford, Bodleian Library MS Buchanan e3, f. 74.

51 Mary of Burgundy and the Veneration of the Virgin and Child. *Hours of Mary of Burgundy*, Vienna, Österreichisches Nationalbibliothek cod. 1857, f. 14^v.

52 St. Thomas the Apostle. Missal, Auckland, Public Library MSS G. 138–39, vol. 1, f. 174^v.

53 The Stoning of St. Stephen. Missal, Auckland, Public Library MSS G. 138–39, vol. 1, f. 15^v.

54 The Transfiguration. Missal, Auckland, Public Library MSS G. 138–39, vol. 2, f. 197.

55 The Conversion of St. Paul. Missal, Auckland, Public Library MSS G. 138–39, vol. 1, f. 184^v.

56 Saints Ferreolus and Ferrucius. Missal, Auckland, Public Library MSS G. 138–39, vol. 2, f. 155^v.

57 St. Antidius. Missal, Auckland, Public Library MSS G. 138–39, vol. 2, f. 157.

58 The Meeting of the Magi. *Très Riches Heures*, Chantilly, Musée Condé f. 51^v.

59 Jacques Daret, Adoration of the Magi. Berlin, Dahlem Staatliche Museum.

60 Jacques Daret, Adoration of the Magi. Detail. Berlin, Dahlem Staatliche Museum.

61 Foliate and vine and tendril patterning (incised). Exeter, Cathedral Library MS 3501, f. 24 ^{v}.

62 Decorated initials and sleeved hands (incised). Exeter, Cathedral Library MS 3501, f. 95 ^{v}.

63 Standing robed figure (incised). Exeter, Cathedral Library MS 3501, f. 96.

64 Standing robed figure (incised). Exeter, Cathedral Library MS 3501, f. 87 ^{v}.

65 Foliate rosette (incised). Exeter, Cathedral Library MS 3501, f. 64 ^{v}.

66 Head of an angel (incised). Exeter, Cathedral Library MS 3501, f. 78.

67 Scribal corrections. Exeter, Cathedral Library MS 3501, f. 17 ^{v}.

68 Scribal corrections. Exeter, Cathedral Library MS 3501, f. 60 ^{v}.

69 Dominican Friar Instructing Young Prince. *Petites Heures*, Paris, Bibliothèque Nationale ms lat. 18014, f. 8.

70 Dominican Friar contrasting Christ as Bread of Angels with Nebuchadnezzar among the beasts. *Petites Heures*, Paris, Bibliothèque Nationale ms lat. 18014, f. 9^v.

71 Calendar for the month of February. *Petites Heures*, Paris, Bibliothèque Nationale ms lat. 18014, f. 1^v.

72 The Annunciation. *Petites Heures*, Paris, Bibliothèque Nationale ms lat. 18014, f. 22.

73	The Baptism of Christ. *Très Belles Heures*, Paris, Bibliothèque Nationale ms Nouv. Acq. lat. 3093, p. 162.
74	The Elevation of the Host. *Petites Heures*, Paris, Bibliothèque Nationale ms lat. 18014, f. 172.
75	Prince Kissing the Paten. *Petites Heures*. Paris, Bibliothèque Nationale ms lat. 18014, f. 173^v.
76	The Annunciation. *Très Belles Heures* (Milan Hours), Turin, Museo Civico, f. 1^v.
77	The Martyrdom of St. John the Baptist. *Belles Heures*, The Metropolitan Museum of Art, The Cloisters, f. 212.
78	Salome with the Head of St. John the Baptist. *Belles Heures*, The Metropolitan Museum of Art, The Cloisters, f. 212^v.
79	The Feeding of the Five Thousand. *Très Riches Heures*, Chantilly, Musée Condé, f. 168^v.
80	The Ascension. *Très Riches Heures*, Chantilly, Musée Condé ms 65 f. 184.
81	The Washing of the Apostles' Feet. Prayer-book, New York, Pierpont Morgan Library MS M. 944, fols. 19^v–20.
82	The Entombment. Prayer-book, New York, Pierpont Morgan Library MS M. 944, fols. 24^v–25.
83	The Ascension. Prayer-book, New York, Pierpont Morgan Library MS M. 944, fols. 35^v–36.
84	St. Katherine. Prayer-book, New York, Pierpont Morgan Library MS M. 944, fols. 83^v–84.

I

Pictures for Aristocrats: The Manuscripts of the *Légende dorée*

Hilary Maddocks

As far as its translation into the vernacular, one wonders what the translators thought they were doing when they made it possible for relatively unsophisticated readers to peruse this particular book by themselves.
. . . the contents of the (vernacular) Legenda must have exerted a profound influence on the religious outlook of many laymen and women.[1]

In her study of the *Legenda aurea,* Jacobus de Voragine's famous thirteenth century compendium of saints' lives, Sherry Reames broke new ground with her suggestion that the work was not simply a repository of colourful, naïve tales written for an equally naïve lay audience. In the past, influential commentators like Emile Mâle successfully promoted the notion that the uncomplicated narrative structures of the saints' lives struck a chord with the simple man and "offered a model after which to fashion his life".[2] Until Reames, this assumption remained unquestioned, despite

---

[1] Sherry L. Reames, *The Legenda Aurea* (Wisconsin: 1985): 86, 208.
Despite the wide influence of the *Legenda aurea* in the Middle Ages, the work had been the subject of few independent studies. See Ernest Cushing Richardson, *Materials for a Life of Jacopo da Voragine* (New York: 1935) and Pierce Butler, *Legenda Aurea—Légende Dorée—Golden Legend* (Baltimore: 1899). The proceedings of a 1983 symposium on aspects of the *Legenda aurea* have been published as B. Dunn-Lardeau, ed., *Legenda Aurea: Sept Siècles de Diffusion* (Montreal and Paris: 1986). The best modern Latin edition is that of T. Graesse, ed., *Jacobi a Voragine Legenda aurea* (Breslau: 1890, reprinted by Otto Zeller, Osnabrück: 1969). The only modern edition of de Vignay's French translation is by Richard Hamer and Vida Russell, "A Critical Edition of Four Chapters from the *Légende Dorée*," *Mediaeval Studies* 51 (1989): 130–204. Apart from an edition of Caxton's version, there is only one (inadequate) English translation by Granger Ryan and Helmut Ripperger, eds., *The Golden Legend of Jacobus de Voragine* (New York: 1941, reprinted by Arno Press, 1969).
[2] Emile Mâle, *The Gothic Image* (New York: 1972, reprint from 1913 edition): 267ff.
Other writers guilty of similar views include the early 20th century Bollandist Hippolyte Delehaye, particularly in *Les légendes hagiographiques*, published in Brussels in 1905, and more recently, Granger Ryan and Helmut Ripperger in their preface to the 1941 English translation. For a discussion

2   HILARY MADDOCKS

the obvious barrier the Latin language presented to the thirteenth century layperson.[3] She has shown that the *Legenda,* like other thirteenth century collections of abbreviated saints' lives arranged according to the order of the Liturgical Year, was written with a clerical audience in mind, and was used as a source book for sermons and readings on important feast days.[4] However, unlike these other compendia, the *Legenda aurea* was used by educated Dominican churchmen as a weapon against heretical and lay challenges to the authority of the thirteenth century Church.[5] Reames supports this assertion with a close study of the text, which reveals emphases on complex, theologically controversial issues and concise accounts of God's harsh retribution.[6] A great many Latin manuscripts of the *Legenda aurea* are extant today—over 1000 compared to around 20 each of its closest rivals—a discrepancy which Reames attributes to deliberate promotion on the part of the Church in the thirteenth century.[7]

The physical appearance of the manuscripts of the *Legenda aurea* and their patterns of early provenance are consistent with Reames' findings. The great majority were owned by clerics and monastic institutions. As a source book for sermons they were essentially utilitarian, and few contain any decoration or illustration.[8]

---

of modern reception of the *Legenda aurea* see Reames chap. 1.

[3] See James Westfall Thomson, *The Literacy of the Laity in the Middle Ages* (New York: 1960).

[4] Two other thirteenth century collections of abridged saints' lives arranged according to the Liturgical Year are the *Abbreviato in gestis miraculis sanctorum* by Jean de Mailly, and Bartholomew of Trent's *Epilogus in gesta sanctorum.* Unlike the *Legenda aurea,* these works include a prologue indicating the intended audience. Bartholomew of Trent's *Epilogus in gesta sanctorum* is designated as a sourcebook for Dominican and other preachers, while Jean de Mailly intended his collection of saints' lives to be used by parish priests for purposes of instruction.

[5] During the thirteenth century the pre-eminence of the Church of Rome was threatened on two fronts. An ongoing power struggle between the Emperor, Frederick II, and the Papacy centered on the Emperor's attempts to unite the North and South of Italy and so diminish the basis of the Pope's power. The second challenge was posed by the emergence of heretical sects such as the Waldenses and Albigensians in Northern Italy and the Languedoc region. For a discussion of the role the Dominican order played in suppressing heresies see Georges Duby, *The Age of the Cathedrals* (Chicago: 1981) chap. 6.

[6] For example, Voragine devotes much attention to the feast of the Assumption of the Virgin in a lengthy, partly apocryphal narrative which culminates in her Coronation in Heaven by Christ. As Ecclesia, a symbol of the Church, the crowned Virgin affirmed the sovereignity of the Church of Rome. In answer to the Albigensians, whose beliefs involved the rejection of all physical matter as evil, it reinforced the Christian dogma of the Incarnation. Many passages also stress the wrath of a vengeful God against detractors. Sinners are severely punished and demonstrations of mercy are few. These sentiments are contained within mainly short, straightforward narratives designed to make these messages as clear as possible.

According to Reames' thesis, only educated clergymen would have understood the implications of the situation and the subtleties of the theologically complex passages. These sophisticated readers would have selected suitable passages for particular purposes, such as to intimidate potential critics.

[7] For a study of the systemization of the Latin manuscripts of the *Legenda aurea* see B. Fleith, "Le classement des quelque 1000 manuscrits de la *Legenda aurea* latine en vue de l'établissement d'une histoire de la tradition," *Legenda Aurea: Sept Siècles de Diffusion,* ed. B. Dunn-Lardeau (Montreal and Paris: 1986) 19–24. Reames, 3 gives these figures for the compendia by Bartholomew of Trent and Jean de Mailly.

[8] One rare exception is a richly illuminated volume in the Glasgow University Library, MS General 1111. Originally illuminated with 106 miniatures by Flemish artists in the early fifteenth century, it was probably made for the Augustinian canons of S. Antonio in Piacenza; see Nigel Thorp, *The Glory of the Page* Glasgow (1987) 114.

Illuminated *Legenda aurea* manuscripts are rarely as splendid as this one. An example in Vienna, Nationalbibl. ms lat. 326 is illustrated with numerous but very simple, technically unremarkable pictures.

MANUSCRIPTS OF THE *LÉGENDE DORÉE* 3

While Reames' argument for the audience and purpose of the *Legenda aurea* is convincing, she is at a loss to explain the almost equal success of the text in translation. Between the thirteenth and fifteenth centuries Voragine's work was translated into all the major European languages.[9] Why was this text, which was written for a sophisticated audience under certain circumstances, such a runaway success in the vernacular during the following two centuries? It is difficult to see why the long, theologically complicated passages and the concise, often non-discursive narratives of the saints' lives should have attracted a large lay audience, particularly when more suitable compendia were available for translation.[10] This is particularly true of the most popular of seven French translations undertaken during the late Middle Ages.[11] Jean de Vignay's *Légende dorée*, which was translated in 1333, was a very close rendition of Voragine's Latin, preserving all his biases and long winded passages.[12] To clarify the attraction the text held for a fourteenth to fifteenth century French audience we must turn to the 34 extant manuscripts of de Vignay's translation and, more specifically, to their illumination.[13]

In the preface to his translation, de Vignay claims that "cest souverain bien faire entendre aux gens qui ne sont pas lettres". Yet there was nothing democratic about de Vignay's intentions. His translation was not popular at all, in the true sense of the word, but targeted to a specifically royal and aristocratic audience. Jean de Vignay was a clergyman who specialized in performing translations for the royal family. He was a particular favourite of the Queen, Jeanne de Bourgogne, for whom

---

[9] Translations appeared in French, English, Spanish, Italian, Provençal, Bohemian, Dutch, and High and Low German. Many printed editions followed. See Robert F. Seybolt, "Fifteenth-Century editions of the Legenda aurea," *Speculum* 21 (1946): 328–38. and B. Dunn-Lardeau and D. Coq "Fifteenth- and Sixteenth-Century editions of the Légende dorée," *Bibliothèque d'humanisme et Renaissance* XLVII (1985): 87–101.

[10] Jean de Mailly's and Bartholomew of Trent's compilations are pitched more to an unlearned audience. They do not include the long and complicated passages which distinguish the *Legenda aurea*, and the text is presented to meet the specific needs of parish priests and preachers. Reames (164ff.) discusses some differences between Voragine's narratives and those of his fellow hagiographers.

[11] These French translations of the *Legenda aurea* are discussed in Paul Meyer, "Notice du MS. Med.-Pal. 141 de la Laurentienne," *Romania* 33 (1904): 1–7.

[12] The best study of Jean de Vignay and his work is by Christine Knowles, "Jean de Vignay, Un Traducteur du XIVe Siècle," *Romania* 75 (1954): 353–383. See also the now outdated study by Pierce Butler (cited in n. 1 above).

[13] Vida Russell and Richard Hamer have identified 32 manuscripts of de Vignay's *Légende dorée*—Hamer and Russell 131–135; see also Richard Hamer, "Jean Golein's Festes Nouvelles: A Caxton Source", *Medium Ævum* LV (1986): 254–60. In addition to the 32 manuscripts, Russell and Hamer have identified but not located two more. One appears as entry 94 in *A Catalogue of Illuminated and other MSS together with some works on Paleography*, Bernard Quaritch Limited, 1931. The other is listed in a Sotheby's sale catalogue, *Catalogue of the Library of Sir John Arthur Brooke*, 25 May 1921, Lot 1470. A fragment in BN ms n.a. fr. 11198 fols. 29–31 may also be a de Vignay translation. I thank Anne van Buren for drawing this to my attention.
A list of the manuscripts of the *Légende dorée*, with the appropriate sigla assigned by Russell and Hamer, is given in the *Appendix* to this article. The suffix 'b' refers to a second version of the text, completed in c. 1402, when the original text was augmented with some 40 saints; see Hamer 254–60. Most of these additional saints were French, or had special significance for a French audience. The 'c' suffix refers to a third version undertaken in the late fifteenth century, in which the order of the contents were changed and some items inserted. This version is represented by only three manuscripts, which were all produced or illuminated in Flanders. This article focuses on the two earlier versions of the text.

he completed four translations, including the *Légende dorée*. This is clearly stated in the translator's preface, where de Vignay pays homage to his "très haulte noble et puissante dame, ma dame de bourgoigne".

It is fitting that the manuscripts of a text prepared for a queen were owned by aristocrats. A good two-thirds of the 34 extant manuscripts of the *Legende dorée* bear arms or signatures indicating that they were commissioned or subsequently owned by royalty or members of the French and Burgundian aristocracy. Among these elite owners were Louis le Bâtard de Bourbon; Philippe le Bon, Duc de Bourgogne; two of Philippe le Bon's counsellors, Jean d'Auxy and Louis de Bruges; Jean du Mas, Seigneur de l'Isle; and, the bibliophile Charles de Croy. At least two manuscripts are decorated with entwined initials, suggesting that they were presented on the occasion of a marriage.[14] Even those manuscripts which do not bear marks of ownership were almost certainly made for or purchased by wealthy clients, as all but four are embellished with marginal decoration and illumination. Of the four surviving unillustrated copies, one is incomplete, with spaces left for miniatures that were never painted, and the miniatures have been excised from another.[15]

From an art historical perspective, the illumination in the manuscripts of the *Légende dorée* represents a stylistic summary of the major Parisian, and to a lesser extent the late Flemish, schools of illumination from the mid-fourteenth to the late fifteenth century. Several artists can be identified by name or by their work in other manuscripts. These include the Pseudo-Jacquemart, the Master of the *Coronation of the Virgin*, the Virgil Master, the Master of the Munich 'Golden Legend', Evrard d'Espinques, Maître François, the Chief Associate of Maître François, the Master of the Harley 'Froissart', and the Master of Margaret of York. Others are distinguished by their stylistic allegiances, and can be called 'follower of' or members of the workshops of influential artists such as the Boqueteaux Master, the Boucicaut Master, Jean Pucelle, the Master of the Duke of Bedford, Simon Marmion, Willem Vrelant, the Master of Jean Rolin II and Loyset Liédet.

The careers of these illuminators relied almost exclusively on the patronage of the wealthy, and most artists appear to have worked in highly organized professional workshops dedicated to furnishing the aristocracy with picture books.[16] Several, like

---

[14] These are BN ms fr. 244–5, several borders of which are decorated with the initials and arms of Antoine de Chourses, Royal Chamberlain, and his wife Catherine de Coëtivy, and Brussels, Bibl. Royale ms 9282–5 which carries the initials of Philippe de Clèves and Françoise de Luxembourg, who were married in 1485.

[15] The several miniatures which decorated BN ms fr. 23113 have been excised, and the numerous illustrations intended for BL MS Egerton 645 were not executed. Both manuscripts appear to date from the early fifteenth century.

[16] Evidence suggests that miniaturists often worked together in a workshop under the artistic direction of a shop master. This appears to be the case with manuscripts such as BN ms fr. 244–5, where the more accomplished artists, the Chief Associate of Maître François possibly aided by Maître François himself, was responsible for the full-page illuminations. Sometimes a manuscript is illuminated by artists working in quite different styles, using unrelated iconography. Here it must be assumed that the overseer of production farmed out sections of a manuscript to several workshops. An example is the *Légende dorée* manuscript now divided between the Pierpont Morgan Library and the Bibliothèque Municipale in Mâcon which was illuminated in five unrelated styles. These workshops

MANUSCRIPTS OF THE *LÉGENDE DORÉE*

the Maître du 'Polycratique' who illuminated a *Légende dorée* just after the turn of the fifteenth century (Geneva, Bibl. Pub. et Univ. ms fr. 57; Plate 1), seem to have worked free-lance, in this case for Charles V and his entourage. Others, such as Evrard d'Espinques, were employed on a semi-permanent basis by one person.[17]

The programme of illumination in a *Légende dorée* manuscript generally opens with a full- or half-page frontispiece depicting Christ in Majesty or *The Coronation of the Virgin*. This is followed by a series of small miniatures, one text column in width, placed at the beginning of each text entry. As there are over 180 different saints and important feasts described in the *Légende dorée* these miniatures are sometimes very numerous. The structure of the programme closely follows the tradition established in liturgical books such as the Lectionary and Breviary, which were similarly arranged according to the Church Calendar, and included prayers in honour of the saints in the Sanctoral.

Like manuscripts of the *Legenda aurea*, most Breviaries were not illuminated, but when they were, the saints were usually represented simply—a facing figure holding an attribute, a traditional, fixed scene from a narrative, or a standard beheading scene. For example, two illustrations from an early fifteenth century *Légende dorée* (BN ms fr. 242, f. 59^v) depict the martyrdom of St. Valentine by beheading and St. Juliana with her symbol, the tethered demon (Figure 2).

In a devotional book these forms had certain advantages. The facing saint, identified by the attribute, invited address in a way reminiscent of the holy icon. The traditional scene, such as St. Agatha's torture, where her breasts are torn off, also aided identification in its reference to a particular miracle associated with the saint or to the saint's martyrdom. The third form, the paradigmatic beheading scene, did not aid specific identification, but in an important sense imparted, as an exemplum for the worshipper, the only information necessary about the life of the saint: he or she was a martyr who had died for the faith.[18]

These three types of representation were not always reliant on an accompanying text for their meaning, which was sometimes determined by factors other than textual tradition. For example, the customary attribute of St. Agnes, the lamb, is

---

are discussed by Jean Caswell, "The Morgan-Mâcon "Golden Legend" and Related Manuscripts," diss., U. of Maryland, 1978. Also see Caswell's "The Wildenstein 'Nativity', a Miniature from the Morgan-Mâcon 'Golden Legend'," *Art Bulletin* LXVII.2 (1985): 311–316.

[17] This *Légende dorée* manuscript and the patrons of the Maître du 'Polycratique' are discussed by B. Gagnebin, *L'enlumineur de Charlemagne à François Ier* (Geneva: 1976) 78–79. Evrard d'Espinques, whose workshop painted the miniatures in BN ms fr. 6448, was employed as 'house artist' by Jacques d'Armagnac, Duc de Nemours, and following his death in 1477, probably by Jean du Mas, Seigneur de l'Isle. See Louis Guibert, "Ce qu'on sait de l'enlumineur Evrard d'Espinques," *Mémoires de la Société des sciences naturelles et archéologiques de la Creuse* 8 (1893–94): 447–468 and A. Thomas, "Un enlumineur Allemand," *Annales du Midi* VII (1895): 219–224.

[18] Charles F. Altman, "Two Types of Opposition and the Structure of Latin Saints' Lives," *Medievalia et Humanistica* ns 6 (1975): 1–11, notes that hagiographic accounts can be divided into two main groups: the *passio* and the *vita*. Each narrative consists of several constant characteristics. The *passio* form for instance involves a dialogue in which a government representative attempts to induce the Christian to recant, persecution involving torture, and finally martyrdom. This narrative does not rely on particulars for a worshipper to appreciate the processes of martyrdom, and a depiction of martyrdom by beheading assumes an understanding of this basic pattern on the part of the viewer.

HILARY MADDOCKS

based on a pun on her name and not on the narrative of her life.[19]

While these conventions of hagiographic illustration are maintained in the manuscripts of the *Légende Dorée,* some of the illustrations represent a departure from such traditions. The illuminating shops which decorated these manuscripts maintained a collection of stock compositions used whenever a picture of a saint was required, regardless of the precise text. The standing figure of St. Andrew by the Pseudo-Jacquemart on f. 9^v of a *Légende dorée* in London (BL MS Royal 19.B.xvii), dated 1382, is repeated by the same artist in the saints of the calendar pages of *Les Grandes Heures* of the Duke of Berry (BN ms lat. 919).[20]

These patterns were also employed by the followers of an artist and other practitioners of the style. The image of St. Christopher painted by the Master of Jean Rolin II in a Book of Hours (Vienna, Nat. Bibl. cod. s. n. 13237 f. 262^v) reappears in two *Légende dorée* manuscripts, one by a coarse follower (Figure 3), the other by the inheritor of the atelier, the Chief Associate of Maître François (Figure 4). It is also used by Maître François himself in Books of Hours like the *Wharncliffe Hours* (Melbourne, National Gallery, Felton MS 1, f. 114^v).[21]

In addition to examples such as these, which abound, the major feasts of the Church Year were also usually accompanied by illustrations drawn from the repertoire of the artist's models. The c. 1380 frontispiece of a *Légende dorée* in Paris (Bibl. Maz. ms 1729, f. 1) illustrating the *Coronation of the Virgin* (Figure 1), also introduces the canonical Hours of the Virgin in the contemporary *Grandes Heures de Philippe le Hardi* (Cambridge, Fitz. MS 3–1954, f. 24^v). The two miniatures were painted by artists associated with the 'Boqueteaux' style which dominated Parisian illumination in the late fourteenth century.[22]

These generalized illustrations derived from the stock repertoire of artistic workshops served the artists of the *Légende dorée* only to a point. At least two factors prompted a need for new iconographic material. Firstly, the 180 or more saints described in the text far exceeded the number usually illustrated in Breviaries or Books of Hours. Consequently, for rarely represented saints source material was

---

[19] Other examples of representations of saints based on extra-textual sources are St. Anthony's attributes of flames and a pig, and the scene of St. Nicholas' raising three boys from a brine tub. The symbols accompanying St. Anthony are probably based on associations with the Antonine order, and the scene of St. Nicholas may have evolved through mistaken interpretation of pictorial representations of the textual narrative of his life. A fuller explanation appears in my article, "Illumination in Jean de Vignay's *Légende Dorée*", B. Dunn-Lardeau, *Légenda Aurea*... 155-170.

[20] Reproduced in Marcel Thomas, *The Grandes Heures of Jean, Duke of Berry* (New York: 1971) Plate 4.

[21] The illumination of St. Christopher by Maître François is reproduced in Margaret Manion, *The Wharncliffe Hours* (London: 1981) 30. The development of the Master of Jean Rolin II-Maître François-Chief Associate of Maître François workshop is discussed by Eleanor Spencer, "L'horloge de sapience, Bruxelles, Bibliothèque Royale, ms IV.111," *Scriptorium* XVII (1963): 277–99; and "Dom Louis de Busco's Psalter," *Gatherings in Honour of Dorothy E. Miner* (Baltimore: 1974) 227–40. See also Margaret Manion, *The Wharncliffe Hours*, Australian Academy of the Humanities, Art Monograph 1 (Sydney: 1972) and *Wharncliffe Hours* (London: 1981) and John Plummer, *The Last Flowering—French Painting in Manuscripts 1420–1530* (New York: 1982) entries 82, 83, 86, 89–91.

[22] See Patrick M. de Winter, "The Grandes Heures of Philip the Bold, Duke of Burgundy: The Copyist Jean L'Avenant and His Patrons at the French Court," *Speculum* 57 (1982): 786–842.

MANUSCRIPTS OF THE *LÉGENDE DORÉE* 7

limited. The other impulse for elaborated iconography emanated from the aristocratic owners of the manuscripts. Like many of their contemporaries, several of these owners had a need for self-aggrandisement which is manifested in their highly decorated and personalized manuscripts. One *Légende dorée,* (BN ms fr. 6448) is adorned with no less than 36 coats of arms of the owner, Jean du Mas (see note 17). These appear in borders, initials and the miniatures themselves. The self-glorification on the part of du Mas and other owners had an effect on the illumination. Richness was emphasized by an ostentatious use of gold hatching, and the very simple scenes of beheadings and saints holding attributes were no longer consistent with the grandiose intentions of the owners. The demand for new iconography was met in several ways.

There is some evidence that the artists were influenced by non-devotional texts in French, which on occasion were decorated with larger and more detailed illustrations of the saints.[23] A miniature from a *Légende dorée* in Paris (Bibl. Ars. ms 3682 f. 8^v; Figure 5) which dates from c. 1480 is based on the large illumination of St. Andrew preaching on the cross in a splendidly illuminated copy of Jean Mansel's chronicle, the *Fleurs des histoires* dating from the early 1450's (Brussels, Bibl. Roy. ms 9232, f. 9; Figure 6).[24] The *Légende dorée* version however, is still only one text column in width, for with only one or two exceptions the hagiographic miniatures in these manuscripts did not exceed this small size. Despite the elaboration of narrative the established convention of one miniature for every text entry also remained. In addition to influence from non-devotional manuscripts, on at least one occasion a *Légende dorée* miniature was influenced by a panel painting. The depiction of the Crucifixion in a *Légende dorée* manuscript now in Brussels (Bibl. Roy. ms 9282 f. 82; Figure 7) by a follower of Simon Marmion was in part based on Marmion's Crucifixion panel in the John C. Johnson Collection in Philadelphia.[25]

The absence of suitable models lead to the adoption of secular iconography in a *Légende dorée* in London (BL MS Phillips loan 36 / 199, f. 1). The single frontispiece was painted by a member of the *Cité des Dames* workshop, which specialized in the illumination of secular texts.[26] It represents Jean de Vignay presenting his

---

[23] Elizabeth Salter and Derek Pearsall, "Pictorial Illustration of late medieval Poetic Texts: the role of the Frontispiece or Prefatory Picture", *Medieval Iconography and Narrative —A Symposium*, eds. Andersen et al. (Odense: 1980) 100–123, discuss the ready interchange between secular and religious iconography, in this case the adoption of the frontispiece of the *Pèlerinage de la Vie Humaine* by the artists of a secular text, a *Troilus.*

[24] This illumination is by an artist known as the Mansel Master who was active during the mid-fifteenth century in Valenciennes. See L.M.J. Delaisse, *La Miniature Flamande—Le Mécénat de Philippe le Bon* (Brussels: 1959) 60–61.

[25] This manuscript is discussed by G. Dogaer, "Miniatures Flamandes ajoutées à une Légende dorée enluminée en France," *Revue des Archéologues et Historiens d'Art de Louvain* IV (1971): 155–63. For the work of Simon Marmion as a miniaturist see Edith Warren Hoffman, "Simon Marmion Reconsidered," *Scriptorium* XXIII (1969): 243–271. The Philadelphia panel is reproduced in Edith Warren Hoffman, "Simon Marmion or 'The Master of the Altarpiece of Saint-Bertin': A Problem in Attribution," *Scriptorium* 27 (1973): 263-270, Plate 20.

[26] The *Cité des Dames* Master was active in Paris during the first two decades of the fifteenth century. He was employed by the poet Christine de Pisan to design miniatures for her work on famous women, the *Cité des Dames*, two copies of which he illuminated for the Dukes of Berry and Burgundy. The artist and his workshop are discussed by Millard Meiss, *French Painting in the Time of Jean de*

8   HILARY MADDOCKS

finished translation to the Queen, Jeanne de Bourgogne. This iconography, used frequently in manuscripts illuminated by the *Cité des Dames* shop, flatters the owner with a pointed reference to the royal patron of the original translation.[27]

While new iconography was derived from non-devotional manuscripts, the principal source for additional illustrative material was the text of the *Légende dorée* itself. The tendency to turn to the text is most marked in large, well organized shops responsible for producing luxury manuscripts for demanding patrons. The illustration of Voragine's narrative presented a challenge for these artists because each text entry was accompanied by only one frame. Techniques were devised like the repeating of characters and the circular motion of the narrative used by the Chief Associate of Maître François (BN ms fr. 245 f. 179^v; Figure 8). This miniature illustrates the life of St. Cecilia, and describes the conversion of her spouse, Valerian. In the left foreground Cecilia bids Valerian to seek out the holy man Urban in the tombs of the martyrs. He is pictured departing on his quest. In the background, the scene encountered by Valerian is represented, complete with the water with which he is subsequently baptized. On his return he recounts his experience to Cecilia and an angel appears, crowning the couple with roses and lilies from Paradise. The figures of Cecilia and Valerian in the left foreground are used again for this final episode so completing the narrative circle. To clarify the sequence the artist has identified the figures with labels and included a speech scroll.

Other methods of encompassing the narrative are not so complex, and involve the juxtaposition of two or more different episodes. A miniature depicting St. Euphemia (Pierpont Morgan MS M. 675, f. 90; Figure 9) is divided by a mound and a church building into background and foreground. Behind, Euphemia withstands torture on the wheel, while her attackers fall, overcome by flames. In the foreground she resists the serpents who pull one of her enemies to his death. The final reward for her faith is also represented—martyrdom, on this occasion by the sword.

The events represented in these pictures are based on a close reading of de Vignay's translation of the text. It could be argued that the interest in amplified narrative represented a move towards naturalistic or mimetic interpretation. The first priority of the artists however, is to provide an illustration appropriate to the particular saint's life, and this is often inconsistent with an Albertian notion of naturalistic representation. For instance, a hagiographic narrative is commonly represented by the selective juxtaposition of two related or contrasting scenes which illustrate an important lesson from the life of the saint for the faithful.

The miniature illustrating the narrative of St. Germain of Auxerre in a *Légende dorée* in the Pierpont Morgan Library (MS M. 674, f. 357^v; Figure 10), is not the spatially and logically coherent picture it may seem at first. Within the walled city of Auxerre at left, Germain, then Governor, is chastised by the Bishop, St. Amator, for pride in his hunting and his habit of hanging the heads of slaughtered animals

---

Berry—The Limbourgs and their Contemporaries (New York: 1974) 7–18 and 377–378.

[27] The significance of the author presentation portrait is discussed by Salter and Pearsall "Pictorial Illustration..."

MANUSCRIPTS OF THE *LÉGENDE DORÉE* 9

from a pine tree. In contrast with this former life is Germain's atonement and elevation to the rank of Bishop of Auxerre, shown at right. The two halves of the picture
bear little mimetic relation to each other; the church is placed illogically outside the
city walls. On both sides the figures are disproportionate to the architectural set-
tings. This diagrammatic as opposed to naturalistic quality is quite intentional on
the part of the artist. Similar juxtapositions which establish certain instructive relationships appear in other hagiographic texts, such as in early medieval illustrations
from *libelli*, single narratives associated with the shrine of a saint.[28]

Clearly the aristocratic readers of the *Légende dorée* placed some importance
on illustration in the manuscripts they owned. The *Légende dorée* is not unique in
this respect; apart from the many well-known examples of lavishly illuminated
Books of Hours, luxury illuminated manuscripts of original or recently translated
vernacular texts were the height of fashion among the French aristocracy. These
texts were usually romances, classical histories or chronicles, such as the famous
Roman de la rose, the *Miroir historial* by Vincent de Beauvais, the *Histoire Ancienne jusqu'à César,* the *Fleur des histoires,* the *Grandes Chroniques de France* and
the *Bible historiale.* Like the *Légende dorée,* many of these texts were written or
translated for aristocratic patrons, and the manuscripts were usually illustrated.

Physically, these vernacular romances and histories were very similar to the
manuscripts of the *Légende dorée.* They were all usually very large, copiously illustrated volumes, written in an elegant cursive hand in double columns, and decorated
by the same groups of artists. The illuminations often took the form of square miniatures set into one column of text, except for larger miniatures introducing important
sections of the text.[29] The hagiographic illustrations decorating histories like the
Miroir historial and the *Grandes Chroniques de France* tend to be rather more
detailed than those of the *Légende dorée* because often more than a single picture is
used to illustrate the life of a saint. The reason for this is the greater emphasis given
to the process of story-telling, and the value of the narrative as entertainment. The
folio divided into a series of six miniatures painted in the Boqueteaux style, which
illustrate the life of St. Louis in the *Grandes Chroniques* (BN ms fr. 2813 f. 265),
glorifies good deeds in the life of a great Frenchman. His birth, unremarkable in
itself, is followed by a depiction of his education and charitable works. The instructive juxtapositions in the *Légende dorée,* which contrast states of ignorance and
grace or strength in torture and salvation through martyrdom, are not found in this

---

[28] The small books known as *libelli* were attached to saints' shrines and contained a description of
the life and miracles of the saint. Most date from the 11th and 12th centuries, and are associated with
the growth of the major abbeys. They played a role in promoting pilgrimage to the burial or resting
site in acting as an authentification of the saint. The miracles and martyrdom of the saint were often
demonstrated in juxtaposed pictures which clearly illustrated the transition from one state to another.
Several *libelli* are illustrated in J. Porcher, *Medieval French Miniatures* (New York: 1959) 12ff.

[29] See M. Alison Stones, "Secular Manuscript Illumination in France," *Medieval Manuscripts and
Textual Criticism,* ed C. Kleinhenz (Chapel Hill: 1976) 83–102, and E. Salter and D. Pearsall "Pictorial Illustration . . ." Also relevant is Lesley Lawton, "The Illustration of Late Medieval Secular Texts,
with special reference to Lydgate's Troy Book," in *Manuscripts and Readers in fifteenth Century England,* ed. D. Pearsall (Bury St. Edmunds: 1983) 41–69.

10 HILARY MADDOCKS

more linear pictorial narrative.

The illustration of the manuscripts of the *Légende dorée* suggests that the text was perceived by the late medieval owners as lying somewhere between an aid to pious devotion and a repository of entertaining narratives. There is an interest in the story-telling potential of the text, reflected in sometimes quite complex pictorial narratives of a sort which do not usually appear in traditional devotional books. While the manuscripts most closely resemble the expensive, illuminated, vernacular romances and histories popular with the French aristocracy in the fourteenth and fifteenth centuries, and were often illuminated by the same artists, there is a marked respect for hagiographical pictorial traditions.[30]

In response to Sherry Reames' notion that the *Legenda aurea* was not a very suitable text for translation several comments can now be made about Jean de Vignay's *Légende dorée*. Reames expected that the responses, negative and positive, of the readers of vernacular manuscripts would be expressed in the form of marginal comments and glosses. She also expected that translators would have made significant changes to the text, in an effort to make the work more accessible to 'relatively unsophisticated readers'.[31] In fact, de Vignay's very faithful translation was preferred to freer versions, and judging by the lack of marginal remarks or corrections, the readers were quite accepting of the contents. Most manuscripts are surprisingly clean, which leads one to wonder how frequently and attentively they were read, particularly given the density of parts of the text.

Certainly to some extent these expensive picture books illuminated by fashionable artists were regarded as aristocratic accessories. They were probably referred to on particular feast days, and the pictures admired, but it is unlikely that these manuscripts were critically studied with the same attention devoted to manuscripts of the *Legenda aurea*. The success of the de Vignay translation above others lies in its claim to authenticity. The work had received the approval of a queen and it was, as de Vignay took care to note, taken from the Latin, which gave it the added authority of the language of Scripture. The 'seriousness' of the text is also reflected in the manuscripts, where the artists maintained several forms of traditional hagiographic representation. The authority and importance given to the *Legenda aurea* by the Church in the thirteenth century was inherited by the close de Vignay translation, but the source manuals used by preachers to proclaim the pre-eminence of the Church had, in the form of elegant picture books, successfully evolved into statements of lay power and prestige.[32]

---

[30] Possibly another symptom of this respect is the absence of representations of owners accompanied by their favourite saint and of emphases given to saints with special significance for the owner. Of course, this could also be the result of mass-production of manuscripts; instead of the manuscript being a special commission, the owner may have had his arms and initials inserted after purchasing the completed work.

[31] Reames 208.

[32] This paper is based on research undertaken as part of work towards a Ph.D. from the University of Melbourne, which was supervised by Margaret Manion and Vida Russell. The thesis is a study of illumination in the manuscripts of Jean de Vignay's translation of the *Légende dorée*.

MANUSCRIPTS OF THE *LÉGENDE DORÉE*

Appendix

Manuscripts of Jean de Vignay's Translation of the 'Légende dorée'[33]

Sig.	Location	Date	Mins.	Artists	Med. Owner
TYPE A					
P1	BN ms fr. 241	1348	143	A conservative Parisian artist	----------
P2	BN ms fr. 244–45	c. 1480	90	Maître François, his Chief Associate and workshop	Antoine de Chourses, Seigneur de Maigne and Catherine de Coëtivy
P3	BN ms fr. 414	1404	80	The Virgil Master and the Medallion Master	Louis de Bruges, Seigneur de la Gruthuyse
P4	BN ms fr. 1535	----	---	----------	----------
P5	BN ms fr. 6448	c. 1480	174	The workshop of Evrard d'Espinques	Jean du Mas, Seigneur de l'Isle
P6	BN ms fr. 17232	----	---	----------	----------
P7	BN ms fr. 23113	c. 1400	---	----------	----------
B1	Brussels, Bibl. Royale ms 9226	c. 1405	78	Follower of Lucan Master and Orosius Master	Charles de Croy
B2	Brussels, Bibl. Royale ms 9227	c. 1400	2	Late follower of Boqueteaux School	Possibly Charles V
C	Chantilly, Musée Condé ms 735	c. 1365	88	Important member of Boqueteaux workshop and inferior followers	----------
F	Cambridge, Fitz. MS McLean 124	c. 1360	49	Late follower of Jean Pucelle	----------
M	Bibl. Maz. ms 1729	c. 1370	15	Master of Coronation of Charles VI (Boqueteaux style)	Possibly Charles V
N	Bibl. Ars. ms 3705	c. 1400	4	Follower of Boqueteaux style	----------

---

[33] See note 13 above for a description of the subdivisions in this table. On a few occasions the formatting programme used here has hyphenated words unconventionally.

Sig.	Location	Date	Mins.	Artists	Med. Owner
Q	BL MS Add. 16907	1375	54	Follower of Boqueteaux style	Charles d'Anjou
R	BL MS Roy. 19.B.xvii	1382	80	Pseudo-Jacquemart and Boqueteaux followers	William Fitzalan, Earl of Arundel
S	Rennes Bibl. Mun. ms 266	c. 1400	159	Follower of Maître du 'Polycratique' and artist under Flemish influence	----------
U	Quaritch 1931	c. 1480	219	Jean Colombe?	Louis le Bâtard de Bourbon
W	Arras, Bibl. de la Ville ms 630	c. 1400	102	Late follower of Boqueteaux style	----------
Z	BL MS Egerton 645	c. 1400	---	----------	----------

TYPE B

Sig.	Location	Date	Mins.	Artists	Med. Owner
Ab	Brussels, Bibl. Royale ms 9228	c. 1420	233	Follower of Bedford style	Appears in the inventory of Philippe le Bon in 1467
Bb	Brussels, Bibl. Royale ms 9282–5	c. 1460–85	62	Follower of Master of Jean Rolin II and follower of Simon Marmion	Philippe de Clèves and Françoise de Luxembourg
Cb	BN ms fr. 184	c. 1400	44	Related to Master of Berry's 'Cleres Femmes'	Raoul de Gaucourt, Chamberlain to Charles VII
Db	BN ms fr. 242	c. 1402	219	Master of the *Coronation of the Virgin* and three inferior followers	----------
Eb	BN ms fr. 243	c. 1415	2	Follower of Boucicaut Master	----------
Fb	BN ms fr. 415–6	c. 1415	27	Member of Boucicaut workshop	----------
Gb	Geneva, Bibl. Publique et Universitaire ms fr. 57	c. 1400	94	Maître du 'Polycratique'	Aymar de Poitiers
Hb	Munich, Staatsbib. ms. Gall. 3	c. 1430	227	Master of the Munich 'Golden Legend'	----------

MANUSCRIPTS OF THE *LÉGENDE DORÉE*

Sig.	Location	Date	Mins.	Artists	Med. Owner
Jb	Jena, Universitätbib. ms Gall. 86	c. 1420	64	Late follower of the Boucicaut Master	Belonged to the collection of the Counts of Nassau
Mb	New York, Pierpont Morgan MS M. 672–5, and Mâcon, Bibl. Mun. ms 3	c. 1470	221	Ten artists based in Bruges, incl. the Master of Margaret of York and the Master of the Harley 'Froissart'	Jean d'Auxy, Chamberlain to Philippe le Bon

TYPE C

Sig.	Location	Date	Mins.	Artists	Med. Owner
Fc	Fitz. MS 22	c. 1500	143	North-eastern French?	Carries arms of the princely Bavarian family of Oettingen
Nc	Bibl. Ars. ms 3682–3	c. 1480	52	Follower of Loyset Liédet	----------
Sc	BL MS Stowe 50–1	c. 1475	1	Flemish	Jacques Losien is recorded as the owner

Figure 1 Member of 'Boqueteaux' workshop: *Légende dorée*, "Coronation of the Virgin." Paris, Bibliothèque Mazarine ms 1729, f. 1; 300×215 mm.

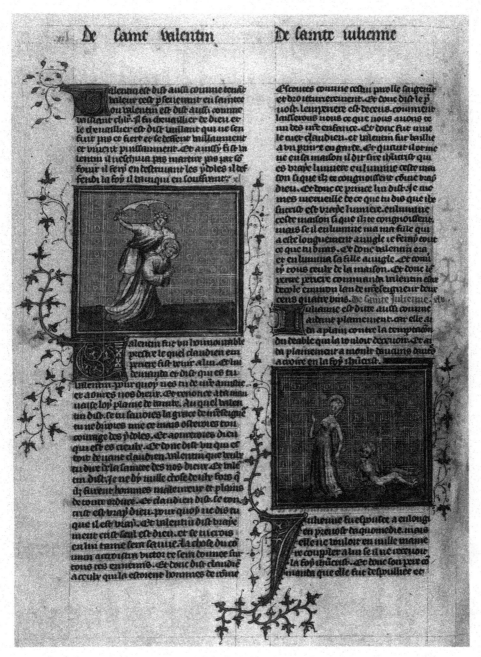

Figure 2 French artist, early fifteenth century: *Légende dorée*, "The Martyrdom of St. Valentine and St. Juliana with a tethered demon." Paris, Bibliothèque Nationale ms fr. 242, f. 59ᵛ; 395×280 mm.

Figure 3 Follower of Master of Jean Rolin II: *Légende dorée*, "St. Christopher." Brussels, Bibliothèque Royale ms fr. 9282–5, f. 161; 372×264 mm.

Figure 4 Chief Associate of Maître François: *Légende dorée*, "St. Christopher." Paris, Bibliothèque Nationale ms fr. 245, f. 5ᵛ; 389×280 mm.

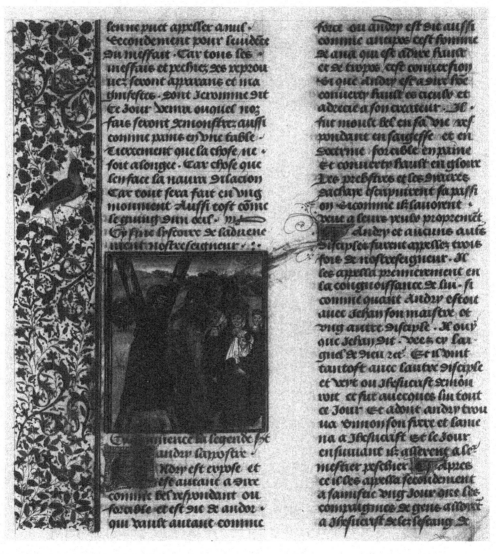

Figure 5 Follower of Loyset Liedet: *Légende dorée*, "The Martyrdom of St. Andrew." Paris, Bibliothèque de L'Arsenal ms 3682, f. 8^v; 431×323 mm.

Figure 6 The Mansel Master: *Fleurs des histoires*, "The Martyrdom of St. Andrew." Brussels, Bibliothèque Royale, ms 9232, f. 9; 430×300 mm.

Figure 7 Follower of Simon Marmion: *Légende dorée*, "The Crucifixion." Brussels, Bibliothèque Royale ms 9282, f. 82; 372×264 mm.

Figure 8 Chief Associate of Maître François: *Légende dorée*,, "St. Cecilia converts her husband Valerian." Paris, Bibliothèque National ms 245, f. 179^v; 389×280 mm.

Figure 9 The Master of Margaret of York: *Légende dorée*, "The Torture and Martyrdom of St. Euphemia." New York, Pierpont Morgan Library MS M. 675, f. 90; 375×270 mm.

Figure 10 Member of workshop of Willem Vrelant: *Légende dorée*, "St. Germain of Auxerre is instructed by St. Amator," "St. Germain becomes Bishop of Auxerre." New York, Pierpont Morgan Library MS M. 674, f. 357^v; 375×270 mm.

II

Liturgy and Image: The Advent Miniature in the Salisbury Breviary

Judith Pearce

In the Salisbury Breviary (BN ms lat. 17294, f. 7; Figure 11), the half-page miniature for Advent was seen by Eleanor Spencer to resemble two late medieval pageants, the *Ordo Prophetarum* and the *Procès du paradis*.[1] The miniature shows Abraham, Isaiah, Jacob, Moses, David and Malachi kneeling or sitting in a landscape, holding scrolls. Above them, encircled by music-making angels, is a version of the *Dixit Dominus* Trinity surrounded by the Heavenly Court. Christ is depicted in his risen form, revealing his wounds and holding the Cross. The third person of the Trinity holds a scroll bearing the words "Ecce venio" (Ps. 39: 8, Ezech. 21: 7). At the bottom of the miniature, Gabriel, with a scroll reading "Spiritus sanctus superveniet in te" (Luke 1: 35), leans down towards the Virgin reading in the initial below.

The main difficulty with the miniature is that it has no standard historical or votive theme. Nor is it related specifically to themes from the prophets like the Tree of Jesse or the Calendar cycle in the *Belleville Breviary* (BN mss lat. 10483–84). Although the Advent miniature also works to demonstrate the concordance between the Old and New Testaments, all the figures except Malachi, who is depicted in the typical pose of a prophet, are kneeling in prayer. In addition, only Malachi's scroll bears a prophetic text, taken from Malachi 3: 1 and reading *Statim veniet dominator* ("Suddenly the Lord will come"). The first scroll, *Domine prestolamur adventum tuum* (cf. Is. 8: 17 "Lord we are awaiting your coming"), held by Jacob, reminds the Lord that his chosen people are ready and waiting for his coming. Moses' scroll, *Obsecro domine mitte quem missurus es* (Exod. 4: 13 "I beseech you Lord, send him who you are about to send"), expresses the urgency with which Christ's Advent

---

[1] "The Master of the Duke of Bedford: The Salisbury Breviary," *Burlington Magazine* 108 (1966): 608.

26   JUDITH PEARCE

is anticipated. The need for penance in preparation for his coming is conveyed by David, whose scroll reads *Ostende nobis domine misericordiam tuam* (Ps. 84: 8 "Show us your mercy Lord'').

Most dramatised versions of the *Ordo prophetarum* draw upon the same exegetical traditions as the Tree of Jesse and the cycle in the *Belleville Breviary*. Prophets, patriarchs and pagans come forward in turn to bear witness to the coming of Christ.[2] Old Testament characters were used in a supplicatory role, however, to preface the Nativity plays in some late medieval French mystery cycles. The earliest extant example occurs in Arnoul Gréban's *Mystère de la passion*, performed first in Paris in 1452.[3] In the play, which is set in Limbo, Adam, Eve, Isaiah, Ezechiel, Jeremiah and David each implore the fulfilment of the prophecies as a preface to the *Procès de paradis*. The *Procès de paradis* was a dramatic dialogue probably first used in the French theatre to frame the four-day long *Passion d'Arras*.[4] Before the opening scenes, the Trinity in the form of God the Father responds to the arguments and pleas of four of the Virtues by sending Gabriel to announce the Incarnation to the Virgin. At the end of the performance, the Heavenly Host, including the dissenting Virtues, rejoice at the return of Christ and give praise to the Trinity.

Spencer was alerted to a connection between the Advent miniature and these two pageants through her familiarity with illustrations of the *Procès du paradis* in a series of Books of Hours painted by the workshop of Maître François in the third quarter of the fifteenth century. The theme was used with *The Annunciation* for Matins of the Hours of the Virgin. In the example in the *Wharncliffe Hours* (Figure 12), probably executed between 1475 and 1480, the artist unites the opening and closing scenes of the play.[5] Whilst the miniature in the Salisbury Breviary does not illustrate the same theme, it is linked in subject with the supplicatory version of the *Ordo Prophetarum* which precedes the *Procès du paradis* in Gréban's play. The role of Gabriel as agent in the salvation of mankind is also emphasized in both miniatures. In addition, the Advent miniature similarly telescopes the events of Christ's life, by depicting the Trinity in all three of its appropriations.

If the iconographic sources for the Advent miniature or its models derive from a play like Gréban's, then it provides strong evidence that the *Procès du paradis* was performed in association with a supplicatory prophet play at a much earlier date than

---

[2] Grace Frank, *The Medieval French Drama* (Oxford: 1954) 39–42, 67, 136–53. The *Ordo Prophetarum* was used as early as the mid-twelfth century as the third part of the *Mystère d'Adam*: Carl J. Odenkirchen, *The Play of Adam (Ordo Representacionis Ade)* (Brookline, Mass. and Leiden: 1976). It also appears in three of the four surviving English Corpus Christi cycles between the Old Testament pageants and the series of Nativity plays: Peter Happe, ed., *English Mystery Plays: A Selection* (Harmondsworth: 1975) 188–215.

[3] Arnoul Gréban, *Le Mystère de la passion d'Arnould Gréban publié d'après les manuscrits de Paris avec une introduction et un glossaire*, ed. Gaston Paris and Gaston Raynard (Paris: 1878) 25–43, lines 1741–3394.

[4] Frank 176–81; Jules-Marie Richard, *Le Mystère de la passion: texte du manuscrit 697 de la Bibliothèque d'Arras* (Arras: 1891). Richard believes the play may have been performed in Paris by the Confrèrie de la Passion et Resurrection soon after 1402.

[5] Margaret Manion, *The Wharncliffe Hours: A Fifteenth Century Illuminated Prayer-book in the Collection of the National Gallery of Victoria, Australia* (London: 1981) 14–16, 58.

THE SALISBURY BREVIARY

the surviving documents suggest. Much remains to be understood, however, about the degree to which liturgically significant themes explored through various media were part of a shared thought world. The dangers of interpreting similarities between art and theatre as evidence of direct influence are particularly great when looking at images in illuminated manuscripts which form part of a larger cycle. It is not sufficient to define the elements which the Advent miniature has in common with the two pageants; one must also explore how it compares with illustrations for Advent in other liturgical manuscripts produced in the same artistic milieu. The Salisbury Breviary, although made for an alien use and patron, was written in Paris a short time after 1424, and decorated by the Paris-based Bedford workshop.[6]

II

In the Temporal of Breviaries made in Paris in the late medieval period, the Offices most frequently emphasized in the hierarchy of decoration include those for the feasts of the Nativity, Circumcision, Epiphany, Resurrection, Ascension, Pentecost, Trinity and Corpus Christi, together with the Dedication of a Church, the first Sunday in Advent, the ten weeks leading up to Easter, and the Sundays opening the post-Epiphany, post-Easter and summer seasons.[7] The emphasis is usually carried by one or at most two initials or column miniatures within the Office, their size depending on the importance of the text. The texts receiving the decorative emphasis vary from Office to Office and from manuscript to manuscript. The Antiphon and Chapter for first Vespers were strong candidates, in competition with the Invitatory and the first Lesson of Matins or its Responsory. In early fifteenth century Breviaries, attempts at standardization are reflected in a preference for the first Lesson. During the second decade of the fifteenth century, there was also some experiment with half-page miniatures for the most highly ranked Offices.[8]

---

[6] The patron was John of Lancaster, Duke of Bedford and Regent of France from 1422–36. The date of the commission is suggested by a note on f. 2ᵛ, giving the dominical letter for 1424. The manuscript was never finished, and may have remained in the workshop until long after the death of Bedford in 1436: see Catherine Reynolds, "The Salisbury Breviary (BN ms lat. 17294) and some related manuscripts," diss., Courtauld Institute of Art, University of London, 1986. The Advent miniature, however, belongs to the period of Bedford's patronage.

[7] The Temporal is the section of the Breviary containing the Offices commemorating the events of Christ's life. A full discussion of the illustration of the Temporal in Paris Breviaries is given in Chapter 4 of my thesis, "Text and Image in the Salisbury Breviary (Paris, BN ms lat. 17294): the decorative cycle and its Paris precursors," diss., Australian National University, Canberra, 1987.

[8] In the Temporal of the Breviary of Jean sans Peur (BL Add. MS 35311 and Harl. MS 2897), half-page miniatures for Good Friday and Ascension survive and there are lacunae for Advent, Easter Sunday, Pentecost and Trinity Sunday (BL MS Add. 35311: fols. 120–21, 333ᵛ, Harl. 2897: fols. 154–55, 188ᵛ, 198–99, 205–06). The Orgemont Breviary (Bibl. de l'Arsenal, ms 660), which only contains the winter Offices, originally had large miniatures for the Nativity, St John's account of the Passion (inserted after the texts for Good Friday), Easter Sunday, Ascension and Pentecost (fols. 145–46, 284–85, 290–91, 321–22, 329–30). The Châteauroux Breviary (Châteauroux, Bibl. Mun. ms 2), which only contains the summer Offices, has a large miniature for Trinity Sunday (Plate 1).

28   JUDITH PEARCE

The subjects used to illustrate these Offices are drawn directly from the text. For the lesser Sundays and weekdays lacking unique texts for first Vespers, this resulted in a range of somewhat arbitrary themes dependent on the first Nocturn Lessons.[9] The case is different for the nine feasts. There were established traditions for the visual interpretation of their themes, many of which were shared by Books of Hours. The versions used in the Breviary, however, were more prescribed than in a para-liturgical manuscript. After the adoption of the feast of the Trinity in 1334, the Office of Trinity Sunday was routinely illustrated in Paris manuscripts by the Mercy Seat version of the Trinity, because the *Dixit Dominus* Trinity was firmly associated with the illustration of Psalm 109 in the Psalter (Figure 13).

Such traditions could be in conflict with the artist's obligation to relate the image directly to the particular text being emphasized. Designers of Breviary cycles were aware that the doctrine of the Trinity epitomized by the first Vespers Antiphon "Gloria tibi trinitas / equalis una deitas" was better expressed pictorially by the *Dixit Dominus* than the Mercy Seat version of the theme. The Psalter tradition was so fixed, however, that it was transferred to the Temporal through the medium of Books of Hours, where images were less firmly connected to individual texts.[10] Thus the miniature for Trinity Sunday in a late fourteenth century summer Breviary in Manchester (Figure 14) borrows its *Dixit Dominus* format and unusual iconography from a model like the one illustrating the memorial of the Trinity in the *Heures de Jeanne de Navarre* (f. 129). The landscape details within the orb in both examples reinforce the idea of the Trinity as *Creator Mundi*.[11]

The first Sunday in Advent posed additional problems for the illustrator because the Office was not directly associated with a particular feast. The complex function of Advent as the season opening the Liturgical Year is reflected in its texts which, directly or through exegesis, predict or implore Christ's coming, or rehearse the moment of incarnation. The main illustration for Advent carried the triple responsibility of giving pictorial form to such texts, of illustrating the Office as a whole, and of opening the Temporal. The synthesizing function of the image was particularly great when the opening rubric was the text receiving pictorial emphasis.

Solutions to this problem were sought in such themes as the Annunciation, references to which are interwoven throughout the Office in the form of musical commentaries to the Chapters and Lessons.[12] Another synthetic theme owed its

---

[9] For example, the Breviary of Charles V (BN ms lat. 1052), dated soon after 1369, has an Old Testament cycle for eight of the nine Sundays preceding Palm Sunday: listed in Robert Calkins, *Illuminated Books of the Middle Ages* (London: 1983) 303. The Lessons for this period were taken from Genesis, Exodus and Jeremiah.

[10] This has also been observed by Don Denny: "The Trinity in Enguerrand Quarton's *Coronation of the Virgin*," *Art Bulletin* (1963): 48–52.

[11] This is now Paris, BN Nouv. Acq. ms lat. 3145. Folio 129 is illustrated in Millard Meiss, *French Painting in the Time of Jean de Berry: The Late XIV Century and the Patronage of the Duke*, 2nd ed., 2 vols. (New York: 1969) II, Figure 601. For the Trinity as *Creator Mundi*, see Adelhard Heimann, "Trinitas creator mundi," *Journal of the Warburg and Courtauld Institutes* 2 (1938–39): 42–52. A winter Breviary produced by the same workshop as the Breviary in Manchester survives as BN ms lat. 1024.

[12] The Annunciation illustrates the rubric in an early fifteenth century Breviary in London (BL Harl. MS 2927, f. 132), and the first Vespers Chapter in a Breviary for Roman Use made for Blanche de

THE SALISBURY BREVIARY

popularity to its use in Italian fourteenth century Antiphonals or Graduals to illustrate the opening Antiphon "Aspiciens a longe" or the Introit "Ad te levavi" (Ps. 24: 1). Old Testament figures occupy the lower half of the opening initial in each case, praying earnestly to the figure of Christ in Majesty or the enthroned Virgin and Child in the upper level.[13] A simple version of this theme may be found opening the rubric for Advent in a late fourteenth century Paris Breviary in Amiens (Bibl. Mun. ms 114, f. 7), where a single figure in biblical robes prays to God the Father before an altar. The exact identification of such figures was less important than the recognition of their role as representative of the whole group of patriarchs and prophets living a life of prayer and penance under God's law before the Incarnation.

The "Aspiciens a longe" tradition also explains the group of men and women in the *bas-de-page* of the folio opening the Chapter from Jeremiah 23: 5 for first Vespers in the *Belleville Breviary* (Figure 15).[14] The reference in the Chapter to David as the ancestor of Christ is directly illustrated in the miniature. The subject is expanded, however, by the depiction, on the bottom right, of the risen Christ in a mandorla, displaying his wounds. The promise of judgment and justice prophesied in the Chapter text and prayed for by the group at the left, is shown to have been fulfilled through the Resurrection of Christ. The designer of the folio thus makes it clear that Advent was seen, not only as a time of preparation before the commemoration and re-enactment of the historical sequence of events initiated by Christ's Birth, but also as a time of anticipation for the second triumphant coming of Christ.

When the first Lesson from Isaiah 1: 1 was illustrated, artists usually depicted Isaiah as prophet of the Incarnation. This is the case in the Breviary of Blanche de France and the *Belleville Breviary*, both of which have two illustrations for Advent. In the former (f. 103^v), Isaiah stands holding an empty scroll looking up at the head of Christ in a blue cloud. In the latter (BN ms lat. 10483, f. 214), he sits at a lectern looking at the head of a dove emerging from a cloud, while in the *bas-de-page*, a crowd of men point upwards. The single miniature in the Breviary of Charles V is slightly more complex.[15] The artist shows Isaiah prophesying to a group of sleeping people, one of whom awakens. The half-length figure of the Virgin, through whom the prophecy is to be fulfilled, appears in her guise as Queen of Heaven in the upper corner of the miniature.

France after 1315 (Bibl. Vat. ms Urb. lat. 603, f. 103).

[13] For examples of both, see Perugia, Bibl. Communale Augusta, ms 2781, f. 1, and ms 2783, f. 3: *Francesco d'Assisi: Documenti e Archivi, Codici e Biblioteche, Miniature* (Electa) 225, 227. I am indebted to Margaret Manion for these examples.

[14] The Chapter reads *Ecce dies veniunt dicit dominus, et suscitabo David germen iustum et regnabit rex et sapiens erit et faciet iudicium in terra* ("Behold, the days come, saith the Lord, that I will raise unto David a righteous Branch, and a King shall reign and prosper, and shall execute judgment and justice in the earth").

[15] Calkins, Plate 125.

30   JUDITH PEARCE

III

The decorative programme of the Salisbury Breviary is exceptional in many regards, not excluding its four border miniatures on each folio and an unprecedented number of half-page miniatures.[16] Bedford's generous patronage had encouraged the workshop to treat the project in the experimental manner of a luxury Book of Hours rather than as a liturgical manuscript. Despite this, the figural cycle of the text relies iconographically on traditional approaches to the illustration of the Breviary. The innovations are those one might expect from the work of the Bedford Master and his assistants: complex exposition of the theme and, particularly in the large miniatures, the inclusion of rich narrative detail.[17]

The Easter Sunday miniature of *The Three Maries at the Tomb* (Figure 16) is a case in point. The standard fourteenth and early fifteenth century theme for Easter Sunday was that of the Resurrection, the feast being celebrated by the Office, but there are a number of precedents for its subordination to the closely related scene of *The Three Maries at the Tomb* under the influence of the first Lesson Gospel extract.[18] In the Salisbury Breviary, the artist used the theme predicated by the emphasized text, but added subsidiary figures in the style of the Master of Flémalle. He also included the risen Christ within the larger pictorial space, thus illustrating in visionary form the words, "Nolite timere...Surrexit...Non est hic" (Matt. 28: 5), spoken by the angel to the Three Maries, and given in contracted form in the scroll.

The use of the half-page format to develop the theme of the feast also informs the miniature for Trinity Sunday (Figure 17), in spite of its surprising subject. The Baptism of Christ rarely appears in Breviary cycles.[19] Its association with the Trinity, however, was firmly fixed by St Augustine, who grouped the voice of God the Father and the descent of the Holy Spirit in the form of a dove with the Incarnation and Pentecost as appropriations of the individual Persons of the Trinity.[20] Although

---

[16] There are forty-six of them, but only ten appear in the Temporal, illustrating Advent, Nativity, Epiphany, Palm Sunday, Easter Sunday, the Monday after the Easter Octave (the following three weeks are devoted to readings from the Apocalypse), Ascension, Pentecost, Trinity Sunday and Corpus Christi (fols. 8, 56^v, 106, 212^v, 228^v, 243, 261^v, 270^v, 278^v and 283^v).

[17] The Bedford Master was responsible for the design of most of the half-page miniatures in the Temporal, although he had a major hand in only four: the Baptism miniature and the Advent, Nativity and Epiphany miniatures. The rest were completed by Spencer's Hand B, "Salisbury Breviary," 611–12.

[18] The latter theme is used in the Paris / Manchester Breviary (BN ms lat. 1024, fol. 248^v). The designer of the Easter Sunday miniature in the *Belleville Breviary* (BN ms lat. 10483, f. 375^v) used the Resurrection in the main miniature above the rubric opening the Lesson, and the Three Maries in the *bas-de-page* space: Victor Leroquais, *Les Bréviaires manuscrits des bibliothèques publiques de France*, 5 vols. and Plates (Paris: 1934) Plate XXXIII.

[19] However, it was used to illustrate the Epiphany Octave in the Breviary of Jean sans Peur (BL Add. MS 35311, f. 216). The first Lesson Gospel extract for the Epiphany Octave was taken from Matthew 3: 13.

[20] St Augustine, *De Trinitate*, I, 4. The nine-miniature pictorial sequence on St Augustine's doctrine of the Trinity illustrating the memorial to the Trinity in the Sobieski Hours (f. 203) includes a much reduced version of the Baptism in the Salisbury Breviary; Eleanor Spencer, *The Sobieski Hours: a Manuscript in the Royal Library at Windsor Castle* (London: 1977).

THE SALISBURY BREVIARY

the use of the theme in the Salisbury Breviary has no direct textual licence from the Antiphon itself, the Baptism is used in the fifth Lesson as the central proof of a scholastic sermon on the doctrine of appropriation, which seeks to reconcile the problem of how the Three Persons of the coequal Trinity may each have individual characteristics:

> quamvis quedam opera dei quibusdam personis specialiter conveniant sicut patri vox illa que de celo sonuit super christum baptizatum: et ad filii personam humanitatis tantummodo pertinet susceptio et spiritus sancti persone proprie congruit illa columba in cuius specie idem spiritus sanctus descendit super eundem filium dei secundum hominem baptizatum: tamen absque omni dubitatione illam vocem et illam columbam et christi humanitatem tota sancta trinitas operata est cuius opera inseparabilia sunt.[21]

The Bedford Master had already experimented with the miniature for Trinity Sunday in the Châteauroux Breviary (Plate 1), a summer Breviary possibly made for the Dauphin, Louis de Guyenne, before his death in December 1415.[22] For the Châteauroux Breviary, he used the *Dixit Dominus* form, but gave the three members of the Trinity the celestial framework of a Christ in Majesty image. This combination had been used by artists to illustrate the memorial of the Trinity in manuscripts like the *Très Belles Heures de Notre Dame*.[23] The Bedford Master modified the model to the demands of the Breviary text, however, by adding a cross to accentuate the physical reunion of the Trinity in Heaven after the Ascension of Christ.

The miniature for the same Office in the Bedford Hours (Figure 18), painted by the Master some four years later, is a confident variant of the theme, in which the *Dixit Dominus* image is used to comment on the transubstantiation issue in the context of an extended version of the *Trinitas creator mundi*.[24] It was a design of this nature which inspired the extraordinary Pentecost miniature in the Salisbury

---

[21] "However, certain operations of God may be particularly suitable to certain Persons, just as the voice which spoke from Heaven over the baptized Christ was to the Father: and only to the person of the Son belongs the taking on of humanity, and to the person particularly of the Holy Spirit corresponds the dove in which form the same Holy Spirit descended upon the same Son of God as he was being baptized in human form: nevertheless, without any doubt, that voice and that dove and the humanity of Christ are the operations of the whole Trinity whose works are inseparable". I have not been able to trace the source of the Lesson, but it echoes thirteenth century conclusions on this issue: see, in particular, Aquinas, *Summa Theologia*, I, QQ xliii, 7; and also Bertrand Margerie, *La Trinité Chrétienne dans l'histoire*, Théologie Historique 31 (Paris: 1975).

[22] The Dauphin's arms appear on f. 430. There were three dauphins during the reign of Charles I: Louis, the eldest; Jean de France, who was Dauphin for only five months; and the future Charles II, who was in exile after 1418. Louis, although not yet nineteen when he died, was a connoisseur of art and spent large sums of money on the furnishings of his private chapel: Léopold Pannier, *Les Joyaux du duc de Guyenne*, Extrait de la Revue Archéologique (Paris: 1873) 8.

[23] Turin, Museo Civico, f. 87 (Memorial of the Trinity): Meiss, II Figure 49.

[24] Janet Backhouse dates the Bedford Hours (BL Add. MS 18850) to 1419, demonstrating with strong supporting evidence that the manuscript was commissioned by Philippe le Bon after the death of his father in that year. Bedford's armorials were added at a later date: "A reappraisal of the Bedford Hours," *British Library Journal* 7 (1981): 47–49.

32   JUDITH PEARCE

Breviary (Figure 19). The miniature, in which the Holy Spirit has left its usual position between Christ and God the Father to hover at the boundary between Heaven and Earth, is a direct illustration of the Invitatory for Pentecost from Wisdom 1: 7, "Spiritus domini replevit orbem terrarum".[25]

Although the Bedford Master may have consulted with theologians concerning the content of such miniatures, it was clearly characteristic of his mature style to explore iconographically rich alternatives to conventional liturgical themes. The by now conventional *Dixit Dominus* Trinity was to be used in another two of the half-page miniatures in the Temporal of the Salisbury Breviary: in the Ascension miniature (f. 261^v), where a small Trinity group watches the full-length figure of the ascending Christ from the arched top of the miniature; and in the Advent miniature. The Baptism, by contrast, was a new and arresting image for the Office of Trinity Sunday. Its use avoided the duplication of themes, and at the same time, encapsulated in pictorial form important twelfth and thirteenth century doctrinal issues preserved in the Lessons for the Office.

IV

Since the large miniatures for Advent have been excised from the Orgemont Breviary and the Breviary of Jean sans Peur, and because no winter equivalent of the Châteauroux Breviary has survived, there are no similarly direct analogues for the pictorial treatment of Advent in the Salisbury Breviary. Nonetheless, it is not necessary to look outside the traditions of Parisian Breviary illumination to find precursors for each of its elements. The designer was clearly aware of the many ways in which the Office could be interpreted in visual terms. The miniature is related to the "Aspiciens a longe" tradition through its hieratic structure and its set of representative Old Testament figures in fervent attitudes of prayer. The Annunciate is incorporated in the initial. David is shown amongst the Old Testament figures as the ancestor of Christ, and Isaiah as the prophet of his Incarnation. The separate figures of Christ in Majesty and the risen Christ illustrating the first Vespers Chapter in the *Belleville Breviary* are combined in an image of the Trinity, which brings together the God of the Old Testament with the risen Christ and the Christ of judgment in a single celestial form.

The artist's authority to use an image of the Trinity to open and close the Liturgical Year also lay in contemporary views of the shape of the liturgy, inherent in the texts for the Office. It was accepted doctrine that the Old Testament revelation was a Trinitarian one. God the Father was usually the agent depicted in such scenes because of the appropriation of this operation by the first Person of the Trinity, but the two images were interchangeable. It was similarly admissable to

---

[25] "For the spirit of the Lord fills the world". The English barge in the seascape is one of the rare topical allusions in the manuscript. A simpler version of a seascape overshadowed by the Holy Spirit may be found in one of the border medallions illustrating the Hours of the Holy Spirit in BL Egerton MS 2019, a mid-fifteenth century manuscript painted by the Bedford workshop, with a conventional Pentecost scene in the main miniature: Janet Backhouse, *Books of Hours* (London: 1985) Plate 43.

THE SALISBURY BREVIARY

exchange the figure of Christ for a Trinity group in the Majesty image used to illustrate Trinity Sunday in the Châteauroux Breviary. The same process occurred in the theatre. In the opening sequence of the *Passion d'Arras* a single actor playing God the Father represents the Trinity according to the doctrinally sound stage direction, *Cy est la Trinité en paradis c'est assavoir Dieu le père.* The English version in the Ludus Coventriae (or N-town) cycle, however, gives speaking roles to all Three Persons of the Trinity.

Such variations on a theme of religious experience in forms approved by the Church all worked from within a shared orthodoxy. The connection between the Advent miniature in the Salisbury Breviary and the two pageants mentioned by Spencer is not coincidental, but neither is it essential to an understanding of the miniature. It is more likely that the Advent miniature indirectly influenced the composition of the miniature in the Wharncliffe Hours, than that they both shared an early fifteenth century model illustrating the *Procès du paradis.* Similarly, both pageants were types for Advent, and borrowed their position in the mystery cycle from the Office.

One important aspect of the Advent miniature still remains unexplained by reference to either pictorial or dramatic precursors. Only two of the scroll texts are taken directly from the Office of Advent. "Obsecro domine" is the pre-Lauds Responsory for the first week in Advent, and "Ostende nobis" is a Versicle, derived from the Penitential Psalm "Miserere mei deus" (Ps. 50: 3) which was used as a Chapter Responsory at Sext during Advent.[26] The meaning of "Statim veniet" (Mal. 3: 1) in the context of the Advent miniature is clear, but the Chapter from Malachi was used only in the Office of the Purification of the Virgin. "Domine prestolamur" is not used in the Breviary at all. Its closest biblical parallel may be found in Isaiah 8: 17, "Et expectabo Dominum...et praestolabor eum," (but see also Judges 6: 18, "Ego prestolabor adventum tuum").

This group of texts, regardless of their exact source, gives to the Advent miniature a fourth, didactic, role. Clerics had an important part to play as intermediaries between the laity and the Divine Office. It can be demonstrated that Bedford's own chaplains worked closely on the decorative programme of the Salisbury Breviary. At least two of his agents prepared lists of subjects for the enormous border cycle. They were not as involved in the main figural cycle, but the use of texts from an external source in the Advent miniature bears witness to the collaboration of a cleric in its design. The main function of the texts is to provide the user of the manuscript with a summary of the spiritual meaning of the Office in words as well as pictures. The overall effect is dramatic to the modern viewer, and the possibility of a theatrical source for the programme cannot be excluded. As late as the 1420s, however, the aim of illustrative art was still to represent the spoken or heard word, of which "both picture and script were the conventional signata".[27]

---

[26] Also as part of the *preces* at Compline, and together with the Psalm during the blessing of the salt and water on Sundays after Prime.

[27] Michael Camille, "Seeing and reading: some visual implications of medieval literacy and illiteracy," *Art History* 8 (1985): 32.

Figure 11 Advent. *Salisbury Breviary*, Paris, Bibliothèque Nationale ms lat. 17294, f. 7; 255×173 mm.

Figure 12 The Annunciation and *Procès du Paradis*. *The Wharncliffe Hours*, Melbourne, National Gallery of Victoria MS Felton 1 (1072–3) 1920, f. 15; 178×125 mm.

Figure 13 The Trinity. Breviary, Paris, Bibliothèque Nationale ms lat. 1052, f. 154; 230×178 mm.

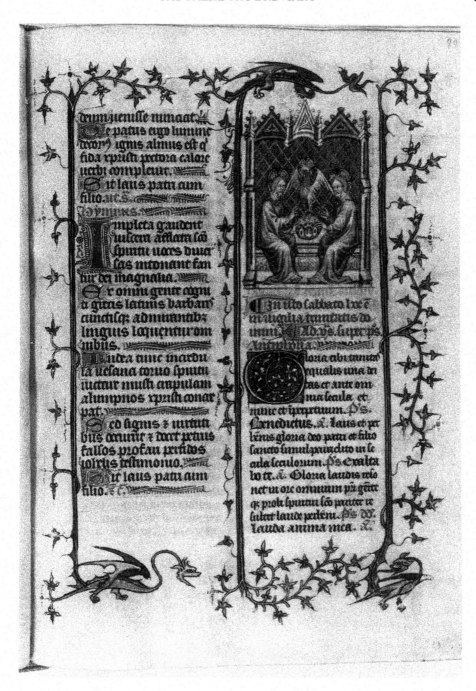

Figure 14 The Trinity. Breviary, Manchester, John Rylands University Library MS 136, f. 90; 182×133 mm.

Figure 15 Advent. Breviary, Paris, Bibliothèque Nationale ms lat. 10483, f. 213; 240×170 mm.

Figure 16 Easter. *Salisbury Breviary*, Paris, Bibliothèque Nationale ms lat. 17294, f. 228ᵛ; 255×173 mm.

Figure 17 Trinity-Baptism of Christ. *Salisbury Breviary*, Paris, Bibliothèque Nationale ms lat. 17294, f. 278^v; 255×173 mm.

THE SALISBURY BREVIARY

Figure 18 The Trinity. *Bedford Hours*, London, British Library MS Add. 18850, f. 113^v; 260×182 mm.

Figure 19 Pentecost. *Salisbury Breviary*, Paris, Bibliothèque Nationale ms lat. 17294, f. 270ᵛ; 255×173 mm.

III

The Significance of Text Scrolls: Towards a Descriptive Terminology

Alison R. Flett

Three small Crucifixion miniatures now held by libraries in Australia and New Zealand have much in common. All are or were found in fifteenth century Books of Hours, those often lavishly illustrated collections of prayers, psalms and devotional texts which constituted "almost a formula for salvation" when recited in private by devout lay men and women.[1] The miniatures therefore share a devotional prayer-book context in which diverse interactions of image and text, of the visual (illustrations of the Gospel story, for example) and the verbal (the accompanying prayers) took place. They also share many compositional features. In Reed Fragment 45,[2] Reed Collection, Dunedin Public Library, Dunedin, New Zealand (Figure 20), a Parisian miniature dated to the third quarter of the fifteenth century,[3] the scene is set in a hilly landscape where figures from the biblical narrative are arranged at each side of the large Cross on which hangs the bleeding figure of Christ. The Cross fills the arched compartment of the miniature, as do the similarly scaled and positioned crosses in the two Crucifixion miniatures of a Southern Netherlandish Book of Hours dated approximately 1450 to 1470,[4] Clifford Collection MS 1097/9, f. 46

---

[1] Christopher de Hamel, *Books of Hours* (Dunedin: 1970) 9.

[2] Although referred to as Reed Fragment 44 in the exhibition catalogue *Medieval Dunedin*, Dunedin Public Art Gallery (1984) 18 and 24, it has been re-catalogued and is now known as Reed Fragment 45.

[3] No precise date has been proposed for this miniature, one of three purchased by the Library in 1983, all from the same Book of Hours. Christopher de Hamel, in unpublished notes made available by the Reed Collection Librarian, merely dates the miniatures to the second half of the fifteenth century, while *Medieval Dunedin* refers to them as being from the late fifteenth century (18). See also M. Manion, V. Vines and C. de Hamel, *Medieval and Renaissance Manuscripts in New Zealand Collections* (London: 1989) 106-107.

[4] M. Manion and V. Vines, *Medieval and Renaissance Illuminated Manuscripts in Australian Collections* (London: 1984) 132.

44 ALISON R. FLETT

(Figure 21) and f. 68^v (Figure 22), National Library of Australia, Canberra. In these compositions biblical figures (albeit reduced in number) again flank the Cross beneath the similarly depicted figure of Christ, set against a landscape background.

While the miniatures are all workshop products of limited aesthetic significance, they share one feature of potential art historical interest. All three include curving white banderoles, those curving scrolls so commonly found in the compositions of Western medieval art, with texts from Gospel accounts of the scenes portrayed. Through these scrolls the verbal penetrates the visual in a process which fuses word and image.[5] Although the miniatures have so much in common their scrolls are markedly different. This is evident in their physical construction, their placement, the positioning of the texts upon their surfaces and the consequent relationship of both scroll and text to the figures in the miniatures and to the reader/viewer.

To describe and categorise these differences and relationships is not easy, for the significance of such composites of word and image has seldom been analysed. Little common ground has existed between the specialist discourses of those interested in the painted texts[6] and art historians concerned with questions of "style" who have studied only scroll forms.[7] Therefore there is no entirely "appropriate interpretive discourse"[8] for evaluating the joint "function, construction and reception"[9] of what are here termed scroll-texts and text-scrolls. There is not even an accepted pictorial vocabulary for describing the forms of the scrolls, let alone an agreed set of terms for distinguishing the often multiple functions of text-scrolls and scroll-texts, their significance in particular compositions, and those internal processes of signification by which their meanings are communicated.

The systems developed by Miecyslaw Wallis and John Sparrow for the classification of inscriptions do however provide sets of descriptive terms which may usefully be applied to scroll-texts.[10] Relevant terms are also found in the

---

[5] Although a detailed study of the specific prayer-book contexts of these miniatures is outside the parameters of this study, they could be examined for possible relationships with the prayers that followed them. S. Hindman in "The Illustrated Book: An Addendum to the State of Research in Northern European Art," *Art Bulletin* 68 (1986): 536–542, summarizes current scholarship on this approach to manuscript studies.

[6] G. Schiller, for example, in her monumental *Iconography of Christian Art,* trans. J. Seligman (London: 1972), provides the complete texts of all inscribed scrolls in the works she discusses but makes no comments about their forms.

[7] B.A. Langer, for example, in "Early Gothic Calvary Scenes of Central Europe," diss., U of Pittsburgh, 1972, 28, examines a scroll in the fourteenth century Klosterneuburg altarpiece as a balancing compositional element, while a second scroll in the same work is seen to integrate a small figure "into the rhythm of the composition".

[8] W.J.T. Mitchell, "The Language of Images," *Critical Inquiry* 6 (1980): 361, discusses the use of language to describe visual images.

[9] M. Camille, "The Book of Signs: Writing and Visual Difference in Gothic Manuscript Illumination," *Word and Image* 1 (1985): 134. Camille argues that such broad theoretical questions are usually ignored in art historical criticism which is largely stylistic. He contends that the value of addressing such questions outweighs the concomitant "danger of de-historicising or denying specific contexts" when applied to individual compositions.

[10] M. Wallis, "Inscriptions in Paintings," *Semiotica* 9 (1973): 1–28. It should however be noted that Wallis in this pioneering article specifically excludes from his analysis those "paintings" found in illuminated codices, claiming that in such contexts "the word is not an adjunct to the image but the im-

THE SIGNIFICANCE OF TEXT SCROLLS   45

language of Peircean semiotics although that system of signs and signifiers has much broader applications than the study of inscriptions.[11]

The scrolls may of course be studied without any reference at all to their texts, using accepted art historical methodology. The curling white configuration of the single text-scroll in the Reed 45 miniature, for example, makes a bold pictorial statement. As this miniature has been described as being "in the style of Maître François", [12] its scroll could, for example, be compared to counterparts in known works by that Master and atelier,[13] an "object" to be used for comparative purposes, just as other "objects" such as trees, faces, hands or items of clothing are routinely compared.

If the text-scroll is however regarded as "subject" rather than "object", that is, as an active agent in those processes of signification by which the total meaning of the Crucifixion miniature is conveyed, its text may not be ignored, but on the contrary, plays a vital role. The scroll-text in the Reed 45 miniature (Figure 20) is still legible though partly worn away. Its words, "Vere filius dei erat iste", are taken from the Gospel of St. Matthew (27: 54) and present the cry of faith made by the Centurion and his men after witnessing the phenomena surrounding the death of Christ. The validity of the visual image of the Crucifixion is here reinforced[14] and extended by the presence of the authoritative "word",[15] in this case the very Word of God, sacred Scripture, here presented in Latin, the language of the Vulgate and of the medieval liturgy.

Word and image combine to convey the totality of Christ's being. That Christ was human is painfully obvious. Rivulets of blood continue to pour down the arms from the wounded hands, blood streams from his side and the skin is stretched taut over muscle and bone. At the same time the brief scroll-text just as clearly asserts Christ's divine nature, his claim to which led to his execution. Its message is

---

age is an adjunct to the word" (2). In contrast, J. Sparrow's broad survey, *Visible Words* (Cambridge: 1969), encompasses not only inscriptions in paintings of all sorts but also those on buildings.

[11] See R. Innis, *Semiotics* (London: 1986), for selections from *The Collected Papers of Charles Sanders Peirce*, ed. C. Hartshorne and P. Weiss (Cambridge, Mass.: 1931).

[12] Sotheby and Co., *Catalogue of Single Leaves and Miniatures from Western Illuminated Manuscripts: 25.4.83*, 218; and Manion, Vines and de Hamel 106-107.

[13] A deeper comparative analysis of its form could also be used in the search for confirming evidence of postulated relationships between the works of Maître François and his atelier and those of other masters such as the Bedford and Horloge de Sapience Masters. For discussion of these relationships see E. Spencer, "L'Horloge de Sapience," *Scriptorium* XVII (1963): 293–296, and "The Master of the Duke of Bedford: The Bedford Hours," *Burlington Magazine* 107 (1965): 498–502, M. Manion, *The Wharncliffe Hours* (Sydney: 1972) 8, and *The Wharncliffe Hours* (London: 1981) 7–12; and Peter R. Monks, "A Study of the Art Work of the Rolin Master in the *Horloge de Sapience*, Brussels, Bibliothèque Royale, ms IV.111 and his other known surviving Works", diss., Melbourne University, 1986. Langer provides a methodological precedent for such a close study of the representations of an individual motif. Asserting that "the appearance of identical or similar patterns in various works of art generally points to a relationship between them" she examines (with the aid of photographic enlargements) the relationships between altarpieces and ateliers as evidenced by their similar treatment of the loincloth of the crucified Christ (5–6).

[14] J. Huizinga, *The Waning of the Middle Ages* (New York: 1954) 165: "The mere presence of a visible image of things holy sufficed to establish their truth."

[15] See M. Camille, "Seeing and Reading: Some Visual Implications of Medieval Literacy and Illiteracy," *Art History* 8 (1985): 33.

46   ALISON R. FLETT

powerfully conveyed in the first instance by the structure of the biblical text itself: the impact of the adverb "Vere" at the beginning of the exclamation is reinforced by the complementary placement of the demonstrative pronoun "iste" at its conclusion. The user of the prayer-book is challenged to make the mental connection between the visible word "iste" and its object, the visible crucified body of the human Christ, whose image is embedded at the heart of the composition just as the words asserting his divinity, "filius dei erat", are embedded at the heart of the scroll-text.[16]

The significance of the text is conveyed not only through the reception of its individual words and phrases and by the recognition of its unique Gospel source, but also by its appearance on the surface of the scroll. The flat shapes of the black Gothic letters are highly visible against the white ground of the three dimensional scroll in a dynamic mix of the second and third dimensions. The impact of this text and scroll combination is intensified by the effort involved in identifying and recognizing the sequence of its Latin words:[17] these cannot be read horizontally from left to right as the scroll, their vehicle, leaps up energetically into the space between the Cross and the standing figure of the Centurion. The eye must travel upwards along the length of the scroll which begins in the Centurion's hand and terminates near the figure of Christ. There must also be a sideways orientation as the letters of the scroll-text are not placed one above the other but retain their conventional side by side, left to right arrangement. In their Gospel context the words of the exclamation seem to be addressed by the members of the group to each other,[18] and in this miniature the figure of the Centurion does turn towards the other figures on the right. The scroll however has its own orientation: it does not turn away from the picture plane but towards it, presenting its exclamatory contents to the user of the prayer-book and, by extension, to all mankind.

Although scroll and text here contribute equally to the impact of the text-scroll, the classificatory system developed by Wallis makes no acknowledgement of such interdependence. Wallis in fact makes no mention of the objects or surfaces on which painted texts appear, defining every such text as a "semantic enclave, which consists of signs of a different kind or from a difference system than the signs in which the main body of that work of art consists".[19] His system for classifying painted inscriptions according to functional type is nevertheless invaluable when attempting to describe and assess the Reed 45 combination of text and scroll.

---

[16] This devotional exercise is entirely consistent with the miniature's position before the text for the hour of None in the Hours of the Cross. The placement of the fragment is given in the sale catalogue of Sotheby and Co., 218 (see note 12 above).

[17] H. Spencer, *The Visible Word* (London: 1969), discusses the receptive processes involved in identifying and reading individual words (18).

[18] "Centurio autem et qui cum eo erant custodientes Iesum, viso terraemotu et his quae fiebant timuerunt valde dicentes: Vere Filius Dei erat iste" (Matthew 27: 54).

[19] Wallis 1. Sparrow distinguishes, however, between what he sees as the potential difficulties of the modern spectator and the response to such composite images of a fifteenth century viewer who "evidently found no difficulty...in looking with one eye while he read with the other" (48).

THE SIGNIFICANCE OF TEXT SCROLLS

Wallis distinguishes between four groups of inscriptions: those which convey information about the figures depicted; texts which present statements made by sacred figures; texts which show invocations to such figures by spectators who are themselves depicted in the compositions; and, finally, inscriptions which record the comments of artists.[20] As the Reed 45 scroll-text presents a "speech-act", it belongs to the second category.[21] Wallis subdivides this group according to temporal context, differentiating between what he terms narrative and representing modes. Specified moments in the lives of the holy figures are depicted in the former, while in the latter the figures are shown statically and outside of the normal time frame "at an unspecified moment of their existence".[22] Sometimes the distinction is unclear as when, for example, a representation of a temporal episode is "petrified" into a fixed figural arrangement, making the image more devotional than narrative.[23]

The Reed 45 scroll-text functions in both modes. The discourse of Gospel-based Christianity is, as Michael Camille points out,[24] essentially narrative in nature, and is based upon such reported statements as this exclamation from St. Matthew's Gospel, here literally presented to the viewer on a scroll.[25]

In supplementary processes of signification involving the Centurion figure and the figure of Christ the scroll-text functions simultaneously in the representing mode as defined by Wallis. The juxtaposition of the hanging static body of the crucified Christ and the insistently upward curling scroll with its declaration of the eternal truth of Christ's divinity distances the iconic figure from its temporal context and enables it to stand alone as a summa of Christian doctrine.

Wallis also claims that in a representing setting a spoken statement acts as the leitmotif of the figure with whom it is associated, and states briefly "that person's role in the history of the world".[26] According to these criteria the Centurion's cry of faith may be regarded as his leitmotif and its utterance as his principal contribution to world history: it actually embodies the most important event in the life of that figure, an unnamed and problematic character not mentioned elsewhere in the canonical books of the Bible.[27]

---

[20] Wallis 6–9.

[21] The term is used by Camille ("The Book of Signs...") to describe "many of the scrolls and inscriptions in medieval pictures" (143).

[22] Wallis 8.

[23] Wallis 8.

[24] Camille, "Seeing and Reading..." 30.

[25] The statement is also represented in the composition by the presence of the figures who participate in that moment of the narrative action in which the statement was made. See S. Alpers, *The Art of Describing* (Chicago: 1983) 236, for this distinction between pictorial presentation and representation.

[26] Wallis 8.

[27] The life of the Centurion after the Crucifixion was however described in some detail in medieval devotional literature and apocryphal texts with wide currency. The Centurion was also often conflated with the figure commonly known as "Longinus" whose lance pierced the side of the dead Christ. See, for example, *The Golden Legend of Jacobus de Voragine* eds. G. Ryan and H. Ripperger (New York: 1941, repr. 1960) 191, and "The Letter of Pilate to Herod", referred to in *The Apocryphal New Testament* ed. M.R. James (Oxford: 1924, repr. 1960) 155. For a discussion of this conflation in Eastern and Western Art see Schiller II.153–155.

The Reed 45 scroll-text may then also be placed in the first of Wallis's categories, that of texts which convey information about the figures with which they are connected, either by identifying them or concentrating on a single feature or life event. It also conveys information about Christ by alluding to his filial relationship to God the Father and, indirectly, to his Death, the circumstances of which prompted the Centurion's cry.

John Sparrow, in an alternative system of classification based on a series of paired oppositions, distinguishes between inscriptions which function as labels and those which act as messages. According to their context he then judges them to have either an internal or imposed relationship to the other elements of the images in which they appear.[28] The Reed 45 scroll-text would be classified by Sparrow as having an internal relationship to its context, for it has not been imposed on its setting but is part of the Gospel Crucifixion narrative. Although the scroll-text presents an emphatic statement it would also be regarded as a label rather than as a message: the similarly emphatic Annunciation text of Gabriel's greeting to the Virgin, is classified as label by Sparrow.[29] That such familiar and routinely expressed texts are designated labels shows that in Sparrow's system they are regarded as having similar characteristics to those physical attributes which often appear in conjunction with certain sacred figures. A statement may therefore be regarded as an attribute, just as a scroll (with or without a scroll-text) may also serve on occasion as an attribute, one which, moreover, often has prophetic overtones.[30]

Sparrow also discusses the processes of connotation and denotation which he connects with such labels and in both of which the Reed 45 scroll-text participates.[31] He does not regard these processes as mutually exclusive but insists, as does the semiotician Roland Barthes,[32] that they occur simultaneously. As Sparrow explains: "Sometimes the label, in the very act of identifying, may intensify for the spectator echoes and associations already evoked by the representation; the label may connote...as well as denote".[33] The process of connotation therefore assumes a degree of prior knowledge and understanding which enables the viewer to grasp the significance of relevant associations and attributes. The Reed 45 scroll-text denotes the spoken statement, made at the site of the narrative Gospel action but at the same time it connotes additional associations and attributes of the figures concerned which are recognised as meaningful by the viewer, namely the dual nature and eternal divinity of Christ and, in the case of the Centurion/scroll combination, the potential role of that figure as witness in the prophetic tradition.[34]

---

[28] Sparrow 48–50.

[29] Sparrow 50.

[30] For the history of the scroll as prophetic attribute in Christian art, see the *New Catholic Encyclopaedia* (New York: 1967–79) XII.966a.

[31] Sparrow 50–51.

[32] R. Barthes, *Image, Music, Text* (Glasgow: 1977) 17.

[33] Sparrow 50–51.

[34] Scroll-bearing prophets in Crucifixion scenes bore witness to the fulfilment of Old Testament prophecies concerning the coming of the Messiah and his subsequent treatment. An example is found in the late thirteenth century *Psalter of Yolande de Soissons*, Pierpont Morgan Library MS M. 729, discussed by E. Panofsky in *Early Netherlandish Painting* (New York: 1971) 1.40. Such scroll-bearing

THE SIGNIFICANCE OF TEXT SCROLLS

The significance of the text-scroll in the Dunedin Crucifixion miniature may also be evaluated according to the specialist terminology of semiotics, that general theory of signs which "deals with meanings and messages in all their forms and in all their contexts"[35] and whose terminology "seeks to describe the underlying systems of conventions that enable objects and activities to have meaning".[36] If the Peircean definition of sign as anything which "stands to somebody for something in some respect or capacity" is adopted,[37] both scroll and text may be seen as meaningful signs and classified as icon, index or symbol according to the nature of their relationship to those things for which they stand.[38] In the Reed 45 miniature the scroll-text combination functions primarily as index. It startles the viewer and focuses the attention of the reader on the scroll as physical object by the contrast it presents between the angular black lettering of the text and the arresting curvilinear scroll form.

Attention is next drawn to the meaning of the text by its use of the demonsrative pronoun "iste" to signify its object, the figure of Christ near which it is placed. This connection is made not by a process of signification based on physical resemblance (as would be the case for an icon) or convention (as for a symbol) but by an existential link "embodied and actuated" in part of the text itself,[39] namely in the demonstrative pronoun, for such pronouns "call upon the hearer to use his powers of observation, and so establish a real connection between his mind and the object".[40] The scroll-text is indexical in a non-reflexive way: it directs attention primarily to its object, the figure of Christ on the Cross, and only secondarily to its source, the figure of the Centurion. The Crucifixion miniatures in Clifford Collection MS 1097/9 also contain text-scrolls and an assessment of their significance is similarly aided by employing the concise descriptive terms of Wallis, Sparrow and Peircean semiotics.

The miniature on f. 46 (Figure 21) prefaces the text for None in the Hours of the Cross and illustrates the same moment from the Gospel narrative as Reed 45.[41] It also includes the same text from St. Matthew's Gospel, here presented on a text-scroll placed over the imposing and richly dressed figure of the Centurion.[42] The

---

prophets also appeared as witnesses to the Christian faith in medieval dramatic presentations such as the *Ordo* or *Processio Prophetarum* (performed in conjunction with the Christmas liturgy) in which they have been described by P. Axton, *European Drama in the Early Middle Ages* (London: 1974) as "icons, pointing to Christ" (72). They also appeared in Easter plays from the late twelfth to early sixteenth centuries, as discussed by O.B. Hardison, *Christian Rite and Christian Drama in the Middle Ages* (Baltimore: 1965) 283, and A.M. Nagler, *The Medieval Religious Stage*, trans. C. Schoolfield (Newhaven and London: 1976) 70.

35 Innis vii.
36 J. Culler, "In Pursuit of Signs," *Daedalus* 106 (1977): 99.
37 Quoted by Innis (1).
38 Innis 2.
39 Innis 2.
40 Innis 2.
41 In this manuscript a short version of the Hours of the Cross is inserted at the end of each of the Hours of the Virgin; see Manion and Vines 132.
42 The Centurion in the Reed 45 fragment is presented as a simply attired layman, not as a Roman military official. Here the figure is more splendidly dressed, again wearing civilian clothing. The lay viewer/reader may, as a result of this portrayal, have identified more closely with the figure, leading in turn to a closer connection with the scroll-text as a personal reaffirmation of faith in the crucified yet

50 ALISON R. FLETT

impact of the profession of faith is nonetheless far less forceful in this miniature. The text-scroll lacks the visual "weight" of many others found in the same manuscript including those in the Crucifixion miniature on f. 68^v (Figure 22). It is merely a slender band of uniform width which extends in a shallow arc above the head of the speaker, passes behind the soldier's upright lance and terminates in a single line which merges confusingly with the line of a path on the hillside. The insignificant form of the scroll, which seems almost to have been added as an afterthought, raises a number of questions. For example, could the scroll have been accidentally or deliberately omitted in the first instance and added later, or could the artist have used as model a Crucifixion scene which lacked a scroll?[43]

The role of the text and scroll combination in the internal structuring processes by which the meaning of this scene is conveyed is however a quite separate issue. Its impact on the reader/viewer is very different from that of the Reed 45 text-scroll. The text here is, firstly, very easy to read, despite the fact that its clear and even letters are proportionately smaller than those in the Dunedin miniature, where the viewer's point of view is controlled by the exigencies of an elaborate upwardly curving vehicle. Here there are no such problems: the text may be assimilated in a single glance as the eye follows the scroll's progress from left to right. Paradoxically the significance of the scroll-text within the composition is diminished precisely because it is so readable. It does not startle or focus the attention on either the Centurion or Christ. Its force as an indexical sign is lost.

Using the descriptive terms of Wallis and Sparrow, this scroll-text, like the Reed 45 scroll-text, appears in a narrative context and is internal to the historical event depicted. It records the Centurion's spoken statement, conveys information about Christ (although the placement of this scroll makes the connection between its content and the actual figure of Christ far less obvious) and so functions simultaneously as label and message.

The less obviously narrative Crucifixion miniature on f. 68^v of the same manuscript (Figure 22) prefaces the text for the devotion of the "Seven Last Words", the seven statements made by Christ from the Cross,[44] in that section of the prayer-book containing "hymns and devotions, including texts in honour of the Virgin and the Passion" and includes two prominent curling text-scrolls on which two of the statements are displayed.[45]

The initial impression (modified when the text-scrolls are examined more closely) is that sacred history is not so much being narrated as celebrated.[46] Although set in a landscape similar to that of f. 46 (Figure 21), the figures of the Virgin and St. John here flank the Cross in those formal standing poses which to Wallis

---

divine Christ.

[43] Conversely, the model could have included a scroll held in the Centurion's right hand which now disappears behind the wood of the Cross, a scroll which would not fit when the figure was transposed from a larger to a smaller compositional format.

[44] The "Seven Last Words" are drawn from all four Gospels: Matthew 27: 46 (or as an alternate reading, Mark 15: 34), Luke 23: 43, 23: 46, John 19: 26, 19: 27, 19: 28 and 19: 30.

[45] Manion and Vines 132.

[46] For this distinction see F.P. Pickering, *Literature and Art in the Middle Ages* (London: 1970) 54.

THE SIGNIFICANCE OF TEXT SCROLLS

signify the removal of such sacred persons and their inscribed statements from their historical narrative setting to an atemporal representing context.[47] The timeless quality of this scene is reinforced by the gesture of the figure of St. John who extends towards the Cross the sacred codex of his own account of the complete Gospel narrative, an account which includes the moment here shown. The dominant impression of a symmetrical pattern is reinforced by the reversed forms of the miniature's text-scrolls. Originating on either side of Christ's upper torso, the scrolls follow the lines of the outstretched arms and billow down into large open curves over the heads of the figures below before curling back towards their source to form reversed and distinctively shaped "key hole" configurations of the type so often found in this manuscript.[48] The curving white scrolls are highlighted against the plain expanse of colour which fills the upper half of the miniature and which is decorated with curvilinear slender golden branches and repeated motifs of tiny golden hooks and curls.[49]

When the figures and text-scroll are considered together, however, the presence of a historical narrative is revealed, for the texts are taken from the Gospel of St. John and record the statements by which the crucified Christ commended his mother and his disciple to each other's care: "Mulier ecce filius tuus...Ecce mater tua" (John 19: 26). These words could be said to produce an active response on the part of the figures. The Virgin crosses her arms on her breast in that gesture of acceptance—so often found in scenes of the Annunciation and in f. 46—while St. John, offering his codex with outstretched arms, appears to dedicate to Christ not only his account of Gospel events but his entire being and future.

At the same time the scroll-texts reinforce what Wallis would term the prevalent representing mode of the scene. Just as the shapes of the scrolls balance each other, so the structure of their textual content and the disposition of that content along the lengths of the scrolls add to the dominant patterning effect. Two of the four words of each scroll-text are, from the reader's point of view, upside down, and the process of perceiving the construction and meaning of the two short statements is not simple. This contrasts strikingly with the easily readable scroll-text of f. 46. Balance and repetition are here actually imposed on the grammatical construction of the scroll-texts, for the name *Johannes* has been inserted before the scriptural words of Christ to St. John. The construction of the second statement is in this way made identical to that of the first which begins with the naming word "Mater".[50] The repetition of the emphatic "Ecce", present in both statements, confirms the role of the texts as indexical signs. It commends and draws attention to the words which

---

[47] Wallis 8.

[48] For example, in the next large miniature, the *Last Judgment,* on f. 73.

[49] Such patterned "skies" are however also routinely found in obviously narrative miniatures such as that of the nailing of Christ to the Cross on f. 65 ᵛ, Figure 115, Manion and Vines 125. The manuscript also includes many examples of what have been termed by Manion and Vines "outmoded diapered grounds" (133), as in the miniature depicting the martyrdom of St. Thomas A'Becket on f. 6, Figure 113, (p. 125).

[50] It is not known whose decision is was to add the word to the biblical text, for the roles and responsibilities of text artists in relation to those of miniaturists and others responsible for the production of such prayer-books are not yet fully understood.

52 ALISON R. FLETT

follow and on the figures to whom the words are addressed in much the same way as did the demonstrative "iste" in the narrative Crucifixion scene of Reed 45.

That scrolls and their texts may function in more than one way is clear when the terms of Wallis and Sparrow are applied to the balancing scroll-texts. In the system developed by Wallis both scroll-texts clearly record spoken statements. At the same time they convey information by stressing the new relationship between the Virgin and St. John. When the composition is viewed as a depiction of a specific moment from the Gospel narrative, and examined according to Sparrow's classification system, the scroll-texts obviously function as messages which vitally affect the immediate futures of both biblical figures. The words "filius tuus" are those placed closest to the Virgin while those nearest to St. John are "mater tua", a visual denotation of that cross-referral of relationships which forms the subject of the messages. The statements could in Sparrow's terms be classified as labels, for, when the scene is regarded as a timeless representation of those figures and relationships identified in the scroll-texts, Mary may be viewed not only as the mother of Christ and, by Christ's express wish, of St. John, but of all mankind including the user of the Book of Hours.[51] That Mary is the eternal mother and St. John the eternal son as well as Evangelist, is connoted by the miniature's combination of figural images and texts. The prominent text-scrolls fix the figures in their new roles, roles signified solely by the scroll-texts, for the figures themselves stand well apart from each other on opposite sides of the Cross, in contrast to more strictly narrative scenes such as that on f. 46 and Reed 45 in which St. John's physical support of the grief-stricken mother attests to some connection between them.

In Sparrow's terms the scroll-texts in f. 68[v] are internal to the depicted moment. They could also be regarded as having been imposed on a "fixed grouping" of sacred figures in a setting which Wallis would describe as representing rather than narrative,[52] a setting in which the miniature could function as a devotional image independently of the text-scrolls. The scene's narrative aspect would, however, be altogether lost without the presence of the scrolls, for no other elements in the composition indicate its narrative content. The two text-scrolls, by their physical and verbal construction, jointly communicate the "chains of significance"[53] present in this miniature which is simultaneously narrative and, as befits its prayer-book context, devotional.

Roland Barthes contends that all images are polysemous unless tied to specific meanings by the presence of accompanying texts which serve "to focus not simply my gaze but also my understanding".[54] However, it could be argued that images such as the three fifteenth century Crucifixion miniatures of Reed 45 and Clifford

---

[51] See *A Catholic Commentary on Holy Scripture* (New York: 1953) 104, concerning the wider implications of the text "Ecce mater tua". The idea of Mary's universal motherhood, "latently in the mind of the Church from earliest times", was not specifically linked to this Gospel text until the tenth and eleventh centuries, but had been long established by the second half of the fifteenth century when this Book of Hours was produced.

[52] Wallis 8.

[53] J.Maquet, *The Aesthetic Experience* (New Haven and London: 1986).

[54] Barthes 17.

THE SIGNIFICANCE OF TEXT SCROLLS

MS 1097/9 seem rather to remain polysemous, in spite (or perhaps because) of the incorporation of texts within the compositions.[55]

By their incorporation into the very fabric of the scrolls the words become images and the verbal becomes visual. The scroll-texts in these miniatures are not "semantic enclaves"[56] or examples of that jarring combination of two distinct visual processes (seeing and reading) which both Hubert and Camille have termed "interference".[57] The significance of text-scrolls as visual signs and carriers of meaning lies as much in their impact as formal compositional elements as in the content and arrangement of the Latin words on their surfaces. Word and image combine for maximum effect in f. 68^v of Clifford MS 1097/9 and in Reed 45, while, conversely, the form, size and placement of both scroll and text diminish the impact of the text-scroll on f. 46 of the Canberra manuscript.

The subject matter of the miniatures lends itself to such a fusion of word and image. As Timothy Verdon points out, the New Testament presents a more "plastic" revelation than the Old: verbal messages to prophets give way to the "total sense experience" of the Incarnation as Christ, the Word made flesh, embodies both the verbal and the visual.[58] The devotional use of Books of Hours also combined verbal and visual as prayers were recited in conjunction with the contemplation of the accompanying images.

Analysis of the multiple functions of scrolls and their texts in such contexts demands a correspondingly complex and subtle discourse, with an agreed and concise terminology, especially when addressing the often multiple and overlapping functions of text and image in text-scrolls. The descriptive terms of Wallis, Sparrow and Peirce may well provide a useful base in the development of such a terminology.

---

[55] The Reed 45 text-scroll for example retains prophetic connotations while serving as the equivalent of a modern "speech balloon".

[56] Wallis 1.

[57] R. Hubert sees this "interference" as being "almost in the acoustical sense": "The Displacement of the Visual and the Verbal," *New Literary History* 15 (1983–84): 577. The term is taken up by Camille, "Seeing and Reading..." 38.

[58] T.G. Verdon, *Monasticism and the Arts* (New York: 1984) 1–2.

Figure 20 The Crucifixion. Book of Hours, Dunedin, Public Library, Reed Fragment 45; 86×60 mm.

Figure 21 The Crucifixion. Book of Hours, Canberra, National Library, Clifford Collection MS 1097/9, f. 46; 195×150 mm.

Figure 22 The Crucifixion. Book of Hours, Canberra, National Library, Clifford Collection MS 1097/9, f. 68^v; 195×150 mm.

IV

The Rolin Master's Hand in London BL MS Additional 25695

Peter Rolfe Monks

It is not uncommon for a French miniaturist's work to present stylistic inconsistencies, but it is often difficult to offer a satisfactory explanation for them. One such artist is the Master of the Brussels *Horloge de Sapience*, better known as the Rolin Master or Master of Jean Rolin II. The *Horloge* in Brussels, Bibliothèque Royale, ms IV. 111 was sumptuously illustrated c. 1450 by this Parisian miniaturist. Its art work affirms his maturity as a master and offers a plenitude of references for his stylistic canon. On the other hand, the Rolin painter's accomplishments in the unassuming Book of Hours that is British Library MS Additional 25695 offer disparate elements which critics have not explored or explained.[1] A closer look at the variations may suggest reasons for their presence.

Three critics have ventured brief comments on the illustrations in the London volume, Eleanor Spencer, John Plummer and Janet Backhouse. Spencer noted that two hands collaborated in its artistic production, the Bedford Master and the Rolin Master, but she did not relate her statement to specific pictures.[2] The identification of one of the hands as that of the Bedford Master is open to question. There are other doubts occasioned by comparisons. Stylistically, none of the miniatures in the

---

[1] The approximately two hundred vellum sheets, small quarto in size, contain the following Latin texts : Calendar (fols. 1–12^v); Gospel Extracts (fols. 13–28^v); Hours of the Virgin (fols. 29–120^v); Hours of the Cross (fols. 121–138^v); Hours of the Holy Spirit (fols. 139–146^v); Office of the Virgin (fols. 147–152^v); Penitential Psalms (f. 153–164^v); Vigils of the Dead (f. 165-end). See *Catalogue of Additions to the Manuscripts in the British Museum in the Years MDCCCLIV–MDCCCLXXV* (London: 1877) II: 223. I should like to thank the Manuscripts Librarian, Mr. M.A.F. Borrie, and the Superintendent and Staff of the Students Room in the British Library for their kindness and co-operation during my inspection of the volume. Janet Backhouse was most generous with her time, and our discussions were fruitful.

[2] See Eleanor Spencer, "*L'Horloge de Sapience*, Bruxelles, Bibliothèque Royale, ms IV.111," *Scriptorium* XVII (1963): 295, n. 44; (hereafter Spencer, *Horloge*).

58   PETER ROLFE MONKS

London Hours contains or mirrors the achievements of the Bedford Master in the two imposing monuments preserved in the Salisbury Breviary (BN ms lat. 17294) and in the Bedford Hours (BL MS Add. 18850).[3] It is, furthermore, curious that Spencer should announce a collaboration between the Bedford and Rolin painters for Additional 25695. She acknowledged herself that the former's hand remains painterly even late in his career, that his hand fades from view at the time work was suspended on the Salisbury Breviary c. 1435, and that his work cannot be confused with that of the Rolin Master.[4] Moreover, the *floruit* years for the Rolin artist are c. 1435–1465, and these dates suggest that collaboration was highly unlikely.[5] A more plausible view is that the Rolin painter shared the decoration of the London Hours with another illuminator, who may be called Hand B, and who had been trained in the Bedford Master's style.

Speaking about Pierpont Morgan Library MS M. 1027, Plummer observed, "Most closely resembling our paintings are perhaps the ones by the Master in a Vienna Horae of about the same size (Öst. Nationalbibl., Codex s.n. 13237) and a larger one at London (BL Add. 25695). These two books contain some of his finest paintings...".[6] Janet Backhouse offered no comment on the views of Spencer and Plummer, nor on the number of hands in Additional 25695. She saw the volume's art work as, "...related stylistically to the work of the fashionable Maître François...".[7] A relationship between the artistic approach of the Rolin Master and that of Maître François had been noticed by Spencer many years ago. She believed that the Rolin painter, "...may well have been the chief formative influence for the style of Maître François...".[8]

As soon as the London Hours are opened at the text pages, evidence of two hands at work strikes the viewer's gaze. The difference in the glow and aura of the matt gold staves which always frame the text on the reverse sides of the large miniatures seems attributable to the individuality of two artists. The irregular staves on the verso of the Rolin Master's illustrations are duller than those for Hand B's paintings. The concave stroke for the gilding at the cleft of the sapling is bland and indistinct for the Rolin artist but clear and bright for Hand B. On the other hand, little personal whim is noticeable in the border decorations of the illuminated folios. It is

---

[3] The volumes were consulted by me when I was recently in Paris and London. I am indebted to the Manuscript curators for according me permission to handle them.

[4] Spencer, *Horloge*, 295, and her two papers "The Master of the Duke of Bedford : the Bedford Hours," *Burlington Magazine* CVII (1965): 495–502 and "The Master of the Duke of Bedford : the Salisbury Breviary," *Burlington Magazine* CVIII (1966): 607–12.

[5] See P.R. Monks, "A Study of the Art Work of the Rolin Master in the *Horloge de Sapience*, Brussels, Bibliothèque Royale, ms IV. 111 and of his other known surviving Works", diss., Melbourne University, 1986, 352–418.

[6] See J. Plummer (with the assistance of G. Clark), *The Last Flowering. French Painting in Manuscripts 1420–1530* (New York: 1982) 63.

[7] Janet Backhouse, *Books of Hours* (London: 1985) 32.

[8] Spencer, *Horloge*, 296. Remarks made by me in this paper about elements of the Maître François style are derived from the same article by Spencer, and from Margaret M. Manion *The Wharncliffe Hours. A Study of a Fifteenth-Century Prayer-book* (Canberra: 1972) and *The Wharncliffe Hours. Facsimile* (London: 1981).

THE ROLIN MASTER'S HAND

of a bold and vigorous kind, featuring flowers, acanthus leaves and assorted berries in red and blue. Other folios almost invariably display pink and white or mauve and white acanthus, liberally highlighted with gold. The plants on the verso of a folio are reversed images of those on the recto side.

Viewed broadly, the artistic interpretation in the London book's twenty-four Calendar vignettes, the historiated initials and the sixteen large miniatures recalls Parisian atelier methods popular between the first and third quarters of the fifteenth century. It was derived mainly from the Boucicaut and Bedford Masters' styles.[9] The same folios, however, present specific traits which point to the presence of the Rolin Master. Both the firm vertical folds of a table-cloth in the *January* interior and a boldly designed Greek palmette configuration overpainted in gold on a dark red background in the *Libra* scene resemble closely their multiple counterparts in the *Horloge* series of miniatures.[10] Again, the finely modelled face within circumscribed lines, and the fluffy hair-ends of the subject in *St. John on Patmos* are characteristics associated with the Rolin painter's skills. By contrast figures in the Zodiac Signs and Labours of the Months are quite doll-like, particularly the female ones. None has the S-curve and sway which the Rolin Master lends to his statuesque forms.

Almost every page of Additional 25695 has at least one illuminated or historiated initial, with many carrying four or five, as well as elaborate and delicately executed line-endings in mauve and white. They feature butterflies, snails, birds, insects or human faces. Of particular interest is a capital *D* on f. 33 that is in the Rolin style. It displays a bust of a young woman who wears a blue truncated hat with gold and black trimmings; a small loop of black cloth rests on her forehead, and a white veil streams from the crown of the hat. A minute section of a blue and white, off-the-shoulder gown is just visible. Both garment and head covering belong to French fashion of the mid-fifteenth century. Other historiated initials bear witness to the Rolin artist's participation in their execution. For example, on folios 32^v, 34, 38 and 39, within an *O*, *V*, *D* and *C*, respectively, appears the head of a man wearing a brown beaver fur and blue hat, identical with the models worn by Daniel and other men in the *Susanna* miniature of the *Horloge* series. Even more apposite is the warrior presented in the *N* on f. 109^v. He is clad in bluish-grey armour, the helmet and shoulders of which accord with the armour on the young Amalekite who severs Saul's head in the *Horloge* painting known as the *Death of Saul*.

Elements of the Rolin Master's hand are also evident in the vignettes which decorate the borders of certain folios. In keeping with his eclectic style, archaisms are not uncommon. They are possibly derived from Bedford trends. One particular form this takes is the positioning outside the frame of the miniature a person or object related to the sequence of events of the pictorial narrative. In the *Annunciation*, for example (f. 129; Figure 23), God the Father, the source of Gabriel's

---

[9] For these two styles, see M. Meiss, *French Painting in the Time of Jean de Berry. The Boucicaut Master* (New York: 1968) *passim* and the two papers by Spencer cited in n. 4 above.

[10] See P.R. Monks, *The Brussels Horloge de Sapience. Iconography and Text of the Brussels, Bibliothèque Royale, ms IV. 111* (Leiden: 1989) chap. 5, and the plates which reproduce all the miniatures.

message stands in the vegetal border at the upper right. He is encircled by orange cherubim and garbed in a blue cope edged with gold, worn over a mauve cassock. His head is crowned with a red and gold triple tiara. His left hand supports a crucigerous golden orb. This treatment may be compared with another instance of archaic placement by the Rolin Master in the *Clock Chamber* miniature (f. 13^v) of the Brussels *Horloge*. Here, a bell cord extends from the body of the painting to the upper border, where it is attached to a small turret, ostensibly on the roof of the building.[11]

The orange used occasionally by the Rolin Master as a contrasting colour for garments or accessories is present too in these marginal vignettes. It is less vibrant than the hue employed later by Maître François in a similar way.[12]

Seven large paintings in the London *Horae* are by the Rolin artist. They are the following: *The Annunciation* f. 29; *The Presentation in the Temple* f. 106; *The Crucifixion* f. 121 (Plate 6); *Pentecost* f. 139; *The Coronation of the Virgin* f. 147 (Figure 25); *David and Nathan* f. 153 (Figure 24); *Wrapping a Corpse* f. 165 (Figure 26).[13] It would be a mistake, however, to imagine that these pictures uniformly mirror the stylistic qualities later found in the Brussels *Horloge* series.

The Virgin and angel's forms in the *Annunciation* are solid and display firm colour; both are traits of the Rolin artist, but the serpentine undulations of which mention has already been made are lacking. To find parallels it is necessary to look further than the *Horloge* illustrations. They occur, to be sure, in another *Annunciation* of a Book of Hours in Baltimore, Walters Art Gallery, MS Walters 251 (Figure 27). A similar bulkiness of form and monumental drapery in garments is clearly present, and the anthropomorphic S-curve is absent.[14]

Both the London and Baltimore *Annunciations* depict intricate architectonic detailings common to the Rolin Master's hand, such as the treatment of Gothic window tracery and scaled-down arcading. The pictures also expose a less felicitous element, the misalignment of a *prie-dieu* and furniture with the perspective chosen for the floor tesserae.

Another trend is apparent in the London *Annunciation*, it is the retention of traits from the Bedford Master's milieu. One is the shallow-ribbed golden dome covering the principal structure; another is the gold-decorated tracery between the forward-placed pendants; a third is the Gothic quatrefoil frieze, which occurs also in the *The Presentation in the Temple* and in *Pentecost*. Small mauve and white statues of prophets set in niches above leading figures are a further indication of that workshop's influence on the Rolin painter.

---

[11] See Monks, *The Brussels Horloge....*

[12] See Manion, *The Wharncliffe Hours. A Study . . .,* 10–11.

[13] Each has a jewelled frame, as does the *Court of Heaven* painting of the *Horloge* series. Such a frame does not seem to be a decorative trait of the Rolin Master, however. The identical embellishment runs across the low wall in the foreground of a second *Court of Heaven* on f. 199^v of the same Brussels *Horloge* volume. See Eleanor Spencer, ''Gerson, Ciboule and the Bedford Master's Shop,'' *Scriptorium* XIX (1965): 104–8 and Plate 12.

[14] For a technical description of MS Walters 251, see R.S. Wieck, *Time Sanctified. The Book of Hours in Medieval Art and Life* (New York: 1988) 188, no. 39.

THE ROLIN MASTER'S HAND 61

Parallel lay-outs for the themes in Additional 25695 are present in other illustrations from his brush. The example of one subject will suffice. Iconographically, the *Crucifixion* in Lyons, Bibliothèque de la Ville ms 517, f. 183^v (Figure 28) recalls the tableau in the London volume. The postures assumed by the tortured Redeemer and the two thieves in both of these lay-outs are repeated in *Christ Offered the Sop* (f. 80; Figure 29) of the *Horloge* series.[15]

Little divergence in technical lay-out and coloration can be found between *David and Nathan* (Figure 24) and *Wrapping a Corpse* (Figure 26) and the other miniatures by the Rolin Master in Additional 25695. The linear clarity already occurs here that will be present in the *Horloge* illuminations. Over the head of the Old Testament prophet in *David and Nathan* are three gold-dusted columns that support a Gothic canopy. One of the columns is a buttress type, with a projecting flange at the summit, at mid-point and at the base of the plinth. This form of architectonic support is, by all appearances, derived from anterior styles, yet, it is an element adopted by the Rolin painter as his own. He employs it, for example, in the portrait of an *Abbot* in London, British Library, MS Egerton 2019, f. 231. Another representation of columns, this time animated and diminutive Gothic ones, complete with slender lancets, supports a frieze surmounting the twin side structures of the proscenium arch in the *Horloge* representation of the *The Repentant in his Cell* (Figure 30).

The stature of the Rolin figures in Additional 25695 is regular, but waists may at times be rather long. Later, in the *Horloge* portraiture of *Lechery and Chastity*, the artist will depict the Virtue as a tall lady with a short waist.[16] The bodies of Christ and the two malefactors in the *The Crucifixion* (Figure 28) of the London book have firm outlines; the faces of the witnesses to the Passion have sharp, bold chins with angular, chiselled jaws and cheeks.

The features of the Virgin and of the angel in the London *The Annunciation* (Figure 23) lack the angular modelling that is salient in the figuration of the *Horloge* pictures. The impression conveyed is one of refined softness, but this may be unintentional. Rubbing of the folios has perhaps softened the distinct linearity of the artist's hand. The visage of Mary in the London *The Coronation of the Virgin* (Figure 25), on the other hand, is identical with that of Sapientia in the *Tree of Life* (f. 20^v) of the Brussels *Horloge*; the hair shows a slight tendency to be less sculptured than its *Horloge* counterpart, especially where it cascades over the right shoulder and falls down her side.[17] Throughout the Rolin Master's works, ears are round, somewhat inelegant, and feature two dots. The trait is exemplified in the *Pentecost* miniature of the London manuscript. Also evident is the artist's

---

[15] This characterization had been customary for a generation or so among French illuminators of the stature of the Rohan, Boucicaut and Bedford Masters. For examples executed in the Rohan workshop see M. Meiss, *French Painting in the Time of Jean de Berry. The Limbourgs and their Contemporaries* (London: 1974) II, Figures 855 and 872. For the Boucicaut Master and his atelier, see Meiss, *Boucicaut Master* Figures 37 and 299. For the Bedford workshop, see the two articles by Spencer cited in n. 4 above.

[16] See Monks, *The Brussels Horloge....*

[17] See Monks, *The Brussels Horloge...*

62 PETER ROLFE MONKS

preference for burnished gold haloes with black rings.

The rendering of architectural elements provides reinforcement for stylistic associations. Silvered windows are a case in point. Several enhance the chamber in the *Pentecost* drama; elsewhere, however, there is a variation in their treatment. In the London *Annunciation* (Figure 23) they have been left uncoloured, while in *David and Nathan* (Figure 24) they display a medium-to-dark grey pigment.[18] A tower with a golden cupola and, nearby, a Gothic porch in *Wrapping a Corpse* (Figure 26) present the painterly lightness of the Bedford Master's style. Maître François will also represent towers with dome-shaped summits. In spite of such parallels in other painters' works, fine detail in the execution of the architectural elements brings us back every time to the Rolin Master's hand. Moreover, the simplified buttresses of the charnel-house, the inverted tulip-shaped arches in the porch, and a diminutive corbel projection on the upper corner of the porch, are features that appear among the architectural structures of the *Horloge* triptych *The Disciple Offering his Heart to Sapientia*, *Sapientia with Faith, Hope and Charity*, and *The Disciple Shutting out Sapientia* (f.49^v; Figure 31).

Thus, although numerous features of the Rolin Master's style are prominently displayed in seven miniatures of the London Book of Hours, they contrast oddly with other elements that recall traits of earlier painters, in particular, the Bedford Master. This lack of uniformity and consistency suggests that the Rolin artist's style had not yet reached the maturity of the Brussels *Horloge* series. He is seen to be still distancing himself from the shadow of the Bedford Master and attempting to assert his own identity. The art work of Additional 25695 was clearly executed some time before that of the Brussels *Horloge de Sapience*.

---

[18] Two clerestory lights may have been silvered here at some time, but confirmation is not forthcoming from the verso of the folio where one would expect to see the stain of the metallic substance employed by the painter.

Figure 23 The Annunciation. Book of Hours, London, British Library MS Additional 25695, f. 29; 190×135 mm.

Figure 24 David and Nathan. Book of Hours, London, British Library MS Additional 25695, f. 153; 190×135 mm.

Figure 25 The Coronation of the Virgin. Book of Hours, London, British Library MS Additional 25695, f. 147; 190×135 mm.

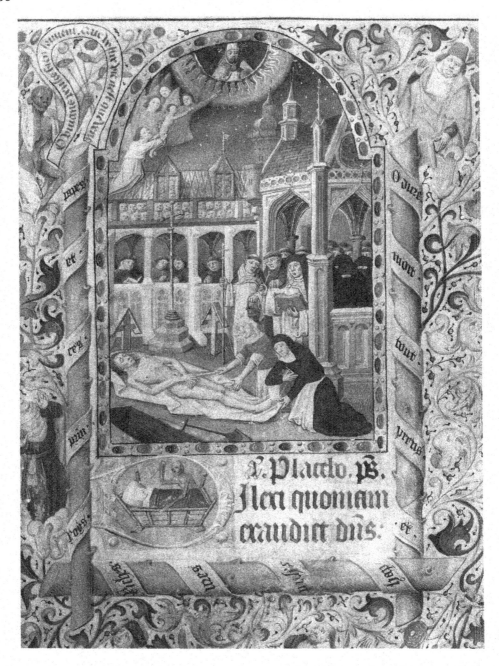

Figure 26 Wrapping a Corpse. Book of Hours, London, British Library MS Additional 25695, f. 165; 190×135 mm.

Figure 27 The Annunciation. Book of Hours, Baltimore, Walters Art Gallery MS Walters 251, f. 26; 191×137 mm.

Figure 28 The Crucifixion. Missal, Lyons, Bibliothèque de la Ville ms 517, f. 183^v; 231×175 mm.

Figure 29 Christ offered the Sop. *Horloge de Sapience*, Brussels, Bibliothèque Royale ms IV. 111, f. 80; 370×260 mm.

Figure 30 Temptations of the Flesh and The Repentant in his Cell. *Horloge de Sapience*, Brussels, Bibliothèque Royale ms IV. 111. f. 18; 370×260 mm.

Figure 31 The Disciple Offering his Heart to Sapientia; Sapientia with Faith, Hope and Charity and The Disciple Shutting out Sapientia. *Horloge de Sapience*, Brussels, Bibliothèque Royale ms IV. 111, f. 49^v; 370×260 mm.

V

Renaissance Books and Raphael's
Disputa : Contextualizing the Image

Cecilia O'Brien

In a recent article Sandra Hindman compared approaches to the study of Italian Renaissance art with those used in the area of Northern European Art.[1] She indicated that Panofsky had bestowed his imprimatur on a methodology which places strong emphasis on the relationship between Franco-Flemish miniatures and Netherlandish panel painting. On the other hand, the study of Italian Quattrocento illumination remains an esoteric preserve, an enclave set apart from the discourses of "mainstream" art history.

But the patrons themselves had different priorities. In forming the famous libraries which best exemplify their particular tastes and ambitions, they spent lavishly on decorated manuscripts. Hence the following examination of the decoration of a Renaissance library attempts to demonstrate the possibility of constructing bridges which link the study of the monumental arts with that of the Renaissance book.

Marshalling archival and archaeological evidence, John Shearman has shown that the so-called *Stanza della Segnatura* was intended to house the private library and study of Julius II.[2] Thus the designation "Segnatura", with its administrative nuances, reflects a later use of the chamber. Shearman has pointed to some aspects of the iconography that are indicative of the room's original function: the presence of Apollo may recall the traditional dedication of libraries to this deity, and the division into disciplines evokes similar categories in contemporary library cataloguing practice.[3] Others have pointed to the sheer number of books depicted in the *Stanza*.

---

[1] S. Hindman, "The Illustrated Book: An Addendum to the State of Research in Northern European Art," *Art Bulletin* 68 (1986): 536.

[2] J. Shearman, *The Vatican Stanze: functions and decorations,* Italian Lecture, British Academy, 1971 (Oxford: 1972).

[3] Shearman 16 and 45 (n. 88).

72   CECILIA O'BRIEN

However, in general terms, the iconography of the ensemble as articulated by Gombrich, who was mistaken about the room's purpose, remains valid. The overall theme is, in his words, "knowledge and virtue as expressions of the divine".[4] Clearly this message is as pertinent to a library as it is to an administrative chamber. Another conclusion based on the older erroneous identification remains valid. The scheme depends on earlier programmes in which personifications of the Virtues and Liberal Arts were linked with depictions of distinguished practitioners of those arts: similar combinations found a place in Renaissance libraries as well as council halls.[5]

Perhaps the fame of the work and its place in the canon of "universally" relevant masterpieces has deterred scholars from assessing the iconography contextually. Why was it employed in the library of this particular patron? Indeed, the *Stanza* scheme is still discussed as if it consisted merely of a generalized visualization of the divine origin of knowledge as lauded in contemporary epideictic oratory. Specific references to the patron—his stemma on the altar cloth in the *Disputa*, his portrait in the scene of the *Decretals* and allusions to his Belvedere and Vatican building programmes in both the *School of Athens* and the *Disputa*—are dismissed as co-incidental, and not treated as conscious allusions to the notion of Pope as priest, ruler and builder, which had been articulated during the preceding century. Jones and Penny, for example, maintain that the inclusion in the ceiling depiction of Urania's orb of the planetary formations which appeared in the Roman sky on the night of Julius' election, is irrelevant to the overall meaning of the ensemble, adding only a minor embellishment.[6] Such an approach does not accord with what is known of the decoration of Renaissance *studioli*. The surviving contents of both Federico da Montefeltro and Isabella D'Este's studies reveal that the commissioned decorations were replete with references to the owner and his or her literary pursuits.[7] Presumably the contents of such schemes were governed by written or oral instructions of some complexity. However, these decorations had other functions besides replicating prior documents. In effect they mapped out the library space, denoted the literary nature of its contents, and most importantly, referred to the patron who

---

[4] E.H. Gombrich, "Raphael's *Stanza della Segnatura* and the Nature of its symbolism," *Symbolic Images* (London: 1972): 88. He bases his conclusion on the fact that the Stanza does not comply with Albertini's description of the library—"quam tua beatitudo construxit signisque planetarum de coelorum exornavit" (*Opusculum*, 1509). Shearman shares the view that this description is incompatible with the actual appearance of the room arguing that it is a "generalised, rhetorical vision of the proper appearance of libraries" (n. 91). However, at least two globes *are* depicted in the scheme. Furthermore, if the conclusions presented in this paper are correct, the horoscope is the major iconographical theme of the first wall.

[5] Shearman 45–46, n. 85. For a summary of nineteenth century scholarship. For a survey of later library decoration and, *inter alia*, discussion of the *Segnatura*, see André Masson, *The Pictorial Catalogue Mural Decoration in Libraries*, The Lyell Lectures, Oxford 1972–73 (Oxford: 1981).

[6] R. Jones and N. Penny, *Raphael* (New Haven and London: 1983): 57. For discussion of fifteenth century Papal theory and the visual arts, see C.W. Westfall, *In this most perfect Paradise: Alberti, Nicholas V, and the Invention of conscious urban planning in Rome* (Pennsylvania State University: 1974) and L. Ettlinger, *The Sistine Chapel before Michelangelo* (Oxford, Clarendon: 1965).

[7] For Urbino, see L. Cheles, *The Studiolo of Urbino: An Iconographic Invesitgation* (Pennsylvania State University: 1986). For the d'Este *studiolo*, see E. Verheyen, *The Paintings in the Studiolo of Isabella d'Este at Mantua* (New York: 1971).

RAPHAEL'S *DISPUTA*   73

would customarily be the surveyor of the room. Thereby the owner was explicitly
located within this private and privileged domain. The decorations functioned deic-
tically like the phrase "dear reader" in the Victorian novel.

A similar index-like quality is evident in Raphael's *Segnatura*. There it is
achieved with clarity and economy through conscious and witty manipulation of the
paradigmatic bibliographical index: the library catalogue itself. If we explore the
relationship between the arrangement of protagonists in Raphael's four frescoes and
the lists of authors in contemporary library catalogues, a close correspondence is
revealed between the ordering of the frescoes and the hierarchy of books found in
the most widely used Renaissance cataloguing system. Developed by Tommaso
Parentucelli, the future Nicholas V, for use by Cosimo de Medici, this form of
catalogue was also employed in the Pesaro, Fiesole, Vatican and Urbino libraries.[8]

The inventory of the Urbino Library furnishes an extant example of such a
catalogue. Moreover, both patron and artist had connections with Urbino.[9]
Raphael's father had composed a panegyric on that library, and in 1508, on becom-
ing the Duke of Urbino, Julius' relative, Francesco Maria della Rovere, had acquired
the library. Let us consider Raphael's *Segnatura* frescoes and the surviving Urbino
inventory in parallel. When this is done it becomes apparent that the usual formula-
like equation of each monumental scene with one of four specific disciplines—
Theology, Philosophy, Jurisprudence and Poetry (for example, of the *School of
Athens* with Philosophy)—is too rigid. At the head of the Urbino catalogue are the
works of Scripture, followed by liturgical books; then come patristics, wherein the
Doctors of the Church— Jerome, Ambrose, Augustine and Gregory—are given pre-
cedence over a mostly chronological list of exegetes and theologians leading up to
Aquinas and Bonaventura. In the *Disputa* the dominance of the Trinity and of biblical figures in the upper tier is notable, as is the centrality of the four doctors in the
lower tier (Plate 8). The monstrance displayed on the altar alludes to liturgical practice. Next the Urbino catalogue lists philosophical works from Aristotle and Plato to
the moderns. Science, Mathematics and Astronomy follow and the section is
rounded off with works on Architecture by Vitruvius and Alberti. The *School of
Athens* includes not just philosophers and mathematical scientists, but portraits of
the contemporary architects Bramante and Michelangelo in the guise of ancients. It
is set against an ideal rendering of the incomplete crossing of the new St. Peter's;
thus Architecture is denoted as a subsidiary theme. Two further disciplines in the
library catalogue—Medicine and Cosmography—are denoted in the *Timaeus* held by
Plato. This text deals with both these natural sciences. Jurisprudence, Imperial History and Biographies of Popes follow in the catalogue. The *Pandects* and *Decretals*
denote Jurisprudence. Moreover, as the only historical scenes in the *Stanza*, they

---

[8] R. Sabbadini, *Le Scoperte dei codici latini e greci ne' secoli XIV e XV* (Florence: 1908) I, 200.

[9] The inventory has been published by C. Guasti, "Inventario della libreria Urbinate compilato nel
secolo XV da Federigo Veterano bibliotecario di Federigo I da Montefeltro Duca d'Urbino", *Giornale
storico degli archivi toscani* VI (1862): 127–247; VII (1863): 46–55, 130–54. For a dating of the inventory after the Borgia sack of 1502, see D. M. Robothan, "Libraries of the Italian Renaissance", *The
Medieval Library*, ed. J. Thompson (New York: 1957): 538–42.

74 CECILIA O'BRIEN

make explicit reference to Papal and Imperial History. Finally Rhetoric, Poetry and Song constitute the last divisions in the catalogue of Urbino's Latin books—the relevance to the *Parnassus* is obvious.

This comparison of the *Stanza's* decorative scheme with the Urbino catalogue suggests that a similar document may have contributed to the *invenzione* of the ensemble. Part of the task of the inventor, most probably Julius,[10] would have been to amalgamate and perhaps omit some disciplines in order to fit those he wanted on to four walls. Personal interest may account for particular emphases found in the decoration and it is known that theological and legal texts formed the bulk of Julius' library holdings.[11] Thus a number of scenes in the ceiling refer to judgement: *The Fall of Man*, the *Flaying of Marsyas* and the *Judgement of Solomon*.

I have drawn attention to the probable fluidity and overlapping of the identities of the disciplines in the four frescos because this calls into question the long-held assumptions that the four *tituli* held by the female figures on the ceiling refer exclusively to the disciplines of Theology, Jurisprudence, Philosophy and Poetry, and that each designates the central theme of the fresco located immediately below.[12] On the contrary, even the literary derivations of the *tituli* employed would suggest that the confluence of knowledge, rather than a rigid stratification into four disciplines is being accentuated. The phrase "causarum cognitio" held by the so-called Philosophy figure above the *School of Athens* is taken, as Rash-Fabbri notes, "from a passage in Cicero's *Topica* devoted to the importance of knowledge of causes not only for jurists and poets, but also for philosophers".[13] Even more suggestive is the derivation of the *titulus* "notitia divinarum rerum", usually held to refer to Theology, from Justinian's definition of Jurisprudence.[14]

Does the term "notitia divinarum rerum" really denote theology *per se*, or something broader? Perhaps as the appearance of non-theologians like Dante and Fra Angelico in the *Disputa* below tends to suggest, this *titulus* should be read quite literally. The knowledge, or concept, of divine matters is not the exclusive property of theologians, but rather of the faithful who constitute the Mystical Body of the Church. Even Aquinas, a professional theologian, placed revelation as in Scripture and tradition, especially the liturgy, above the discourses of theologians. "Theology as the science of which God is the subject argues from the divine knowledge of God contained in the Scriptures, whose main aspects are summarized under specific articles of faith."[15] "The defining of the faith in articles is the office of the Roman

---

[10] "Pinxit in Vaticano nec adhuc stabili autoritate cubicula *ad praescriptum* Julii Pontificis"— Jovius, *Raphael Urbinatis vita*, cited in L. Pastor, *The History of the Popes* Vol. VI, 1843, ed. F.I. Antrobus (London: 1950) 580.

[11] Robothan 565.

[12] These assumptions originated in G. P. Bellori, *Descrizzione delle imagini dipinte da Raffaelle d'Urbino nelle Camera del Palazzo Apostolico Vaticano* (Rome: 1695).

[13] N. Rash-Fabbri, "A Note on the Stanza della Segnatura," *Gazette des Beaux-Arts* 94 (1979): 98.

[14] Rash-Fabbri 98. In the corners of the ceiling, the scenes in the rectangles— the Fall, the Judgement of Solomon and the Flaying of Marsyas— also seem to point to a blending of the disciplines of Law, Theology and Poetry. See Jones and Penny 52–55.

[15] Abstracted from Thomas Aquinas, *Summa Theologia* II-II q. 1, a 10, c, as cited in *An Aquinas Reader*, ed. M.T. Clark (New York: 1972) 409; and on Scripture, *Summa Theologia* II-II, a. 9, ad. 1. (408); and for tradition, *Exposition of I Corinthians 11: 25* (408–09).

RAPHAEL'S *DISPUTA*

Pontiff" [as stated in the Decretals].[16] Thus Julius had legal status as final arbiter of "notitia divinarum rerum", hence the appropriateness of a *titulus* taken from a legal text. Rash-Fabbri has argued that other allusions to the law discernible in the *Stanza* are indicative of a general theme of "an age when all knowledge is united in the service of Justice".[17]

The notion that "Theology" is presented in the *Disputa* has led to various interpretations of the work. Many of these have as a starting point Vasari's misconception that the figures depicted are discoursing or disputing on the real presence, "e sopra l'ostia, che è sullo altare, disputano".[18] This reading is apparently grounded in Vasari's experience of the Counter Reformation and led to the assigning of the misappelation *Disputa* to the work.

In the decades which separated Vasari from Raphael a fundamental shift in religious practice had occurred. As Kavanagh has argued, the sixteenth century saw a variety of factors, including printing, humanism, and doctrinal dissent, contribute to an up-ending or inversion of the patristic maxim *legem credendi lex statuat supplicandi* ("the law of worshipping is based upon the law of believing").[19] "Rite became less a means than an obstacle for the new textual piety . . . The truth now lies exclusively in the text, no longer on the walls, or in the windows, or in the liturgical activity of those who occupy the churches."[20]

This new hegemony of the learned text informed Vasari's alternate description or interpretation of the *Disputa* as representing saints "ordering" or "writing" the Mass. Correction of liturgy by committee consensus post-dated Raphael's *Stanza* by some decades. "The technology of printing...greatly speeded up liturgical change by giving this previously labyrinthine and long-term process over to committees of experts whose work was predominantly textual and theological rather than ritual and symbolic."[21] As I argue below, Raphael's image utilizes the earlier ritual tradition to convey a specifically Julian theme: neither Julius nor Raphael could have anticipated the revolution which would make the painting's meaning less than patent.

Iconographers, the heirs to the triumph of literary expertise, often base their interpretations of Christian art of the pre-Reformation on the *dicta* of exegetes and commentators, ignoring the liturgical bedrock on which these images rested. Even when a precise "text" rather than an oral, visual or ritual tradition may be relevant to the interpretation of a work of art, the emphasis placed by modern scholars on certain types of texts seems lop-sided. On a purely pragmatic level, the question as to whether the kinds of texts now enshrined in Migne were readily and widely available is rarely addressed.[22] Despite an exponential rise in the number of books produced

---

[16] Aquinas, *Exposition of I Corinthians 11: 25*: 409.

[17] Rash-Fabbri 101.

[18] Giorgio Vasari, *Le Vite de' piu eccellenti pittori, scultori, ed architettori*, 9 vols., ed. G. Milanese, (Florence: 1878–85) 4: 336.

[19] A. Kavanagh, *On Liturgical Theology*. The Hale Memorial Lectures of Seabury-Western Theological Seminary, 1981 (New York: 1984) chaps. 5–7.

[20] Kavanagh 104.

[21] Kavanagh 105.

[22] For this "Mignomania" see S. Sinding-Larsen, *Iconography and Ritual: a Study of Analytical Perspectives* (Oslo: 1984) 198.

76 CECILIA O'BRIEN

in the fifteenth century, Renaissance libraries were usually extremely limited in stock. It is extraordinary that the Breviary and Missal, the very texts which were commonly available to clerics and often known by heart, are so infrequently used today as sources for iconographical studies.

Vasari's familiarity with post-Reformation revisions of the liturgy seems to have influenced his conclusion, which is not unnatural, but certainly anachronistic, that the image referred to composition or revision of the liturgy by a group of scholars. He recognized elements of the Mass liturgy in the work. In particular, it seems to evoke the "Suscipe, sancta Trinitas" of the Offertory.

> Receive, O Holy Trinity, this offering, which we make to Thee in memory of the Passion, Resurrection, and Ascension of our Lord Jesus Christ, and in honour of the blessed Mary ever Virgin, of blessed John the Baptist, of the holy Apostles Peter and Paul, of these and of all the Saints.

A similar reading led some nineteenth century apologists to conclude that the image was actually derived from such prayers.[23] But from the demeanours of the personages shown, from the lack of typical Mass furnishings on the altar (as seen, for example, in the *Mass at Bolsena*), and from the presence of the monstrance on the altar, Vasari rightly concluded that *no* actual Mass was depicted here.[24]

Perhaps Vasari was also reminded of the Mass because the image belongs to a rather fluid class of "Presence" images usually employed in liturgical contexts. Shearman points to the work's typological and compositional affinities with a number of late fifteenth century altarpieces.[25] As de Campos has noted, the image has overtones of the type of Paradise depiction found in earlier medieval apse programmes.[26] Garzelli has recently published a similar image which appears in a Florentine Missal illuminated by Attavante in 1487. In this book the risen Christ

---

[23] Pastor 563.

[24] The reservation of the Host in a monstrance on side altars dates from the fourteenth century in Northern Europe; see A.A. King, *Eucharistic Reservation in the Western Church* (London: 1965) 137. Wall and altar tabernacles were used for reservation in fifteenth century Italy; see H. Van Os, "Painting in a house of glass the altarpieces of Pienza", *Simiolus* 17 (1987): 21–38. However, contemporary illustrations show that monstrances were also used, as the Corpus Christi image in at least one Breviary reveals (Vat. B.A.V. ms lat. 7235, f. 200—Gubbio, c. 1470). These exposures were later formalized in the rite of Benediction. However the exposure of the monstrance during Mass and on High altars seems to post-date Raphael's work. Its use during Mass was interdicted by Paris de Grassis, papal Master of Ceremonies (King 194). The ritual wherein the exposed Host was allowed on the altar during Mass—the Forty Hours prayer—was fostered in Counter-Reformation Northern Italy by Carlo Borromeo; see R. Cabie, *The Eucharist*, The Church at Prayer, ed. A.G. Martimort (Collegeville: 1986) II, 248–49; and with regard to the same ritual up until Vatican II, "Without necessity, grave cause or special indult, Mass may not be said at an altar on which the Sanctissimum is exposed", Adrian Fortescue, *The Ceremonies of the Roman Rite Described*, ed. J. O'Connell, 7th ed. rev. (London: 1943) 61.

[25] J. Shearman, "Raphael's Unexecuted Projects for the Stanze," *Walter Friedlaender zum 90. Geburtstag* (Berlin: 1965) 162, 159. For other liturgical works similar in composition and meaning, see H. Pfeiffer, *Zur Ikonographie von Raffael's Disputa* (Rome: 1975) Plates 17–38.

[26] D. Redig de Campos, *Raphael in the Stanze*, trans. J. Guthrie (Milan: 1973) 10.

RAPHAEL'S *DISPUTA* 77

showing his wounds, surrounded by figures seated in a *synthronos* arrangement above a scene of the *Resurrection of the Flesh,* accompanies the "Te Igitur" of the Canon (Figure 32).[27] This depiction in fact preceded Fra Bartolomeo's *Last Judgement* rendering, so often cited as Raphael's source. In evoking such earlier images Raphael could have scarcely avoided some form of tacit reference to the Canon of the Mass which would provoke recognition in a viewer familiar with the eucharistic liturgy. However, as noted above, the image explicitly confutes such readings; a different focus is intended.

The evidence of contemporary liturgical books indicates that the Court of Heaven with the Trinity and other related images—including the Coronation of the Virgin, the *Maiestas Domini* and the Last Judgment—also appear in a variety of liturgical contexts other than the Canon.[28] These include the feasts of the Assumption and All Saints and the first Sunday of Advent.[29] Elaborate Trinitarian imagery like that found in the *Disputa* can occur in a variety of contexts. In the Breviary of

---

[27] A. Garzelli and A.C. de la Mare, *Miniatura Fiorentina del Rinascimento 1440–1525: Un Primo Censimento,* 2 vols. (Florence: 1985) 1: 226. The Missal is that of Matthias Corvinus (Brussels, Bibliothèque Royale Albert 1er de Belgique ms 9008, f. 206). Related images by Attavante occur in the Missal of Thomas James, Bishop of Dol, now in Lyon, f. 206; see V. Leroquais, *Les Sacramentaires et les Missels Manuscrits des Bibliothèques Publiques de France,* (Paris: 1927) 3: no. 802. A variant appears in a Missal of 1509 for the future Leo X. There Christ showing his wounds is accompanied by border medallions of prophets and evangelists (BN ms lat. 17323, f. 178; Leroquais no. 850).

[28] The explanation for this lies in the liturgy. All these images are parousial and demonstrate the culmination of a salvation achieved through the Eucharist. The liturgies of Advent, All Saints, the Assumption and the Canon of the Mass have a *summa*-like quality. Office and Mass texts for the feast days overlap. The Office readings for the Assumption were, for example, not concerned with the historical event, but with the resurrection of the flesh in general as discussed in Jerome's letter "Cogitis me o Paula". It is thus related to both the First Sunday in Advent and to the feast of All Saints in theme. Thus a Coronation image might feasibly be replaced with a resurrection of the flesh image without much change in meaning. This is precisely what occurs later in the altar wall of the Sistine Chapel (which had a double dedication to the Virgin Assumptive and to All Saints).

[29] For example, the *Coronation* frequently introduces Advent in French Breviaries and *Golden Legends.* One Italian example appears in a Milanese breviary of c. 1450 (Vat. ms lat. 9217). The image is used for All Saints in two French Breviaries: the Salisbury Breviary (BN ms lat. 17294, f. 618); and Châteauroux (Bibl. Mun. ms 2, f. 387 ^v). For knowledge of the French Breviaries cited in this article I am grateful to Judith Pearce, who allowed me to consult her *Text and Image in the Salisbury Breviary,* diss., Australian National University, 1987.
The *Virgin and Child and Saints* appears in two *Golden Legends* for the feast of All Saints (BL MS Add. 19907 and Munich, Bayerische Staatsbibliothek ms Gall 3). I am indebted here to Hilary Maddocks who allowed me to consult her unpublished material on the *Légende Dorée.*
The *Trinity and Saints* appears in the following *Golden Legends*: at Advent (BN ms fr. 243); and at All Saints (BN ms fr. 244–45, BN ms fr. 6448, and Mâcon, Bibl. Mun. ms 3).
The *Resurrection of the Dead* sometimes appears at Advent in Florentine books; examples occur in an Evangelistry (Firenze, Bibl. Medicea Laurenziana edili 115, f.1—for illustrations, see Garzelli Plates 180 & 181), and in a Breviary (Firenze, Museo Nazionale ms 68, f. 17—Garzelli Plate 417). It occurs at the "Te igitur" in fifteenth century French Missals, including Bibl. Mun. d'Évreux, ms 99 (Leroquais no. 806) and BN ms lat. 16827 (Leroquais no. 836)
The *Maiestas Domini* occurs at Advent in a French *Golden Legend* (BN ms fr. 244–5) and at All Saints in a Tuscan Breviary (Vat. ms lat. 4761, f. 348^v) which bears the arms of Julius II (on a folio inserted some decades later). It commonly appeared at the Preface or "Vere dignum" in earlier Missals; see Staale Sinding-Larsen "Some observations on liturgical imagery of the twelfth century," *Acta ad Archaeologiam et Artium Historiam Pertinentia* 8 (1978): 198–201, and O. Pächt, *Book Illumination in the Middle Ages* (London: 1986) 39–44.

78   CECILIA O'BRIEN

Matthias Corvinus (Figure 34) Attavante includes a *Dixit Dominus* Trinity (that is, one where the Son and Father are side by side, as indicated in the opening words of Psalm 109) surrounded by the Virgin, John the Baptist and the Apostles seated in a semi-circle in the upper section of the illustration; they are praised by scroll-bearing prophets arrayed beneath.[30] On the opposite page, gesticulating figures are ranged about an altar on which is placed the *incipit* of the text. Above the altar is the half-length figure of God the Father making a gesture of blessing and holding an orb, as he does in the *Disputa* (Figure 33). These configurations appear frequently in liturgical books illuminated by Attavante, and are related to the traditional *Aspiciens a longe* schema used in the illustration of Advent. To a certain extent, Raphael's work represents a conflation of two images commonly found in contemporary liturgical books. The context of Attavante's Trinity is worth noting:[31] its position at the beginning of the Common of Saints indicates its status as an All Saints' picture.

Vasari, it will be remembered, described the protagonists in Raphael's work not as theologians, but as *un numero infinito di Santi*.[32] His comment, I propose, is the key to the work. But before pursuing this, some iconographical cobwebs must be cleared away. As Sinding-Larsen has trenchantly argued, traditional iconography comes unstuck when dealing with "Paradise" images because of an underlying assumption that one morphological type necessarily conveys one fixed meaning.[33] Christian imagery, because it is embedded within the rich web of the liturgy, is not amenable to such treatment. Illustrations in contemporary Missals, Breviaries, and vernacular versions of the *Golden Legend,* both north and south of the Alps, do not support the Panofskian proposition that pictorial emulation of that day's Mass liturgy with its vision of the Lamb is the sole way of representing All Saints.[34] Scenes of Paradise with images such as the Coronation of the Virgin and Christ as *Maiestas Domini* also occur, as do representations of the Trinity in various guises.[35] The Trinity can take on a Throne of Grace format, a *Dixit Dominus* format, or be represented as Three Persons seated side by side.[36] Alternately, one figure can indicate the Trinity: the notion of Christ seated at the Father's right hand is, for example,

---

[30] Vat. Urb. ms lat. 112, fols. 555^v–556, c. 1487–92; the Breviary was commissioned by Matthias Corvinus, King of Hungary.

[31] The *Blessing God the Father (with orb)* recurs in Matthias' Missal (Brussels, Bibl. Roy. Albert 1er de Belgique ms 9008, f. 8 ^{v}). Doubtless the "Dixit Dominus" format was chosen because Vespers of the Office begins with Psalm 109.

[32] Vasari 335.

[33] Sinding-Larsen, *Iconography and Ritual (passim),* and also his "The 'Paradise Controversy': a Note on Argumentation," *Interpretazioni veneziane: Studi in onore di Michelangelo Muraro,* ed. D. Rosand (New York and Venice: 1984) 363–70.

[34] E. Panofsky, *Early Netherlandish Painting,* 2 vols. (New York: 1971) 1: 214–17. For example, he could not see the liturgical relevance of the Just Judges in the Ghent altarpiece, but both Office and Mass are shot through with references to Justice and the Sermon on the Mount; see also the critique in Sinding-Larsen's "The 'Paradise . . .'" 368–69.

[35] Instances are cited in n. 29 above.

[36] For example the "Dixit Dominus" version in Vat. Urb. ms lat. 112 discussed above. A representation of the Trinity as three persons introduces the feast of All Saints in Caxton's 1527 English edition of the *Golden Legend* (illustrated in *The Golden Legend of Jacobus de Voragine,* trans. and adapted by G. Ryan and H. Ripperger (New York, London, Toronto: 1941) Plate XIII).

RAPHAEL'S *DISPUTA*   79

implicit in the *Maiestas Domini* image which sometimes accompanies the feast.[37] In its All Saints' image, a fifteenth century Breviary from Treviso evokes the celestial liturgy of the Communion of Saints by showing God, between Mary and John the Baptist surrounded by a mandorla of seraphim, one of whom holds the Host.[38] This is a clear reference to the "Supplices te rogamus" of the Canon, "command these offerings to be borne by the hands of the holy Angel to Thine altar on high, in the sight of Thy divine majesty". Traditionally, there is cross-fertilization of the imagery of the Canon with that of All Saints' because of the relationship between their texts.[39] There is no standard way of depicting *all* the saints—Old Testament figures such as Adam, Eve, Moses and David may find a place, or the scheme can be extremely truncated showing only one class of saints, such as Virgin Martyrs or the Apostles.[40] Limitations of space, personal preference, workshop patterns and local litanic significance all bear on the choice of saints.

These observations are offered as a prologue to a reading of Raphael's *Disputa* as an All Saints' image, not because any direct visual relationship between these sources and his image will be posited, but to demonstrate that the pictorial treatment of All Saints is variable, that the notion of All Saints is inherent in the late Quattrocento altarpieces which Raphael "quotes" in his work, and that because of the latitude found in the deployment of specific figures and compositional arrangements in All Saints pictures, there is very little iconographical significance to be attached to the so-called "radical" changes found in Raphael's working sketches. Some have argued that these changes, which concern the number and placement of figures, imply that any programme for the work must have been ill-defined, vague and mutable.[41] But as Shearman demonstrates, the central germ of the picture—figures clustered in two tiers about the Trinity in an architectural setting—is apparent in the earliest study.[42]

While Gombrich has employed the analogy of a musician setting libretto to score in speaking of Raphael's achievement in the *Segnatura*, I shall use that of the stage director interpreting a script.[43] Raphael has "told" us as much. On the left side of the fresco the artist, his head still wrapped in the cloth which protects his hair from paint, stands poring over a book. His colleague Bramante turns to look at the

---

[37] Instances are cited in n. 29 above.

[38] Vat. ms Rossiani 125, f. 212^v (c. 1440).

[39] This is a point stressed by Sinding-Larsen, but worth re-iterating. The Ordinary of the Mass contains the following prayers referring to All Saints: *Confiteor*, "Oremus te Domine", "Per intercessionem", "Suspice sancta Trinitas", "Communicantes", "Nobis quoque peccatoribus", and "Libera nos". The Proper of All Saints recalls the Ordinary of the Mass in the Epistle (Apocalypse 7: 2–12) which relates the vision of the Lamb (i.e., the Eucharist), and in the Secret "Munera tibi", which recalls the Offertory. In the All Saints' Office the kinship with the whole Church Year is stressed and elements are taken from many other festal liturgies.

[40] Adam, Eve, Moses and David appear at All Saints in a *Golden Legend*, BN ms fr. 244–5. Female saints are accentuated in the Advent page of a Breviary from Treviso (Vat. ms Rossiani 125, f. 12) but frequently in Italian Breviaries only male saints are depicted at All Saints.

[41] Gombrich 97; Jones and Penny 60.

[42] Shearman, "Raphael's Unexecuted Projects...", 159.

[43] Gombrich 97.

80 CECILIA O'BRIEN

finished painting and gesticulates, indicating that it corresponds to the text. As a parallel reading of the text and image will show, the book is a Breviary, and Raphael's script is the Office for Matins of the Feast of All Saints; his task was to assemble its textual motifs into a visual whole.[44]

First let us turn to location or set. The actors are positioned within a sanctuary surrounding a high altar; in the background is a building under construction, most likely Julius' Belvedere. On the right-hand side is a massive incomplete pier, probably part of the new St. Peter's, the foundations of which had been hastily laid by Julius in 1506—much to the chagrin of some of the curia.[45] The figures, both terrestrial and celestial, fill the apse, made of the living stones of the Church as in Ephesians 2: 19–20, "You are citizens with the Saints and members of God's household; you are built upon the foundation of the Apostles and Prophets with Jesus Christ himself as the chief cornerstone".[46]

The location is the high altar of St. Peter's, a church associated with the institution of the Feast of All Saints by Gregory III, who had an oratory built there in honour of "all the holy Martyrs and Confessors and all the just who have reached their consummation".[47] As recounted in the *Golden Legend*, the high altar of this church was the site of the warden's vision of the celestial liturgy during Matins of the Feast of All Saints.[48] Turning to the Matins Office itself, we find an emphasis on church dedication. The legend of the Pantheon's conversion into a church for All Saints is narrated in its first Lesson from Pseudo-Bede, "Legimus in ecclesiasticis historiis". The theme of dedication is reiterated in the Response, "In dedicatione templi". In the fifteenth century in Northern Europe, the monstrance was similarly displayed on the altar during feasts of dedication.[49] The image of the Church founded atop a mountain, which occurs a number of times in the Office, is used in the Versicle and may be alluded to in the construction works in the left background of the *Disputa*.

The second Matins reading concerns the "knowledge of things divine" and is Trinitarian in essence, quoting Romans 11: 33–36, "O altitudo divitiarum sapientiae

---

[44] The Office is found in Vat. ms Urbinates lat. 112, a Roman curial Breviary. It replicates exactly the Franciscan *ordo* of Haymo of Faversham, which was derived from the thirteenth century curial Office and was standard for the use of Rome at least until the mid-sixteenth century; see S.J. Van Dijk, *The Sources of the Modern Roman Liturgy: The Ordinals of Haymo of Faversham and related documents (1243–1307)*, 2 vols., (Leiden: 1963) 2: 167–69. The text from which the first eight Matins Lessons are extracted is edited by J.E. Cross, "'Legimus in ecclesiasticis historiis': a Sermon for All Saints, and its Use in Old English Prose," *Traditio* 33 (1977): 101–35. The Responses and Versicles—which, naturally, do not occur in the sermon edited by Cross—are recorded below in the *Appendix*.

[45] For identification of the buildings, see Jones and Penny 60.

[46] This verse, the little chapter for Vespers of the Common of an Apostle, may be consciously evoked in the large cornerstone.

[47] P. Jounel, "The Year," *Liturgy and Time*, vol. 4 of *The Church at Prayer. An Introduction to the Liturgy*, eds. I.H. Dalmais, P. Jounel and A.G. Martimort (Collegeville: 1985) 115. For the cult at the Vatican, see P. Jounel, *Le Culte des Saints dans les Basiliques du Latran et du Vatican au douzième siècle*, Collection de l'École Française de Rome 26 (Rome: 1977) 397–98.

[48] The *Golden Legend* 647–48.

[49] King 137.

RAPHAEL'S *DISPUTA* 81

et scientie dei...'". This text was also the capitulum for the Office of the feast of Trinity Sunday. Above Raphael's Trinity are the numerous stars mentioned in the reading. The Response, "I saw the Lord sitting upon a high throne", evokes a Majesty theme, and in depicting the enthroned Christ showing his wounds, Raphael is using a type of *Maiestas* image common in Florentine liturgical manuscripts. In these, artists depict the Christ of the Second Coming as the Christ of the Ascension out of deference to the text of Acts 1: 11, "This Jesus, who was taken up from you into heaven, will come again in the same way as you saw him go."[50] Above Christ in the *Disputa* are the seraphim invoked in the Versicle. The third reading lauds the Virgin. Her worthiness to bear God, is emphasized in the Response. She sits, head inclined, as if awaiting the Coronation which is her reward. The fourth reading concerns the angelic hosts, liberally represented in Raphael's work—and refers consistently to their knowledge of divine matters echoing the *titulus* above the painting. Its Response weaves together the motifs of angels and dedication: "In the presence of the Angels, I will sing your praise; I will worship at your holy Temple". The angels venerate the Lord of Hosts in Julius' new basilica. The next Lesson deals with the prophets and patriarchs who "see God face to face". The relaxed pose of Adam conveys precisely this type of intimacy. The Response, "Precursor Domini", is taken from the liturgy of the feast of John the Baptist and stresses his primacy, "Nullus maior inter natos mulierum...'". Raphael has placed him on a dais elevated above the prophets and patriarchs and on the same level as the Virgin. The following reading describes the athletes of God, the apostles. The Response, "Iste sunt viventes...'", emphasizes their foundation of the Church and their reward in Heaven, *not* on earth. They are followed by the Martyrs.

The cast for the upper tier is complete. Representatives of each class seem to be chosen on account of their importance in Papal liturgy, their status as priests and prototypes of Julius, and because those depicted had been credited with direct vision of God and this is appropriate to their position in the picture.[51]

---

[50] Some Italian examples of the risen Christ as Christ of the Ascension are found in the following Breviaries in the Vatican Library: Chigiani C IV 108, f. 262^v (Florence, c. 1465); Rossiani 85, f. 130 (Modena, 1404); and Vat. lat. 4761, f. 132 (Tuscany, mid-fifteenth century). The image appears in Quattrocento Italy in the context of the Second Coming in the Canon of the Missal (e.g. Brussels, Bibl. Roy. Albert 1er de Belgique ms 9008) and in Advent in Evangelistaries (e.g. Firenze, Bibl. Medicea Laurenziana edili 115) and Missals (e.g. Aosta, Collegiati di Sant' Orso); see n. 29 above.

[51] The images are polysemous. For priesthood, the relevance of the apostles and deacons is obvious. Moses, David and Abraham are prototypes of Christ the priest and, as such, accompany "Te igitur" illustrations in Missals like that of Cardinal Bernadino de Carvajal (Sotheby's, *Western Manuscripts and Miniatures, Sale Tuesday 11th December, 1984;* lot 44). De Campos' tentative identification of the first figure on the right hand side as Judas Maccabeus would fit as the Maccabees are associated with priesthood and church dedication in the Roman liturgy.
With respect to papal and Roman liturgy, Saints Peter, Paul, John the Evangelist, Stephen and Lawrence were all a particular focus of the old Lateran liturgy. Saints Peter and Stephen were venerated at the Vatican; see Jounel, *Culte* 369. Judas Maccabeus recalls the martyred Maccabees venerated on Julius II's titular feast, S. Pietro in Vincoli (August 1). Peter's Liberation and a scene from Maccabees are juxtaposed in the *Stanza d'Eliodoro*.
With respect to seeing God: Saints Peter and John correspond to the Transfiguration, Moses to the Burning Bush, David to the Vision in the Wilderness, Abraham to the Vision of the Three Angels, and Paul to the Transport into third Heaven. Stephen and Lawrence are credited with seeing God in their liturgies (in the Responses to the third Lesson of Matins in their respective Offices).

82   CECILIA O'BRIEN

Pastor proposed a division between actual sight in the upper register—associating this with the Church triumphant—and unillumined faith in the lower register—associated with the faith of the Church militant on earth.[52] However, this distinction seems improbable because the lower register contains only deceased persons who would normally be regarded as saints or members of the Church Triumphant. The actions of the figures below are rather related to their identity as a class.

The penultimate Lesson of the Office and the last drawn from Pseudo-Bede deals with priests, Doctors and Confessors, the last of which was an extraordinarily loose category, accommodating any male who did not fit into another category of sainthood.[53] The Lesson tells us what the figures in the lower registrar are doing:

> Quorum mens lucidissima, manus vero plene sunt munditia; eo quod in mensa altaris sacrosancta Christi corporis et sanguinis mysteria celebrantes et in sui cordis penetrabilibus hostiam vivam, deoque placentem, id est semet ipsos sine macula atque amixtione pravi operis offere non desistant.[54]

The figures in the *Disputa*, holding their works—books—participate in the discourses of the terrestrial world but, nonetheless, continuously turn their lucid minds to the sacrifice on the altar. The visual disjunction between the static centre-point of the Host on its unadorned altar and the turbulent periphery with its animated figures captures this division between outer appearance and inner thought. Raphael has shown, as is appropriate in a library, the workings of the mind. The monstrance perfectly conveys the notion of a Mass which is not a Mass, for the monstrance was removed from the altar during papal Solemn Mass, as Paris de Grassis considered its exposition inappropriate when bishops would be seated and wearing mitres.[55] This explicit negation of "Canon of the Mass" content separates this image from other All Saints depictions in which there is a great deal of overlap permissible because they occur in multifunctional liturgical contexts, such as Missals and altarpieces. Greater clarity was required of Raphael's image because any ambiguity would distort the explicit meaning which, as will be argued, pertains to the patron.[56] Perhaps others contributed ideas which enriched the basic *invenzione*, among them Dominican court officials, as Ettlinger suggests.[57] It may even be that the artist himself

---

[52] Pastor 575–76.

[53] The cult of the Confessors (i.e., those who had endured torture, but not death, for the faith) constituted one of the first inroads into the Christian cult of the Martyrs; see Jounel, *The Year* 111. The term was then associated with local bishops. During the high Middle Ages the rise of the mendicants and the concomitant burgeoning of the Sanctoral saw an increase in the number of saints in this class.

[54] "Their minds are most pure and truly their hands are clean; on which account let them not cease to offer in celebration on the table of the altar the most holy sacrament of the body and blood of Christ and also in their inmost hearts the living victim, also pleasing to God—that is, themselves—without stain or taint of sin."

[55] See n. 24 above.

[56] In this context it is pertinent to note that the exposed Host was also a personal emblem of Julius, who had it carried before him in processional entries and triumphs. F. Hartt, "*Lignum Vitae* in Medio Paradisi: The *Stanza d'Eliodoro* and the Sistine Ceiling," *Art Bulletin* (1950): 120.

[57] H. S. Ettlinger, "Dominican Influences in the *Stanza della Segnatura* and the *Stanza*

RAPHAEL'S *DISPUTA* 83

augmented the invention.[58]

Whatever the nature and context of such additions, the central theme remains unmistakable. The focus here is on the Confessors and Doctors and priests with whom Julius identified as priest and arbiter of the faith, on those he honoured as authors of his religious library.[59]

There are a number of reasons why Julius may have selected this All Saints' text for illustration, among them the historical and apocryphal association of the feast with St. Peter's, the church which was to be his mausoleum. The choice may have been guided by familial piety, since his uncle Sixtus IV had raised the rank of the feast in the curial Calendar, endowing it with an octave.[60] Similar dynastic manipulation of liturgy has been observed by Gaston in his study of the Medici dealings in San Lorenzo, Florence.[61] But in the final analysis, the choice is in the best tradition of Renaissance library decoration—for the image is truly "all about Julius". The feast was central to his personal history, for it was in 1503 during the Vigil of All Saints that he was elected to the Papacy. Officially his reign dates from 1 November, thus the recitation of Matins ushered in the Julian "Golden Age".[62] Recorded on Urania's orb on the ceiling is the configuration of the constellations and planets seen in the Roman sky on that momentous and auspicious night in 1503.[63] By depicting the Matins Office of All Saint's Day in the *Disputa* Raphael shows, in a different guise, the state of the heavens at the time Julius was elected.

The astrological conceit leads us into a labyrinth constructed of yet more texts and enmeshes us in a description of another Imperial residence. In his rooms on the Palatine Septimius Severus had his birth stars painted on the ceilings and there, Dio Cassius relates, the Imperial horoscope was also depicted in other guises.[64] As we

---

d'Eliodoro," *Zeitschrift für kunstgeschichte* 46 (1983): 176–86. In the *Disputa* the inclusion of Fra Angelico and Savanorola may indicate Dominican influence. The juxtaposition of the work with the *School of Athens* recalls the preacher's *Triumphus crucis*: "Now just as the philosophers, by having before their eyes the order of the universe...arrived at an understanding of the divine Majesty...so we too, if we were to examine as closely as possible the image of the Triumph...we would gradually attain cognition of Christ's divinity." Translation from Sinding- Larsen, "Titian's Triumph of Faith and the medieval tradition of the Glory of Christ," *Acta ad Archaeologiam et Artium Historiam Pertinenta* 6 (1975): 320. Obviously the Vatican librarian and Paris de Grassis should also be considered as possible advisers.

[58] The inclusion of Dante is suggestive. His *Paradiso* is echoed in the work, but it is interesting to note that Raphael's activities as a poet coincide with the execution of the *Disputa*. He appears to have gone to some "trouble to demonstrate the equivalence of painting and poetry" at this time (John Onians, "On How to Listen to High Renaissance Art," *Art History* 7 (1984): 429).

[59] One could speculate that the warrior prelate, himself so enmeshed in profane concerns, was asserting that his heart, too, was "in the right place".

[60] A.A. King, *Liturgy of the Roman Church* (London, New York, Toronto: 1957) 206.

[61] R. Gaston, "Liturgy and Patronage in San Lorenzo, Florence, 1350–1650," *Patronage, Art and Society in Renaissance Italy*, eds. F.W. Kent and P. Simons (Clarendon: 1987) 111–34.

[62] *New Catholic Encyclopedia* (New York: 1967) 8: 52.

[63] Rash-Fabbri 100.

[64] *Dio's Roman History*, trans. E. Cary, Loeb Classical Library, vol. 9 (London: 1927) 260–61. A fifteenth century manuscript of the *Epitome* is the source of all extant versions of this particular passage—it is one of the treasures of the Vatican Library.
The conceit also seems to inform the decorative scheme of Isabella d'Este's study. Her wedding horoscope is enshrined in Mantegna's *Parnassus;* see P.W. Lehmann and K. Lehmann *Samothracian Reflections: Aspects of the Revival of the Antique* Bollingen Series CXII (Princeton: 1973).

turn to leave the *Stanza* and this literary maze, we face the *School of Athens* and see Ptolemy holding a globe marked with constellations. Do the mute philosophers also contribute to a discourse on intellectual and political *renovatio*? Is this, the most famous yet paradoxically silent, conversation in Western culture, all about Julius II and his stars?[65]

---

[65] I am especially grateful to Vera Vines for the invaluable advice and encouragement she has given me during the preparation of this article. Thanks are also due to Judith Collard and Russell Staiff, who commented on it earlier while in draft form.

RAPHAEL'S *DISPUTA* 85

Appendix

Feast Day of All Saints: Responses to Matins Lessons

First Nocturn

1st Response[66]
In dedicatione temple decantabant populus laudem. Et in ore eorum dulcis resonabat sonus ("At the dedication of the temple the people sang songs of praise. And the sweet music resounded in their mouths").
Versicle
Fundata est domus Domini supra verticem montium, et veniet ad eam omnes gentes ("The House of the Lord is established on top of the mountains, and to it all nations shall come").
2nd Response[67]
Vidi Dominum sedentem super solium excelsum et elevatum et plena erat omnis terra maiestate eius. Et ea, quae sub ipso erant, replebant templum ("I saw the Lord sitting upon a high and lofty throne, and all the earth was full of his majesty. And that which was beneath him filled the temple").
Versicle
Seraphim stabant super illud: sex ale uni: et sex ale alteri ("The Seraphim were standing above that: one had six wings and so did the other").
3rd Response[68]
Sancta et immaculata virginitas quibus te laudibus efferam nescio. Quia quem celi capere non poterant tuo gremio contulisti ("Holy and immaculate Virginity, I know not how to offer your praises. For you carried in your womb the One whom the heavens are not able to contain").
Versicle
Benedicta tu in mulieribus et benedictus fructus ventris tui. ("Blessed art thou among women and blessed is the fruit of thy womb.")

Second Nocturn

1st Response[69]
In conspectu Angelorum psallam tibi et adorabo ad templum sanctum tuum. Et confitebor nomini tuo, Domine. ("In the presence of the angels I will sing your praise; I will worship at your holy temple and give thanks to your name, O Lord.")

---

[66] *Source:* Office for the Dedication of a Church.
[67] *Source:* Office for the First Sunday of November.
[68] *Source:* Office for Christmas Day.
[69] *Source:* Office for the Feast of St. Michael the Archangel (Sept. 29).

86 CECILIA O'BRIEN

Versicle

Super misericordia tua et veritate tua quoniam magnificasti super nos nomen sanctum tuum. ("Because of your kindness and your truth; because you have made great your holy name before us.")

2nd Response[70]

Precursor Domini venit de quo ipse testatur. Nullus maior inter natos mulierum Iohanne Baptista. ("The Precursor of the Lord has come, about whom the Lord testifies. Among those born of women there is not a greater prophet than John the Baptist.")

Versicle

Hic est enim propheta, et plus quam propheta, de quo Salvator ait nullus. ("For this is a prophet, and he is more than a prophet, of whom the Saviour says, There is none...")

3rd Response[71]

Isti sunt viventes in carne plantaverant Ecclesiam sanguine suo. Calicem domini biberunt, et amici Dei facti sunt. ("Now we meet those who during their earthly lives planted the Church with their own blood. They drank the Chalice of the Lord and became God's friends.")

Versicle

In omnem terram exivit sonus eorum et in fines orbis terre verba eorum. ("Through all the earth their voices resound. And to the ends of the world, their message.")

Third Nocturn

1st Response[72]

Sancti mei, qui in carne positi certamen habuistis. Mercedem laboris ego reddam vobis. ("You, my holy ones, bitter conflict was your lot in the days of your mortal life. Now I will grant you reward for your sufferings.")

Versicle

Venite benedicti Patris mei percipite regnum. ("Come, blessed of my Father, take possession of the kingdom.")

2nd Response[73]

Sint lumbi vestri precincti et lucerne ardentes in manibus vestris. Et vos similes hominibus exspectantibus dominum suum quando revertatur a nuptiis. ("Your loins should be girt, and your hands should be holding lighted lamps. You should resemble servants who are awaiting their master as he returns from a wedding feast.")

Versicle

Vigilate ergo qui nescitis qua hora Dominus vester venturus sit. ("Be vigilant, for you do not know the hour at which your Lord will return.")

---

[70] *Source:* Office for the Birth of John the Baptist (June 24).

[71] *Source:* Office for the Common of an Apostle.

[72] *Source:* Office for the Common of several Martyrs.

[73] *Source:* Office for the Common of a Confessor not a Bishop.

Figure 32 Christ in Judgment. *Missal of Matthias Corvinus*, Brussels, Bibliothèque Royale ms 9008, f. 206; 400×280 mm.

Figure 33 Common of the Saints. *Breviary of Matthias Corvinus*, Vatican Urb. ms lat. 112, f. 555[v]; 272×393 mm.

Figure 34 Common of the Saints. *Breviary of Matthias Corvinus*, Vatican Urb. ms lat. 112, f. 556; 272×393 mm.

VI

An Unusual Pentecost Cycle in a Fourteenth Century Missal

Veronica Condon

Among the manuscripts left by Francis Douce to the Bodleian Library is a Fourteenth Century Franciscan Missal (Douce 313) which is remarkable for a number of reasons. Of particular interest is its exceptionally large programme of illustration: in addition to six full-page miniatures, it has twenty-four Calendar miniatures, some nine hundred and twenty smaller miniatures and many hundreds of figures of apostles, prophets and evangelist symbols which identify the authors of the texts.[1]

The manuscript is remarkable not only because of the extremely large number of illustrations it contains, but also because many of the smaller miniatures relate to subjects that were seldom illustrated in contemporary manuscripts. The head of the atelier—the artist who was responsible for the programme—must have had some help from a cleric, almost certainly a Franciscan priest, and although he followed many long-established artistic traditions, he often had to be both original and ingenious to keep each scene close to the words of the text. Each miniature depicts either an incident from the text, its opening words, its principal subject or its author. Nothing in the illustration of the manuscript is irrelevant or merely decorative.

This relationship between the miniature and the text is one of the most outstanding features of the Missal. It was intentional because the artist's objective was not only to illustrate the manuscript but to identify the texts so that they would be easy to find. Fully illustrated Missals like MS Douce 313 are rare: throughout the thirteenth and most of the fourteenth centuries the usual form of Missal illustration is a single full-page miniature or a very small number of historiated initials.[2]

---

[1] There are many miniatures which are divided into parts or placed in the margin as an appendage to the principal miniature. This makes it difficult to be precise as to their number; see Veronica Condon, *MS Douce 313, A Fourteenth Century Missal in the Bodleian Library, Oxford* (Melbourne, 1984) 77.

[2] Condon Chap. I, 1–4.

91

92   VERONICA CONDON

Although a small group of artists worked on the illustration of the Missal, it would have taken a long time to finish, and it must have been an important commission for the atelier.[3] Possibly it was ordered by a confrère who belonged to the Third Order of St. Francis and wanted a Missal for the church where he worshipped.[4] Figures of Franciscan priests who say Mass, preach, chant, pray and tend to the needs of their people recur throughout the series of miniatures. In addition, many of the Collects and a few of the Introit miniatures depict men who are not tonsured, but wear a form of religious habit. They are not all young, so it seems unlikely that they are intended to be novices of the First Order of St. Francis. While the depiction of such clothing could merely reflect the artist's desire to vary the appearance of the laity, it is evident that these figures do not occur in random fashion and that they usually occur in miniatures beside texts which could relate to the spiritual life and duties of a confrère. They are seen in Lent, Holy Week and during the season of Pentecost as well as at other times throughout the Liturgical Year. If these figures do represent confrères, they add even greater historical interest to the Missal because they give some insight into their lives. By contrast with the abundance of surviving documentation about Italian confraternities, very little can be found concerning Franciscan confraternities in medieval France.

There is little evidence for the very early provenance of MS Douce 313.[5] It is not until the sixteenth and seventeenth centuries that one can find definite links with Bonneval-les-Thouars and the great Benedictine Abbey of St. Jean. This evidence is a scribbled reference to Isabeau de Châtillon de Vivonne (Abbess of St. Jean, 1590–1632) on f. cccxxxix, an inscription on the front flyleaf to Elizabeth de Châtillon (Abbess, 1646–1668), and a note on the back flyleaf which records that the second last of the long line of the de Châtillon abbesses, Madeleine-Angelique-Marie (Abbess, 1676–1708) gave the manuscript to the provincial administrator F.J. Foucault in 1703.[6]

Manuscript Douce 313 would not have been commissioned for use in a large Benedictine Abbey such as St. Jean. Both its Sanctoral and its rubrics are inadequate for such a purpose, and even the scribbled marginal notes and cross-references add nothing specifically Benedictine to the text.[7]

How it came to the Abbey is still a mystery. One definite lead is in the history of the families of some of the abbesses: their names survive, but unfortunately there are no records of any other members of the community. These abbesses came from great families—de Sully, de Thouars, de Parthenay, de Brézé, de Rochechouart, de Chasteigner, de Maillé, de Vivonne, de Châtillon, and many others. Their lands often included towns and villages where a Franciscan house had been established

---

[3] Condon Chap. X, 68–72.

[4] I have argued this elsewhere: "The Franciscan Confrères in the Illustration of a Fourteenth Century Missal (MS Douce 313)," *Bodleian Library Record* (1988): 18–29.

[5] I have examined the evidence for the provenance in "The Mystery of the Provenance of a Fourteenth Century Missal," *Scriptorium* XXXV (1981): 295–303, and in "The Franciscan Confrères...," 18–29.

[6] See A.C. de la Mare in *The Douce Legacy*. (Bodleian Library: Oxford, 1984) 45.

[7] Condon, *MS Douce 313...*, 16.

AN UNUSUAL PENTECOST CYCLE 93

during the thirteenth and fourteenth centuries, either long before or at about the time the manuscript was illustrated.[8]

A Franciscan church, particularly when situated in a town, often had a lay confraternity attached to it. It is likely that many members of these noble families were Franciscan tertiaries and that one of them might have considered a Missal like MS Douce 313 a suitable offering to the church. The Missal need not have been presented to the friars. It may have been intended for use in the church but still been retained by the family. If, on the other hand, it had been presented to the friars, it may have been taken by them from one place to another since nothing in its text restricts its use to a particular church, diocese or Franciscan province.

The manuscript is unusual in that it illustrates almost all the Introits, Lessons, Epistles and Gospels of the Liturgical Year and the Commons of the Saints, Votive Masses and Requiem Masses. In the Sanctoral only the more important feasts have three miniatures. The minor feasts have only an Introit miniature because their Masses are largely comprised of cross-references to other texts. For each Votive Collect there is also a illustration. It is well worth examining the style and iconography of these miniatures to see how the artist in charge of the programme set about the task of illustrating such a vast number of texts without any duplication. His understanding of the text is not always good and he was limited by the comparatively small number of types of figures, faces, buildings, trees, animals (etc.) in the repertoire of the artists who worked with him on the manuscript. However, such is his ingenuity that, though some miniatures are similar, no two are exactly alike. I focus here on the Pentecost Cycle. It is rare for a Missal to have so many miniatures for the Vigil, Feast and Octave of Pentecost.

The Pentecost Cycle of MS Douce 313 [9]

MS Douce 313 illustrates the following texts:[10]

---

[8] See the relevant entries in J.H. Moorman's *Medieval Franciscan Houses* (New York, 1986). The following notes suggest areas, but not their precise lands which, of course, could be altered greatly either by war or by marriage contract:

Sully: it is doubtful that there was a Franciscan foundation here.
Thouars: founded either 1330 or 1358.
Parthenay: founded before 1269.
(de Chasteigner) Fountenay-le-Comte: founded before 1389.
(de Brézé) Saumur: founded before 1229.
(de Rochechouart) Soissons: founded in 1228.
(de Maillé) Fontenay-le-Comte and Tours, founded c. 1267.
(de Vivonne) Angôuleme: founded c. 1230, and Poitiers, founded in either 1248 or 1267.
(de Châtillon) Blois: founded by 1233. Châtillon (Burgundy) was founded in 1226, but there is no record of a Franciscan foundation in Châtillon-sur-Loire or in Montleon.
Brive: founded 1224.
Bourges: founded 1228.

[9] The comparative material which is cited here is only a small part of the material which has been studied.

[10] See Condon, *MS Douce 313...* 122–167 for the full catalogue.

Folio	Type	Incipit
clxxvii^v	Collect	(Vigil of Pentecost) Deus, qui in Abrahae famuli tui opere
clxxvii^a	Collect	Deus, qui primis temporibus implete miracula novi testamenti luce reserasti
clxxvii^b	Collect	Deus, glorificatio fidelium et vita justorum
clxxvii^{va}	Collect	Omnipotens sempiterne Deus, qui per unicum Filium tuum
clxxvii^{vb}	Collect	Deus, qui nobis per prophetarum
clxxviii^a	Collect	Domine Deus virtutum, qui collapsa reparas
clxxviii^b	Collect	Concede, quaesumus, omnipotens Deus: ut qui solemnitatem
clxxviii^{va}	Collect	Praesta, quaesumus, omnipotens Deus, ut claritatis tuae super nos splendor effulgeat
clxxviii^{vb}	Lesson	Factum est, cum Apollo esset Corinthi, et Paulus peragratis. Acts 19: 1–8
clxxix	Gospel	Si diligitis me. John 14: 15–21
clxxx (top)	Introit	(Pentecost) Spiritus Domini replevit orbem terrarum. Wisdom 1: 7
clxxx (bot.)	Lesson	Cum complerentur dies Pentecostes erant omnes discipuli pariter in eodem loco. Acts 2: 1–11
clxxx^v	Gospel	Si quis diligit me, sermonem meum servabit. John 14: 23–31
clxxxi	Introit	(Whit Monday) Cibavit eos ex adipe frumenti, alleluia. Ps. 80: 17
clxxxi^v	Lesson	Aperiens Petrus os suum, dixit: Viri fratres. Acts 10: 34, 42–48
clxxxii	Gospel	Sic Deus dilexit mundum. John 3: 16–21
clxxxii^{va}	Introit	(Whit Tuesday) Accipite jucunditatem gloriae vestrae, alleluia. 4 Esdras 2: 36–37
clxxxii^{vb}	Lesson	Cum audissent Apostoli, qui erant Jerosolymis. Acts 8: 14–17
clxxxiii	Gospel	Amen, amen, dico vobis, qui non intret per ostium in ovile ovium. John 10: 1–10
clxxxiii^{va}	Introit	(Whit Wednesday) Deus, dum egredereris coram populo tuo, iter faciens eis. Ps. 67: 8–9
clxxxiii^{vb}	Lesson	Simon Petrus cum undecim levavit vocem. Acts 2: 14–21
clxxxiv	Collect	Praesta, quaesumus, omnipotens et misericors Deus
clxxxiv^{va}	Lesson	Per manus autem Apostolorum. Acts 5: 12–16
clxxxiv^{vb}	Gospel	Nemo potest venire ad me, nisi Pater. John 6: 44–52
clxxxv	Introit	(Whit Thursday) Spiritus Domini replevit orbem terrarum. Wisdom 1–7

AN UNUSUAL PENTECOST CYCLE

Folio	Type	Incipit
clxxxv^{va}	Lesson	Philippus descendens in civitatem Samariae. Acts 8: 5–9
clxxxv^{vb}	Gospel	Convocatis Jesus duodecim Apostolis, dedit illus virtutum. Luke 9: 1–6. Note that the evangelist symbol for this Gospel is St. John's eagle and words before the miniature refer to St. John.
clxxxvi	Introit	(Ember Friday after Pentecost) Repleatur os meum laude tua, alleluia: ut possim cantare, alleluia. Ps. 70: 8, 23
clxxxvi^{va}	Lesson	Haec dixit Dominus Deus: Exsultate, filii Sion. Joel 2: 23–24, 26–27
clxxxvi^{vb}	Gospel	Factum est in una dierum, et Jesus sedebat docens. Luke 5: 17–26. The text is on the following page.
clxxxvii^{va}	Introit	(Whit Saturday) Caritas Dei diffusa est in cordibus nostris, alleluia. Romans 5: 5
clxxxvii^{vb}	1st Lesson	Haec dicit Dominus Deus: Effundam Spiritum meum super omnem carnem. Joel 2: 28–32
clxxxviii	2nd Lesson	Locutus est Dominus ad Moysen, dicens: Loquere filiis Israel. Levit. 28: 9–11, 15–17, 21
clxxxviii	3rd Lesson	Dixit Moyses filiis Israel: Audi, Israel, quae ego praecipio tibi hodie. Deut. 26: 1–3, 7–11
clxxxix	4th Lesson	Dixit Dominus ad Moysen: Loquere filiis Israel, et dices ad eos: Si in praeceptis meis. Levit. 26: 3–12
clxxxix^v	5th Lesson	Angelus Domini descendit cum Azaria et sociis ejus in fornacem. Daniel 3: 47–51
cxc^a	Collect	Deus, qui tribus pueris
cxc^b	Epistle	Justificati ex fide, pacem habeamus ad Deum. Romans 5: 1–5
cxc^v	Gospel	Surgens Jesus de synagoga, introivit in domum Simonis. Luke 4: 38–44

The Collects

Similar types of liturgical scenes to those which occur in MS Douce 313 are to be found in many manuscripts, but they do not usually illustrate Collects.[11]

There are ten Collect miniatures in the Pentecost Cycle of the Missal, eight for the Vigil, one for Pentecost Wednesday and one for Pentecost Saturday. These are quite simple scenes showing a priest before an altar with one or two of his congregation. These miniatures give no indication of the words of the prayer, and in this they differ from the illustration of the Votive Collects and the Collects of the Requiem

---

[11] Compare *Paris*, BN ms fr. 13342, a Fourteenth Century Anglo-Norman treatise on the Mass which has many miniatures that indicate what the congregation should do at various parts of the Mass. Compare also the numerous examples of miniatures of a priest before an altar that illustrate "Ad te levavi", the Introit for the first Sunday of Advent, or the Adoration of the Host at the "Te igitur".

96 VERONICA CONDON

Masses which always include either the subject or the object of the prayer. There are dozens of Collect miniatures throughout the Missal, but no two are alike. The artist varies the shape of the altar, the position of the chalice or book, the placement of the people; and he may add the Hand of God or the Dove of the Holy Spirit. He also varies the number and the clothing of the laymen. The miniatures for the Vigil (Figure 35) and Pentecost Wednesday include men who wear a form of religious habit indicating, presumably, that they are confrères—if it is true that MS Douce 313 was prepared for a Franciscan confraternity, then it would be appropriate for confrères to be depicted as present at Mass during the major seasons of the Liturgical Year.

The Introits

Some of the Introits of the Pentecost cycle are of subjects which were seldom illustrated, while others are based on earlier traditions which occur most frequently in Psalters or Bibles.

The first verse of the Introit of Pentecost Sunday is taken from the Book of Wisdom, where it was usual to illustrate the text with the figure of King Solomon. However, the artist of MS Douce 313 has sought to relate the miniature to the feast rather than to the author of the text. He has drawn a conventional Pentecost scene with the Dove of the Holy Spirit and with flames coming from it onto two groups of apostles below; his arrangement of the apostles into sharply divided groups separated by a central v-shaped space is reminiscent of some much earlier Psalter and biblical traditions.[12]

A more unusual subject is that of Pentecost Monday (Figure 36). The artist has followed the text exactly: "He fed them with the finest wheat, alleluia, and filled them with honey from the rock" (Ps. 80: 17), verses which were also used and illustrated for the Introit of the comparatively new feast of Corpus Christi. In the Pentecost Monday miniature the men are given the grains of wheat by the Hand of God and bees fly near a hive at the top of a rocky hill, while in the Corpus Christi miniature the same images are drawn and arranged quite differently.[13] There are several traditions for illustrating this Psalm, though not necessarily this verse; by far the most common illustration is that of David playing bells or another musical instrument. Other illustrations showed Jacob wrestling with an angel or men carrying the Ark of the Covenant, none of which the artist would have found appropriate when

---

[12] Compare, for example:
Paris, BN ms lat. 11560; Moralized Bible, f. 94, 12th century.
London, Collection of E.G. Millar, *Le Somme de Roi*; f. 10 ͮ, 14th century.
Munich, Staatsbibl. cod. lat. 15903; Gospel Book, f. 63, 14th century.
Lyons, Bibl. de la Ville ms 5122; Missal of the Sainte-Chapelle, f. 179, 14th century.
Brussels, Bibl. Royale ms 25513–25517; Breviary of Mary of Burgundy, f. 118, 14th century.
New York, Spencer Library MS 2; Psalter, f. 8ͮ, 14th century.
Paris, BN ms lat. 10483–84; Belleville Breviary, f. 422, 14th century.
Some miniatures include the Virgin Mary:
Avignon, Musée Calvet ms 121; Hours-Psalter, f. 40, 14th century.
Baltimore, Walters Gallery MS 62; Responsorial, f. 126, 14th century.
[13] Corpus Christi, f. cxci.

AN UNUSUAL PENTECOST CYCLE

the text was used to symbolise Holy Communion.[14]

Occasionally the artist makes mistakes, as he has done in the miniature for Pentecost Tuesday. Here he has substituted David for Esdras, the author of the text. Esdras was often illustrated, particularly in Bibles and moralized Bibles, but the artist has chosen to focus on the words "God has called you to a heavenly kingdom" (4 Esdras 2: 36–37), and has drawn David with a crown, holding a harp and gazing up to God who is commanding an angel to place crowns on the heads of the two people who stand before him (Figure 37).[15]

Another unusual miniature is that for Pentecost Wednesday: Christ and a small group of people watch as a little crowned figure climbs a ladder towards an angel in heaven. The Introit begins "Oh God! When thou didst go forth in the sight of thy people, making a passage for them" (Ps. 67: 8–9). It is difficult to relate this scene to any other miniature, although it is likely that the ladder goes back to a tradition where this Psalm was illustrated with the story of Jacob's Ladder.[16] The king climbing the ladder is probably David, since the artist rarely omits the author or introduces an irrelevant figure. Another possibility is that he is St. Louis, King of France, who was a great benefactor to the Order of Friars Minor. He has omitted the author again in the Introit for Pentecost Friday. Here a priest chants, thus depicting the words of the Introit: "Let my mouth be filled with Thy praise, alleluia, that I may sing" (Ps. 70: 8, 23).

In the last of this group of Introits, that of Pentecost Saturday, the artist has mistakenly drawn St. John instead of St. Paul who usually appears beside passages from his Epistles. Here the identification of the feast must have seemed of more importance since the image of the Holy Spirit is shown with its rays falling down upon the Romans to illustrate the verse "The charity of God is poured forth in our hearts, alleluia, by his Spirit dwelling in us" (Romans 5: 5).[17]

The Lessons

The miniatures for the Lessons illustrate subjects from both the Old and New Testaments; they vary considerably in the amount of detail they take from the text. The

---

[14] Examples occur in the following manuscripts:
"David playing bells": Cambridge, Fitz. MS 369; Breviary-Missal, part 1. f. 121ᵛ, 14th century; and Lausanne Bibl. Cant. and Univ. ms 964; Bible, f. 213ᵛ, 13th century.
"Ark of the Covenant": CUL MS Ee.4.24; Psalter, f. 22, second half of the 13th century.
"Jacob wrestling with an angel": Baltimore, Walters Gallery MS 34; Psalter and Hours, f. 55, 13th century; and Belvoir Castle, Library of the Duke of Rutland; Psalter, f. 84, 13th century.

[15] *The Bylling Bible* (BN ms. lat. 11935, f. 222) illustrates the book of Esdras with a detailed scene quite unrelated to the miniature of MS Douce 313.

[16] There are many illustrative traditions for this Psalm; they include the "Mouth of Hell", "Christ trampling on the gates of Hell", "Moses with Aaron", and "Jacob's Ladder". "Jacob's Ladder" is employed quite frequently; see, for example:
Brussels, Bibl. Royale ms 9961–62; Psalter, f. 90 ᵛ, 13th century.
New York, Spencer Library, Public MS 22; Miscellany, f. 25, c. 1300.
Paris, BN ms lat. 10525; Psalter of St. Louis, f. 3ᵛ, c. 1270.

[17] An example where the miniature includes the Holy Spirit is BN ms lat. 11534–35; Bible II, f. 300 ᵛ, 12th century.

98   VERONICA CONDON

first of these Lessons, that for the Vigil of Pentecost, depicts St. Paul speaking boldly in the synagogue of Ephesus (Figure 38). The traditional illustration for this text is *Apollo at Corinth*, who is referred to at the beginning of the Lesson, while St. Paul in the synagogue is not mentioned until the end. It is unusual for the artist to take an image from the last part of the text. For the Lesson for Pentecost he has drawn the City of Jerusalem, the seated apostles, a few of the devout of every nation and the coming of the mighty wind— all of which are mentioned in the text (Figure 39). The wind is blown from a trumpet, which is characteristic of apocalyptic illustrations (from time to time throughout the Missal the artist reveals his dependence on such manuscripts).[18]

The Lesson for Pentecost Monday is again a subject which was not often illustrated; once more the images are taken directly from the text: St. Peter opening his mouth, God commanding him to speak to the people, God as the judge of the living and the dead, the grace of the Holy Spirit poured down upon the gentiles, and St. Paul baptizing in the name of the Lord. The illustration for Pentecost Tuesday is almost as detailed, for it includes the apostles, the messenger who tells them that Samaria has received the word of the Lord, and St. Paul and St. John in Samaria laying their hands on the people so that they may receive the Holy Spirit. By contrast, the illustration for Pentecost Wednesday is a simple didactic scene. Here too the artist has made a mistake: St. Peter is described as standing with the eleven; but the artist has included too many haloes in the group of apostles. He follows tradition in his inclusion of the People of Judea.

The miniature for Pentecost Thursday shows St. Philip healing the man who had an unclean spirit. This particular text is seldom illustrated, though there are numerous examples of miniatures which depict similar cures. The artist frequently uses the image of a devil to indicate unclean spirits or evil deeds and temptations— for example, on Thursday of Holy Week a devil clings to Judas' back as the High Priests give him the thirty pieces of silver.[19]

In the miniature for Pentecost Friday the artist depicts Joel telling the Children of Sion to "be joyful and to rejoice in the Lord" (Joel 2: 23–24, 26–27). This admonition was rather too hard for the artist to convey, though it is surprising that he did not read more of the text and find images that were easy to draw, such as rain, wheat, or the presses overflowing with wine and oil. However, as with Esdras, comparable miniatures of Joel are mostly in Bibles and moralized Bibles and indicate the beginning of a book of the Old Testament rather than an episode from it.

Pentecost Saturday is an Ember Saturday, and a larger number of Lessons than usual are read at Mass. In the first of these the artist has been careless once more. The miniature illustrates the text which alludes to the young men who see visions

---

[18] The similarities are in scenes of hillsides strewn with bones or with animals grazing on them; in details such as trumpets, flames, clouds, islands, and streams of water. See, for example:

f. xcv^a: Introit, Saturday, 4th week in Lent.

f. cxl: 1st Prophecy, Holy Saturday.

f. xxlviii^v: 7th Prophecy, Holy Saturday.

[19] Folio cxxv^v: Gospel, Wednesday in Holy Week.

AN UNUSUAL PENTECOST CYCLE

and the old men who dream dreams, but here all the men on the hillside are young (Figure 40). The second Lesson begins: "The Lord spoke to Moses saying: Speak to the Children of Sion" (Levit. 28: 9–11, 15–17, 21). There are many comparable miniatures where God speaks to Moses, but none (to my knowledge) where God leans out of a temple window to do so. The scene does not appear to be dependent on another manuscript; rather it is an adaptation of another miniature in MS Douce 313, where St. John the Baptist leans out of his prison window to speak to some of his disciples.[20] The third Lesson is a very simple scene with Moses and the Children of Israel standing by sheaves, the first fruits of their harvest. The miniature for the fourth Lesson is another didactic scene, which illustrates the text "The Lord said to Moses: Speak to the Children of Israel" (Levit. 26: 3–12). The artist has placed the Children of Israel behind Moses, but he has not included any of the other textual images such as the harvest or the vintage.

The last of these Lessons tells the story of Azarias and his companions in the fiery furnace. It is a subject which was often illustrated, sometimes simply and sometimes in detail. Two versions appear in MS Douce 313, a simpler one for Saturday of Ember Week in Advent, while the miniature for Pentecost Saturday takes a number of precise images from the text: "The angel of the Lord went down with Azarias and his companions into the furnace... he drew the flame of the fire our of the furnace and made the midst of the furnace like a blowing wind...and the flames mounted up above the furnace...and it broke forth and burned such of the Chaldeans as it found near the furnace, the servants of the king" (Dan. 3: 46–50).[21]

The Epistles

With few exceptions, the artist illustrates St. Paul's Epistles with the figure of St. Paul, his messenger, and the people to whom he addresses his letter (Figure 41). This is the traditional way of illustrating the Epistles.[22] What is so interesting about these particular miniatures is the way in which the artist has managed to vary the clothes, gestures, stance, background and general arrangement of the scenes so that no two miniatures are alike. In Figure 41 St. Paul is that strange, distorted figure

---

[20] Folio 11: Gospel, Second Sunday in Advent.
[21] Some other simple versions are:
  Geneva, Bibl. Publique et Univ. ms fr. 2; Bible Historiale, f. 189, 14th century.
  Cambridge, Fitz. MS 43–1950; *Speculum humanae salvationis,* no. 24, 14th century.
Some more detailed versions are found in the following:
  Manchester, John Rylands Library MS 17; Bible, f. 231, 13th century.
  BN ms lat. 11560; Moralized Bible f. 204, 13th century.
  Dijon, Bibl. Communale ms 12–15; Bible III, f. 64, 12th century.
[22] See, for example:
  BL Harl. MS 1526–27; Moralized Bible, II, fols. 95 and 108, 13th century.
  BL Burney MS 3; Bible of Robert of Battle, f. 496, 13th century.
  Geneva, Bibl. Publique et Univ. ms fr. 2; Bible Historiale, fols. 436, 442, 443^v, 444^v, 446, 448^v, 14th century.
  BN ms lat. 11935, *The Bylling Bible*; fols. 570, 577 ^{v}, 584, 588^v, 590, 600, 602, 602^v, 14th century.

100 VERONICA CONDON

that appears frequently throughout the illustration of the Missal and also occasionally in *The Bylling Bible, The Hours of Jeanne d'Évreux, The Belleville Breviary* and the Geneva Bible Historiale. The long waisted gown of the messenger does not suggest a date of the 1360s, since similar figures are also seen occasionally in the Pucelle manuscripts of the 1320s and 1330s. One should keep in mind the tenuous link between MS Douce 313 and Pucelle's atelier.[23]

The Gospels

Among the eight Gospels of the Pentecost Cycle there are three with miniatures which give no indication of the text, apart from showing that Christ is speaking to the apostles. For the Vigil and the Feast of Pentecost it would have been difficult for the artist to convey the admonitions that begin these Gospels: "If you love me, keep my commandments" (John 14: 15) and "If anyone love me, he will keep my word" (John 14: 23). However, he could have introduced Nicodemus into the miniature for Pentecost Monday, since his name occurs at its very beginning and he is often included in illustrations of this text in other manuscripts.[24]

A gateway behind the apostles is the only indication that the Gospel for Pentecost Tuesday tells the Parable of the Sheepfold. The artist has either ignored or perhaps not known the imagery traditionally used for this theme—Christ the Good Shepherd, scenes with sheepfolds or fields of grazing sheep tended by shepherds.[25] Nor has he followed any of the traditions of quite detailed illustration of the Gospel for Pentecost Thursday, where Christ gives power and authority to the disciples and sends them forth on their mission.[26] Perhaps the artist had not realized that this was a passage from St. Luke, for the eagle of St. John is mistakenly included in the miniature.

He went back to his usual practice of following the first words very literally when he illustrated the text "No man can come to the Father except the Father who has sent me draw him" (John 6: 44), words which introduce the Gospel for Pentecost Wednesday. Here Christ watches as God the Father leans down from a heavenly cloud to gather into his arms St. John, St. Peter and a small group of the apostles (Figure 42).[27]

Only two of the Gospels of this cycle show any dependence on popular tradition. The story of the man stricken with palsy is told in the Gospel of Pentecost Friday. Here Christ is seated as the sick man is brought before him in a little two-wheeled cart (Figure 43). This contrasts with the usual scenes where the man's bed

---

[23] See Condon, *MS Douce 313...* Chap. IX, 51–57, "MS Douce 313 and the problems of its relationship to the atelier of Jean Pucelle".

[24] For example, in BL Add. MS 47692, the Holkham Bible Picture Book; f. 20 ᵛ, 14th century.

[25] Examples are found in:
BL Add MS 17341, Gospel book of the Sainte-Chapelle; f. 97 (two scenes), 13th century.
BN ms lat. 17326, Gospel book of the Sainte-Chapelle; f. 99, 13th century.
Munich, Staatsbibl. cod. Clm. 15903, Pericope; f. 51, 14th century.

[26] An example is found in Florence, Bibl. Laur. ms Plut. VII.23, Gospel Book; f. 19, 11th century.

[27] Other illustrations of this text generally show Christ teaching.

AN UNUSUAL PENTECOST CYCLE

is either let down from the roof of a building, or he is carried in his bed to Christ, or else he is shown carrying his bed away after he is cured.[28]

The Gospel of Pentecost Saturday tells of the cure of Simon Peter's wife's mother.[29] The images are drawn directly from the narrative—Christ leaving the synagogue and entering the house where the mother is seated in bed. However the artist has ignored the tradition of including St. Peter and his wife or some of the apostles, substituting for them two of the people who have come to him to be cured of disease. They do not belong to this part of the Gospel, but to a later passage from it.

The artist seems to be both limited and uneven in his understanding of the Gospels of the Pentecost Cycle. Twice he has kept to the narrative and once he has followed the text in a literal and imaginative way, but he appears to be less concerned with the relevance of the Gospel miniatures for the text than he was with those of the Introits and the Lessons.

These miniatures of the Pentecost Cycle reflect the way in which the artist has approached his task of preparing miniatures for the whole of the manuscript. He is aware of traditions, he keeps closely to the text, yet he is inconsistent in his understanding of it.

Very little of the programme of MS Douce 313 is reminiscent of the relatively small number of profusely illustrated Missals that have survived from the middle of the Fourteenth Century.[30] Comparison, for example, with the *Missal of St. Denis* in the Victoria and Albert Museum, the Lyon Missal for the Use of Paris and the somewhat later Franciscan Missal and Book of Hours in the Bibliothèque Nationale reveals great differences in style, iconography and in the choice of texts for illustration.[31] It is also rare to find a detailed programme for Pentecost and its Octave in Missals with a much smaller number of miniatures.

Since the artist had so many subjects to illustrate he had to turn to a number of sources—Gospel Books, Bibles, Psalters and many others—to find scenes he could copy or adapt. When these failed him he had to improvise, and in this he was successful. Just as the miniatures were intended to make it easy for the priest to find his place in the Missal during Mass, so also they make it possible for us, some six hundred years later, to find our way quite easily amongst the Introits, Collects, Lessons, Epistles and Gospels of a Fourteenth Century manuscript.[32]

---

[28] Examples are found in: BN ms ital. 115, Pseudo-Bonaventure; fols. 88 and 88^v, 14th century; Stockholm, Mus. Nat. ms B.1713, a miniature from a Gospel Book, 13th century.

[29] Other examples of illustration of this text are found in: BL Harl. MS 1526–27, Moralized Bible II; f. 25, 13th century; BN ms gr. 54, Gospel Book; f. 114^v, 13th-14th century; BN ms ital. 115, Pseudo-Bonaventure; f. 89^v, 14th century.

[30] See Isa Ragusa, "The Missal of Cardinal Roselli," *Scriptorium* XXX (1975): 47.

[31] London, Victoria and Albert Museum MS A.M. 1346–1891, 14th century; Lyons, Bibl. de la Ville ms 5122; 14th century; and BN ms lat. 757, 14th century.

[32] I should like to thank the librarians of the following institutions for allowing me to consult manuscripts in their collections: the Bodleian Library, the British Library, the Bibliothèque Royale, Brussels, the Bibliothèque Publique et Universitaire, Geneva, the Bibliothèque Nationale, and the Pierpont Morgan Library. I am grateful also for having been given access to the resources of the Index of Early Christian Art at Princeton University, and to Dr. Isa Ragusa, Dr. Adelaide Bennett and Miss Jean Preston who have given to me so much help and encouragement.

Figure 35 Collect for the Vigil of Pentecost. Oxford, Bodleian Library MS Douce 313, f. clxxviiᵃ; 273×216 mm.

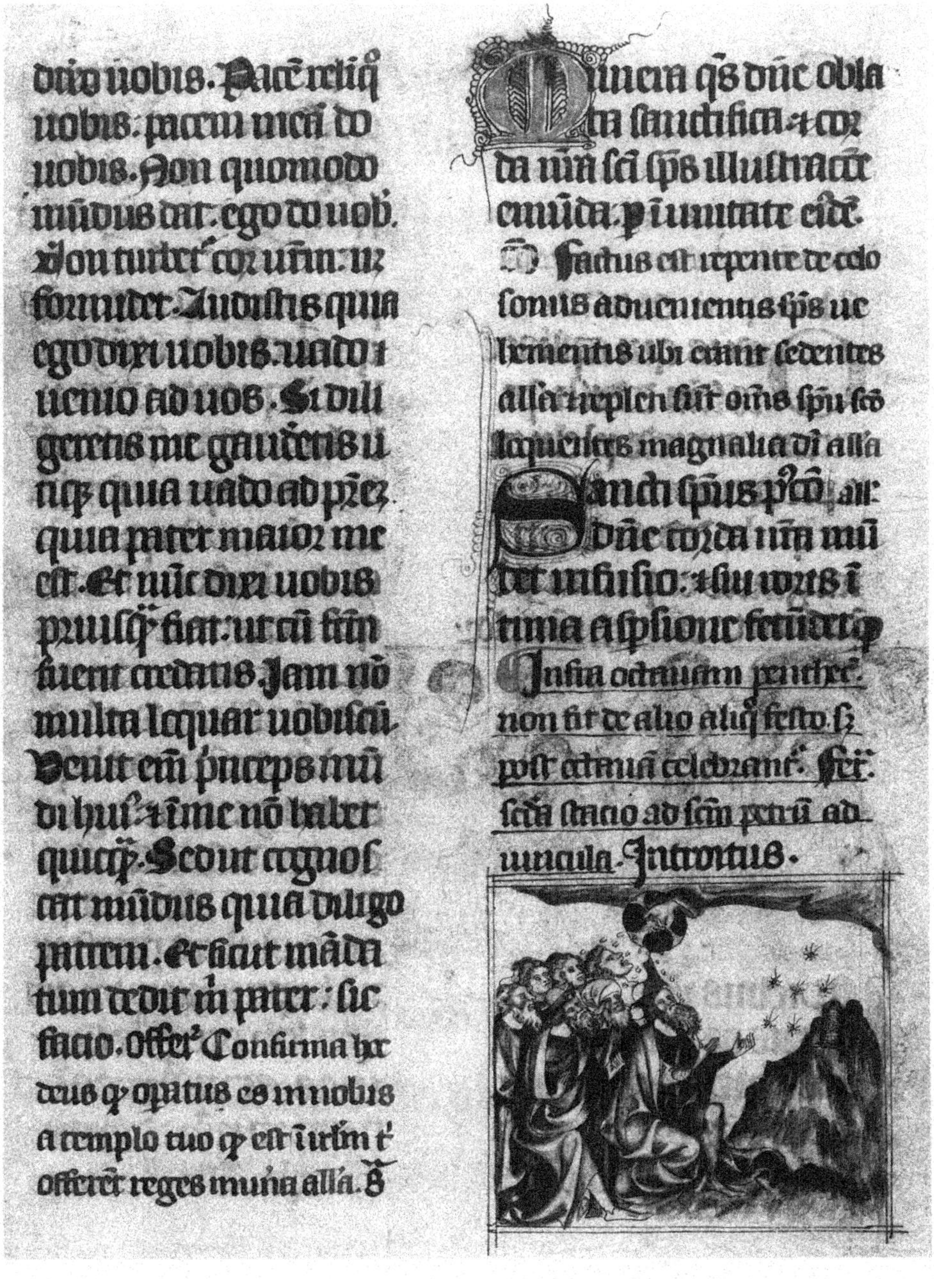

Figure 36 Introit for Pentecost Monday. Oxford, Bodleian Library MS Douce 313, f. clxxxi; 273×216 mm.

Figure 37 Introit for Pentecost Tuesday. Oxford, Bodleian Library MS Douce 313, f. clxxxii[va]; 273×216 mm.

Figure 38 Lesson for the Vigil of Pentecost. Oxford, Bodleian Library MS Douce 313, f. clxxviii[vb]; 273×216 mm.

Figure 39 Lesson for the Feast of Pentecost. Oxford, Bodleian Library MS Douce 313, f. clxxx[a] (bottom); 273×216 mm.

Figure 40 Lesson for Pentecost Saturday. Oxford, Bodleian Library MS Douce 313, f. clxxxvii[vb]; 273×216 mm.

Figure 41 Epistle for Pentecost Saturday. Oxford, Bodleian Library MS Douce 313, f. cxc[b]; 273×216 mm.

Figure 42 Gospel for Pentecost Wednesday. Oxford, Bodleian Library MS Douce 313, f. clxxxiv[vb]; 273×216 mm.

Figure 43 Gospel for Pentecost Tuesday. Oxford, Bodleian Library MS Douce 313, f. clxxxvi[vb]; 273×216 mm.

VII

A Minimally-intrusive Presence: Portraits in Illustrations for Prayers to the Virgin

Joan Naughton

The extra-liturgical prayers in honour of Mary most frequently illustrated in fifteenth-century French and Flemish Books of Hours are the *Obsecro te, O intemerata* and "The Fifteen Joys of the Virgin".[1] Based often on the theme of the Virgin and Child their illumination is relatively free of the narrative emphasis that characterizes the illustration of the Offices in these manuscripts.[2] The accent is rather on the pictures' devotional function. Placed at the beginning of the prayer, they focus attention on Mary, to whom the text is addressed, and serve to arouse in the devotee an appropriate contemplative mood, either through their invitation to shared intimacy with a tenderly accessible Mother and Child,[3] or through their presentation of a devotional exemplar.[4] Affective elements inform even the most hieratic themes

---

[1] The texts of the *Obsecro te* and one of the two distinctly different prayers beginning *O intemerata* (to the Virgin and St. John the Evangelist) are translated in R.S. Wieck, *Time Sanctified: The Book of Hours in Medieval Art and Life* (New York: 1988) 163ff. For the text of the other *O intemerata* (to the Virgin only) and "The Fifteen Joys of the Virgin" see V. Leroquais, *Les Livres d'Heures* (Paris: 1927) 3: 336ff. and 310ff. respectively.

[2] From a consideration of more than a thousand Books of Hours, Wieck lists the broad variety of illumination which most frequently encompasses the theme of Virgin and Child: the Virgin may be depicted as Virgin of Humility, *Virgo lactans* or Virgin of Mercy; she may offer the Christ Child fruit; the theme may be widened to include St. Joseph. Pietà and Lamentation scenes are also common (Wieck 94–96, 103). My own study is revealing an extraordinary breadth of thematic material and detail associated with this theme; the illustrations appear to be accorded a considerable freedom, sometimes moving well away from the content of the prayer. For illustrations of the Hours of the Virgin and other Offices in Books of Hours see J. Harthan, *Books of Hours and their Owners* (London: 1977); and R.S. Wieck.

[3] S. Ringbom, *Icon to Narrative: The Rise of the Dramatic Close-Up in Fifteenth-Century Devotional Painting* 2nd ed. (Doornspijk: 1984) 12ff.; J.H. Marrow, "Symbol and Meaning in Northern European Art of the Late Middle Ages and the Early Renaissance," *Simiolus* 16 (1986): 151–53.

[4] C. Harbison, "Visions and Meditations in Early Flemish Painting," *Simiolus* 15 (1985): 101.

112 JOAN NAUGHTON

such as the Apocalyptic Woman "clothed with the sun, the moon under her feet" (Figure 45),[5] and the Christ Child often exhibits a playful interest in his surroundings, as for example in his preoccupation with the instruments of attendant angel musicians. Most emotive, perhaps, and allied to the continued reiteration of Christ's humanity, are the implied references to his impending Passion in the sad, foreknowing expression of the Virgin (Plate 3) and the naked body of the Child with stiffly-hanging arm presaging scenes of the Deposition and Lamentation (Figure 49).[6]

Just as the illustration of the Hours of the Virgin serves to mark the canonical divisions of this Office, so also the illumination which accompanies the Marian prayers helps to clarify the hierarchical ordering of particular elements within the book.[7] Thus, the frequency with which the prayers attract large miniatures indicates their importance to the patron, relative to other devotional texts. While these illustrations clearly serve the double function of devotional aid and significant bookmark, it is more difficult to ascertain the precise nature of their relationship to the prayers they precede. Are the two necessarily linked, or can the image function independently of its textual accompaniment? Are these paintings essentially equivalent to the very similar miniatures of Virgin and Child which occur in Books of Hours as free-standing 'frontispieces', presumably intended as an aid to purely imaginative contemplation rather than to a devotion which is largely verbal?[8] The rubrics to these prayers always refer to the efficacy of saying (or even just carrying) the prayer itself. An appropriate emotional state is suggested less often, and then the rubric merely states that the prayer should be said *devote*[9] or *dévotemente*[10] or *bono et puro corde;*[11] or it may comment that Thomas of Canterbury recited such prayers *cum magna devotione.*[12] It would seem, therefore, that for their recitation no specific

---

[5] Revelations 12:1. More emotive still is the conflation of this imagery or the majestic theme of the Virgin and Child in a Glory with that of the Eleousa-type Virgin and Child, where the Child's arms are affectionately placed around his mother's neck while their faces gently touch, a popular amalgamation appearing early in fifteenth century Paris (M. Meiss, *French Painting in the Time of Jean de Berry. The Limbourgs and their Contemporaries* (London: 1974) Figures 388–391, pp. 138–140, 268).

[6] For discussion of the equivalence of sleeping Child and Pietà in both text and image see E. Panofsky, "Reintegration of a Book of Hours executed in the workshop of the 'Maître des Grandes Heures de Rohan'," *Medieval Studies in the Memory of A. Kingsley Porter*, ed. W.R.W. Koeler (Cambridge, Mass.: 1939) 2: 490ff.

[7] See M.B. Parkes' discussion of the development of the ordering of the contents of books by careful compilation and by separating items by illustrative means: "The Influence of the Concepts of Ordinatio and Compilatio on the Development of the Book," *Medieval Learning and Literature: Essays Presented to Richard William Hunt*, eds. J.J.G. Alexander and M.T. Gibson (Oxford: 1976) 115–41.

[8] For medieval theory concerning devotional technique, and the compromise regarding the superiority of non-corporeal devotion by theologians such as Jean Gerson in early fifteenth century Paris at a time when contemplative meditation was increasingly being taken up by the laity, see S. Ringbom "Devotional Images and Imaginative Devotions: Notes on the Place of Art in Late Medieval Private Piety," *Gazette des Beaux-Arts* 6th ser. 73 (1969): 162–66.

[9] See, for example, Cambridge, Fitz. MS 9–1951, f. 110, a Book of Hours; and Paris, BN Donation Smith-Lesouëf, ms lat. 759, f. 78 ^{V}, a Book of Hours and Missal.

[10] See, for example, Cambridge, Fitz. MS 3–1954, f. 263, a Book of Hours; and Besançon, Bibl. Mun. ms 140, f. 218, a Psalter and Book of Hours.

[11] See, for example, Paris, BN ms lat. 757, f. 427 ^{V}, a Book of Hours and Missal; and Cambridge, Fitz. MS 338, f. 154, a Book of Hours.

[12] See Vienna, Öst. cod. 1857, f. 15, a Book of Hours.

A MINIMALLY INTRUSIVE PRESENCE

devotional mood was recommended. This allowed scope for varied illumination and for an even greater variety of associative thought on the part of the reader.

There is, however, a complication. In these compositions the patron is frequently portrayed at prayer. This involves a change in reference on the part of the user of the book. Such imagery may be logically interpreted as reflecting a devotional state already attained as the result of the contemplative exercise. Indeed, the patron is almost invariably depicted with unfocused gaze; the religious image thus becomes an extension of his / her inner thoughts, while the book, the initial impetus leading to this state, lies open but unheeded on the *prie-dieu* (Figure 45).[13]

Illustrations in which the patron appears, therefore, as well as acting as a devotional stimulus also direct the attention of the reader (whether the original patron or later user) to the achievement of this activity. They are both a means to devotion and the visualisation of its result.

There is yet another aspect to consider. The Virgin and Child in such scenes are often shown interacting with the patron. The Christ Child may finger the patron's rosary or accept a banderole which invokes the Virgin's aid "O mater Dei memento mei" (Plate 3) in the same playful fashion as he treats the angel musicians.[14] The sacred pair may also acknowledge the presence of the patron with a glance or gesture (Figure 50). A complex set of relationships is thus set up by the introduction of the patron into this type of affective illustration. Not only do the Virgin and Child interact with the portrayed patron; but also to be taken into account is the relationship between the user of the book and the portrait, as well as the nature of the affective response invited by the religious image. How then did the artist deal with the challenge of including the patron in these illustrations? Was it possible in such circumstances to maintain the viewer-directed devotional nature of the Virgin and Child? One means of answering this question is to examine closely how the pictures function visually. To this end I shall discuss a number of illustrations which I consider to offer a variety of artistic solutions to the problem.

Confronted by the folio which introduces the *Obsecro te* in the *Hours of Isabella Stuart* (Plate 3) from the Rohan Master's workshop, the viewer's attention is immediately claimed by the image of the Virgin and Child, situated near the top of the miniature which itself occupies the upper part of the page. The conspicuous lapis lazuli blue of the introductory rubric "Oracio beate Marie" overwhelms the sepia text below, and forces a link with the large mass of matching rich colour in the Virgin's mantle, while the three dimensional pattern of the intervening floor mounts inexorably and uni-directionally towards the sacred pair. Once arrived the viewer stays easily with the devotional image: the three-quarter frontal rendering of both

---

[13] The interpretation of devotional images which include owner or patron participation as a reflection of his or her contemplative state of mind is argued in Ringbom, "Devotional Images" 164–66; A. H. van Buren, "The Canonical Office in Renaissance Painting, Part II: More About the Rolin Madonna," *Art Bulletin* 60 (1978): 624–26; and Harbison 96–105.

[14] See, for example, the miniatures related to the Boucicaut Master in Paris, BN ms Lat. 1161 f. 130 ᵛ and Nouv. Acq. ms lat. 3107 f. 232 ᵛ (M. Meiss, *French Painting in the Time of Jean de Berry. The Boucicaut Master.* (London: 1968) Figures 204 and 220).

JOAN NAUGHTON

Virgin and Child together with their shared golden tones of flesh, hair, haloes and dress, reinforces their centrality. The flowing diagonal rhythm, which passes from the Virgin through Christ to the rosary and the banderole which he holds, is halted before reaching the patron and St. Catherine by the gap which isolates their visual plane from that of the dominant Virgin and Child. Patron and saint, smaller in size and crowded into the corner, occupy less space than the Virgin and Child. Their forms are sketchy, especially that of the patron, whose garment is given a disconcertingly piecemeal heraldic pattern.[15] They offer little visual challenge to the monumental shape and richly shadowed modelling of the drapery which describes the devotional pair. Even the banderole, though conceptually a link between the two groups, visually isolates them by forming a delimiting line. As a result the patron's space in the picture is rendered as separate from that apportioned to the sacred pair. Nor does it impede the viewer's access to them. Thus, while the inclusion of the patron's portrait means that the Virgin and Child may be read as a depiction of her own contemplative experience, and despite the depicted interaction between the two groups, the devotional image can still function, in association with the text, as an uninterrupted stimulus to all future contemplation whether undertaken by the patron or other users of the book.

Other formal devices are employed with like effect in the miniature above beginning of the *Obsecro te* in the Book of Hours belonging to Amadée de Saluces (Figure 44). As she kneels at her devotions, Saints Dominic and Bernardino of Siena commend her to the Virgin, who, crowned and enthroned holds out a daisy spray before the Child. The composition is derived from depictions of the Epiphany with the kneeling Amadée substituting for the worshipping oldest Magus and the saints standing behind her completing the traditional trio.[16] The hieratic conception of Mary as Queen of Heaven and *sedes sapientiae* is tempered by the genre-like gestures and softly human forms of Mother and Child.[17]

In compositional terms, as emphasized in the black and white reproduction (Figure 44), the patron, by virtue of her size and foreground placement, commands equal attention with the Virgin and Child. But this is to reckon without the element of colour, through which visual dominance is gained for the object of devotion in this picture.[18] The form of the patron, and particularly the most expressive aspect,

---

[15] The heraldry, if not the portrait as well, seems to have been added to the miniature when Isabella became the owner of the book. This, however, does not affect our argument, which refers to viewer involvement with the altered folio. For discussion of the likely previous owner see M.R. Toynbee, "The Portraiture of Isabella Stuart, Duchess of Brittany (c. 1427– after 1494)," *Burlington Magazine* 88 (1946): 303ff., and G. Ring, *A Century of French Painting 1400–1500* (1949; New York: 1979) 204.

[16] The similarity between depictions of the Epiphany and the donor with Virgin and Child in van Eyck's Rolin Madonna has been noted by E. Michel, *Musée Nationale du Louvre, Catalogue Raisonée des Peintures du Moyen-âge, de la Renaissance et des Temps Modernes. Peintures Flamandes du XVe et du XVIe Siècle* (Paris: 1953) 116.

[17] For the incorporation of sculptured hieratic images of the Virgin and Child into depictions of the Epiphany, see I.H. Forsyth, "Magi and Majesty: A Study of Romanesque Sculpture and Liturgical Drama," *Art Bulletin* 50 (1968): 217–19. For their similar use in devotional pictures with owner, see Van Buren 622–26.

[18] There is an excellent colour reproduction on the front cover of J. Backhouse, *Books of Hours* (London: 1985).

A MINIMALLY INTRUSIVE PRESENCE

her face, is disturbed by its placement against a background cloth which is disconcertingly patterned in small multi-coloured squares. Moreover, her red garment lacks both the fullness and spatial coverage of the arresting lapis-coloured gown of the Virgin, which backed only by the unobtrusive brown throne, forms an appropriate setting for the Child. The image of Mary also exerts a certain magnetism through expression and gesture which stand out against the unified tones of halo and throne, unobscured by any intermediary object. Once attention has been claimed, it is difficult to leave the sacred pair whose gestures and frontal presentation make them so accessible. The patron's *prie-dieu*, linked to the throne by colour and perspectival direction, encloses the space to the side of the Virgin, effectively barring the viewer's access to the less peaceful right hand side of the picture. Again the immediacy and availability of the Mother and Child as a devotional image are preserved, despite the relationship with the depicted patron. Both here and in the *Hours of Isabella Stuart* the unfocused contemplative gaze of the patron further isolates her from the viewer's engagement with the devotional image.

A common device used by illuminators throughout the fifteenth century was the formal separation of patron and sacred image. In the *Boucicaut Hours*, "The Seven Heavenly Joys of the Virgin" are introduced by a miniature which shows the Marechal Boucicaut and his wife kneeling beneath a visionary depiction of the Apocalyptic Woman and Child (Figure 45).[19] The division of the composition into an upper and lower half by the curtain behind the patrons allows the viewer to respond directly to the sacred image. Indeed, the kneeling patrons serve to direct attention upwards, functioning as an exemplar.[20]

In contrast to this simple, almost harsh separation, the contemporary *Belles Heures*, made by the Limbourg Brothers for the Duc de Berry, uses the elements of the text itself to relate portrait and image which are placed several pages apart. In "The Fifteen Joys of the Virgin", the description of each Joy is followed by a request to the Virgin to intercede with her Son to help the devotee to lead a good life and achieve salvation after death.[21] This prayer in the *Belles Heures* is illuminated on its first and last pages. The devotional image is placed in the quarter-page above the beginning of the prayer "Doulce dame de misericorde" ("Sweet Lady of Mercy", Figure 46). In the quadrant diagonally below, linked to the image only by their upward glances, are the Faithful at prayer. The vision they share is the Assumption of the Virgin; with hands joined in prayer she is conducted by angels to God the Father above, whose blessing and glance appear to be directed as much toward the viewer as at the Virgin. This opening illumination occurs on folio 88; but the specific aspect of the prayer to which it is tied, the Assumption, is the final

---

[19] For comment on the visionary type of image in devotional books, see Ringbom, "Devotional Images" 166 and "Some Pictorial Conventions for the Recounting of Thoughts and Experiences in Late Medieval Art," *Medieval Iconography and Narrative: A Symposium* (Odense: 1980) 56–60, and Harbison 91ff.

[20] This purpose may also be served by the placement of the patron's portrait in an initial or border well separated from the devotional image, towards which the patron conspicuously directs his or her devotion.

[21] See Leroquais (note 2 above).

116   JOAN NAUGHTON

Joy in the series. And it is beside this text, three leaves further on, that the Duc de Berry is portrayed (f. 91; (Figure 47). His positioning in the lower quadrant corresponds to that of the Faithful on folio 88. He looks upwards, just as they do, in his case toward the textual description of the Assumption, whereas they look towards the visual image of this Joy.[22] The artistic conceit continues over the page on folio 91^v where, beside the space which her surprisingly youthful husband occupies on the previous page, is his second, younger duchess in a similar attitude of prayer.

The presentation of a religious image on the page opposite the patron at prayer resembles the devotional panel diptych common in fifteenth-century Flanders. *The Brussels Hours* of the Duc de Berry provides an early example of this format in a manuscript; there it serves as a frontispiece, independent of text.[23] Later in the century, Jean Fouquet in the *Hours of Etienne Chevalier* links the adjacent pages by implying a background continuum of Renaissance interior and celebrating angels.[24] Potentially the viewer may choose to take a distant view and observe the whole. However this is difficult from reading distance. Moreover there is a conceptual difference in the environments of each group; the Virgin and Child are shown in a close spatial relationship to the Gothic portal which acts as an isolating niche, whereas the patron is more loosely associated with his Renaissance-style environment. Again, the viewer is encouraged to concentrate on the devotional Virgin and Child.

In the late fifteenth-century *Hours of Joanna of Castile*, the beginning of the prayer to the Virgin is faced by a full-page *Virgo lactans* within a narrow frame (Figure 48). The three-quarter slightly turned figure of the Virgin, finely featured and with high forehead, who, in offering her breast to the Child presents its salvific potential directly to the viewer,[25] derives from Flemish panel painting near to

---

[22] Meiss suggests that the leader of the Faithful is David, who is said to have composed the Psalms in a chapel at the site of the Assumption in Jerusalem (M. Meiss and E.H.Beatson, *Les Belles Heures de Jean Duc de Berry* (London: 1974) 255). However David in this book is invariably depicted with dark brown hair (though it is white in the later *Très Riches Heures*, made by the same artists for the same patron). The leader has grey hair, causing him to resemble more closely the depiction of Emperor Augustus on folio 26 ^{v}; the dress and bodily shape of David and Augustus are identical. This identification would fit with the observation that leaders at the time, including Berry, tended to identify with Augustus (Harbison 91f; M. Meiss, *French Painting in the Time of Jean de Berry. Late Fourteenth Century and the Patronage of the Duke* (London: 1967) 234ff.). The identification, frequently played out in manuscripts by Berry and Augustus wearing similar dress, may here be alluded to by their similar praying attitudes before the Assumption, the one allied to the illumination, the other to the text it illustrates.

[23] Meiss, II, Plates 179 and 180.

[24] C. Sterling, *The Hours of Etienne Chevalier* (London: 1972) Plates 4 and 5.

[25] The role of the Virgin in human salvation as intercessor before Christ is frequently spelt out in medieval texts. Her requests rely on her motherhood. It is incumbent upon him to submit to her because she was the source of Christ's human flesh and provided his nourishment as a child: "Remember, Beloved, that Thou didst receive of my substance, my visible, tangible and sensible substance...", to which he replies, "It is impossible for me to deny thee anything" (Miracle L in Johannes Hérolt, called Discipulus (1435–1440), *Miracles of the Virgin Mary*, trans. C.C. Swinton Bland (London: 1928) 76). Indeed, it is this special role of the Virgin, as the most effective intercessor of all, being nearer to God than the saints and angels, but sufficiently close to mankind so that she might hear its pleas, which leads to the importance in medieval books of personal prayer to her.

A MINIMALLY INTRUSIVE PRESENCE

Rogier van der Weyden.[26] The way this book is bound causes the large Virgin and Child image on the verso to lie at a higher level, closer to the viewer than the patron and St. John the Evangelist on the opposite page. Being smaller in size, and removed further by their placement in a plane at some depth behind the page, the patron group is subsidiary to the devotional image which pushes forward from its frame toward the viewer. Interestingly, the patron and the Evangelist look out to the Virgin across real space—the viewer's space—between the leaves of the book.

The depiction of the patron as smaller in size than the sacred protagonists was an obvious means of minimizing competition for viewer attention. This traditional device is used in the miniature which illustrates "The Fifteen Joys of the Virgin" in a Book of Hours from Rouen (Figure 49). Here the patron kneels close to the knee of the Virgin who glances in her direction. At the same time, her inferior placement and small size allows the viewer unencumbered access to the physical presence and quiet mood of the Holy Family. The expressions, postures and gestures of the devotional group freely communicate the means of salvation through the Virgin's role in the Incarnation and Christ's redemptive sacrifice.[27] The Christ Child, his stiff right arm presumptive of the Crucifixion, calls attention to his mother's breast, while St. Joseph and the Virgin regard him with tender sadness.

In a small Book of Hours from Rouen, the Virgin and Child occupy the picture space immediately behind the frame of the miniature and the incipit of the prayer which begins "Mère de dieu..." (Figure 50). The close-up rendering of Mary, displaying her Child on the parapet behind which she stands, offers an immediate and inescapable presence which is directed outwards. The image acts both as the object of supplication and as exemplar, as the Virgin turns the pages of the book by the Christ Child's feet while he himself has a rosary around his shoulders. Almost unnoticed is the distant, unnaturally small figure of the patron at the rear of the room towards whom the Virgin almost imperceptibly inclines her head.

Even the competition from a portrait considerably larger than the devotional image is to a large extent annulled by the complex play on separate focal planes used in the full-page miniature facing the beginning of "The Seven Joys of the Virgin" in *The Hours of Mary of Burgundy* (Figure 51). As Ringbom has remarked, the viewer is placed inside, rather than outside the picture space.[28] The force of the trompe-l'œil illusion at reading distance transports one immediately into the interior of the

---

[26] A number of panels attributed to Rogier or his workshop display aspects closely related to this miniature, most particularly the Virgin and Child in *St. Luke Drawing a Portrait of the Virgin* (Boston, Museum of Fine Arts, reproduced in Martin Davies, *Rogier van der Weyden* (London: 1972) Plate 76). Noteworthy is the Virgin's left hand, the fingers of which press above and below her breast, as are the Christ Child's distinctively stretched out toes and fingers, common also to the centre panel of the Bladelin Altarpiece, Berlin-Dahlem, Staatliche Museen, and the panels of the Virgin and Child in Chicago, Art Institute and Tournai, Musée des Beaux-Arts (Davies Plates 31, 83 and 91). Equally distinctive are the features of the Virgin and the way her veil comes forward from underneath her mantle to cross her breast and engage the mantle on the opposite side; the latter two panels also share this aspect.

[27] See note 25 and the double intercession for mankind by the Virgin who beseeches Christ with exposed breast, while Christ in turn displays his wounds before God, discussed by B.G. Lane in "The 'Symbolic Crucifixion' in the Hours of Catherine of Cleves," *Oud Holland* 86 (1973): 4–11.

[28] Ringbom, *Icon to Narrative* 199.

JOAN NAUGHTON

church, into the presence of the hieratically frontal Virgin. Centrally placed, she presents the Child upon her lap as though on an altar, directly before the high altar of the church. Her monumental form clad in rich blue holds one's attention, and it requires conscious effort to move back to the separate plane where the patron is seated. Despite the relatively large size of the latter and her proximity to the viewer, she is effectively relegated to an unimportant border position outside the viewer's focus. Nor does the second portrayal of the patron, kneeling in profile and far to the side of the frontal Virgin and Child within the compelling trompe-l'œil, vie for attention.[29]

It appears, then, that fifteenth-century illuminators made use of a number of artistic devices to ensure that the portrayal of a patron before a devotional image would not interfere with the potential efficacy of that image as an aid to contemplation. The devotional group itself is invariably fairly frontal. It dominates attention and provides an interactive experience, promoting an appropriate state of mind for recitation of the prayer which follows. Viewer interest is maintained by the activities of the group, especially those of the Christ Child. Although these always refer to salvation, they are frequently unexpected, involving an apparently genre-like playful randomness. What might be seen as obligatory for the devotional group—to show some acknowledgement of the portrayed patron *and* to be fully available to the viewer—is fulfilled by the image's near frontality. This allows for involvement in two directions at once. There is a minimal interaction, usually involving only one member of the devotional group, with the patron who may be placed to the side or back; this has a negligible effect on the availability of the devotional image to the viewer directly before it. The patron's presence is also rendered unobtrusive in other ways. The portrait may be physically distant on another page or part of the page, or it may be reduced in size and placed in an obscure corner of the composition. The intrusion of the portrait could also be moderated by manipulating colour and degrees of compositional clarity, or by locating the portrait within a different focal range from the devotional group.

In conclusion, it is apposite to compare a portrait of an owner not in the presence of the depicted result of contemplation, but before a material devotional object. A miniature by the Master of Mary of Burgundy in a collection of religious treatises shows Margaret of York praying before a small panel.[30] Here the patron, and her retinue, are allowed free movement throughout the picture space; they are large in size and command the viewer's attention and curiosity, overwhelming and thus reducing to a mere accessory the small panel before which they pray. This representation virtually amounts to a secular portrait of a devout patron. It points up by contrast the artists' formal attempts to minimise the possibly intrusive effects of the portrait in the devotional compositions examined in this study.

---

[29] The use of the contrasting frontal and profile forms is discussed in M. Schapiro, *Words and Pictures: On the Literal and the Symbolic in the Illustration of a Text* (The Hague and Paris: 1973) 37–49. The frontal figure in Schapiro's analysis indicates a direct 'I-you' relationship with the viewer, whereas the profile involves an indirect 'he' or 'she' experience.

[30] O. Pächt, *The Master of Mary of Burgundy* (London: 1948) Plate 2.

Figure 44 Amadée de Saluces and saints with the Virgin and Child. *Saluces Hours*. London, British Library MS Additional 27697, f. 19; 280×190 mm.

Figure 45 The Boucicaut patrons beneath and vision of the Virgin and Child. *Boucicaut Hours*, Paris, Musée Jacquemart-André ms 2, f. 26^v; 274×190 mm.

Figure 46 The Assumption of the Virgin; and The Faithful at worship. *Belles Heures*, New York, Metropolitan Museum of Art, The Cloisters, f. 88. 238×170 mm.

Figure 47 Jean de Berry at prayer. *Belles Heures*, New York, Metropolitan Museum of Art, The Cloisters, f. 91; 238×170 mm.

A MINIMALLY INTRUSIVE PRESENCE 123

Figure 48 Virgo lactans; Joanna of Castile and St. John the Evangelist. *Hours of Joanna of Castile.* London, British Library MS Additional 18852, fols. 287^v–288; 110×75 mm.

Figure 49 The Holy Family and angels with the patron at prayer. Book of Hours, Vienna, Österreichisches Nationalbibliothek, cod. 1954, f. 63; 153×108 mm.

Figure 50 The Virgin and Child with the patron at prayer. Book of Hours, Oxford, Bodleian Library MS Buchanan e3, f. 74; 192×114 mm.

Figure 51 Mary of Burgundy and the Veneration of the Virgin and Child. *Hours of Mary of Burgundy*. Vienna, Österreichisches Nationalbibliothek cod. 1857, f. 14^v; 225×150 mm.

VIII

Reading Medieval Images: Two Miniatures in a Fifteenth-Century Missal

Vera F. Vines

As recent writers have reminded us, pictures performed a range of functions in medieval books.[1] They sharpened the visual interest of the page by interrupting the flow of the written word: cartoon-like, at times they provided the viewer with near-substitutes for the text; alternatively, they could communicate meaning by furnishing stories with descriptive explanations or moralizing commentaries, to heighten the impact of the text. Picture and word were in conversation with one another, collaborating in intricate ways and there is still much to unravel about the nature of these interactions, about the kinds of information transmitted by narrative images, for example, and how contemporary viewers responded to such information.

The term "narrative" applied to an individual visual image suggests a number of things—the content or the story behind the image and its interpretation, the compositional form involving style and design, and the implied element of time which presupposes movement and progress from beginning to end. When fifteenth century artists portrayed a "narrative" through the medium of a single composition they used certain formal devices to convey a sense of transitoriness.[2] Thus diagonals

---

[1] H.L. Kessler, "Reading ancient and medieval art," *Word and Image* 5.1 (1989): i. Sixten Ringbom, "Some pictorial conventions for the recounting of thoughts and experiences in late medieval art," in *Medieval Iconography and Narrative. A Symposium* (Odense: 1980) 38–69; see especially 38–41. See also James H. Marrow, "Symbol and Meaning in Northern European Art of the late Middle Ages and the early Renaissance," *Simiolus* 18 (1988): 150–69; Craig Harbison "Response to James Marrow," *Simiolus* 18 (1988): 170–72. There are relevant remarks in R. Brilliant, *Visual Narratives: Storytelling in Etruscan and Roman Art* (Cornell: 1984) Introduction and 53ff.

[2] With the onset of the fifteenth century, the demands of naturalism no longer favoured the use of "continuous narrative" devices to signify the time-flow of events. Thus, for example, in the depiction of Adam dispatching Seth to Paradise in the *Hours of Catherine of Clèves* the presence of two Seth figures in the same pictorial space detracts from the veracity of the narrative image (Pierpont Morgan Library MS M. 917, p. 75).

128   VERA F. VINES

might suggest movement, figures describe incomplete gestures, or assume animated expressions, or their directed gaze could signal the climactic moment of the story.

Such ploys are part of any artist's repertoire, providing clusters of visual metaphors to activate the informed viewer's imagination, alerting it to make associations which set the episode into a temporal context. But unless there is familiarity with the story in question, a visual composition cannot signify unequivocal meaning even though its forms are recognizable objects: of itself, a narrative picture cannot "tell" a tale. But to the spectator already acquainted with a particular context, an image can be recognized and "read". Meanings will unfold, resonances will be set up in the mind forging linkages and interactions with remembered words or appropriate text, and, perhaps, with the observer's own contextual associations.

* * * * *

This study focuses on two "narrative" images in a fifteenth century French Missal which contain novel responses to the accompanying liturgical text. The themes are rare enough to invite study, and in seeking to establish their significance in terms of a specific historical context the discussion addresses some general questions about the nature of narrative painting in late-medieval manuscripts. The two-volume Missal in question was designed for use in Besançon and was probably made in about 1464 by a local workshop for Charles de Neufchâtel (1439–1498), Archbishop of that city. The Calendar contains several local feasts, including the Translation of Saints Ferreolus and Ferrucius (May 29), their Feast Day (June 16), and the Invention of their Relics (September 5), and St. Antidius (June 17). It is an elaborate book, with every feast in the Liturgical Year marked by a large illuminated initial accompanied by a finely executed border, while the major Temporal feasts and all the Masses in the Sanctoral are introduced by rectangular single-column miniatures. Two full-page paintings prefix the Canon in both volumes.[3] The miniatures are the work of two artists coming from different stylistic traditions, one of whom was probably trained in Provence, while the second displays affinities with the North-Netherlandish centre of illumination in Utrecht.

Temporal and Sanctoral illustrations are mostly developed from familiar models with the saints conventionally identified. Saint Thomas the Apostle, as depicted by the Provençal artist, is a traditional iconic figure who holds a book in one hand and in the other a builder's T-square—an attribute which stems from the apocryphal claim that he built a palace for an Indian king (Figure 52).[4] Nevertheless, the saint's portrait gains conviction through its background, a tranquil scene stretching into the distance, shafted with light and shadow—demonstrating the Provençal

---

[3] See Margaret M. Manion, Vera F. Vines and Christopher de Hamel, *Medieval and Renaissance Manuscripts in New Zealand Collections* (London, 1989) 55–58 for a detailed description of the codicology of the volumes, a stylistic analysis of the contributing artists and a brief account of the historical context. The Missal is in the Grey Collection (Med. MSS. G138–39).

[4] D.H. Farmer, *The Oxford Dictionary of the Saints* (Oxford: 1982) 374ff.

READING MEDIEVAL IMAGES 129

miniaturist's talent for painting naturalistic landscape. To mark the Feast of Ferreolus and Ferrucius the Northern artist too has depicted the saints as iconic figures. They stand side by side confronting the viewer from an interior architectural space, each holding his decapitated head with a halo incongruously placed behind the neck stump (Figure 56).[5] Such images would have presented few problems to the artists who had atelier models to call on as part of their stock-in-trade.

Despite their different figurative and compositional styles, the two miniaturists shared an ability to interpret well-known narrative themes in lively ways. In the *Stoning of Stephen*, for example, the Provençal artist provides realistic anecdotal details which invite the audience to project in imagination beyond the moment treated (Figure 53). The malefactors appear as if interrupted in their task. One stands with rumpled leggings and head inclined, his gaze fixed on the back of the saint, his right arm raised, stone clenched in hand. Rolling up his sleeve, a second figure postures threateningly, his right arm and leg held taut, as he presses forward. The captors' murderous intent is in stark contrast to the saint's compliant stillness as he kneels awaiting martyrdom. The dramatic nature of this narrative is reinforced by the contrasting elements of the landscape—rugged boulders with a dead tree project the three figures into relief, while a line of greenery leading to still water reflects, it seems, St. Stephen's self-abnegation.

The Northern artist has a different approach to narrative depiction. His compositions, although lacking the expressive subtleties of the Provençal artist's interpretation, nevertheless gain in energy and conviction through their spatial realism and the warm palette which animate the stocky, almost comic-strip figures. Thus, for the *Transfiguration*, an event of psychological intensity, the tableau is in a plausible three dimensional setting which separates each figure by colour and form to convey the apostles' awe-stricken response to their moment of enlightenment (see Figure 54). In the *Conversion of St. Paul* (Figure 55), a narrative with a more physical climax, the Northern artist has again used form and colour with dramatic effect—employing a large patch of scarlet for Paul's rumpled jacket and another to frame the vision of Christ above, with the heavenly and earthly zones being connected by a stream of golden rays. By placing the horse and rider before a line of asymmetric hillocks, he has emphasized the animal's solid rump, a dead weight upon the ground. Confronted by such an energy-charged image, the literate viewer cannot fail to be reminded of the strange circumstances leading to Saul's conversion.

* * * * *

In addition to such illustrations based on readily recognizable iconographical patterns, the Besançon Missal contains two images for which there appear to be no established models. These compositions demonstrate the powers of invention of both

---

[5] The miniature is in vol.2, f. 155 ᵛ. For Ferreolus and Ferrucius see *Biblioteca Sanctorum Instituto Giovanni XXIII, Pontifica Universita Lateranense* (Rome: 1964) vol. 5, 652–53.

130 VERA F. VINES

artists, in response it would seem, to the specific interests of the patron.[6] They introduce the Mass for St. Antidius (volume I, f. 22) and the Feast of the Epiphany (volume II, f. 157). Unlike the static iconic representation of many of the other saints, including Ferreolus and Ferrucius (Figure 56) who were of major importance in the Besançon calendar, St. Antidius is accorded a lively narrative reference. Seated astride a devil, he is shown flying over a landscape, intent upon his journey (Figure 57). The saint's determined expression and the energy of the demon—with its limbs extended, claws splayed out, and eyes turned towards the viewer—communicate a sense of movement and single-minded purpose. Antidius was supposedly a bishop, martyred in about A.D. 411, and, although of doubtful historical authenticity, his name appeared in the episcopal lists of Besançon compiled in the eleventh century. It was claimed that he was murdered by Crocus, a king of the Vandals, and buried some eleven miles from the city. In 1042 his relics were discovered and transferred to St. Paul's Church in Besançon, after which his cult became popular. Miracles were attributed to the saint and fanciful legends proliferated, the most remarkable of which is the one commemorated in the Sanctoral miniature.[7] The holy man was credited with making a journey to Rome on the back of a (supposedly benevolent) devil, because he was disturbed by rumours that the Pope had committed fornication. Arriving in Rome as the Pope was about to say Mass, Antidius called him aside and charged him with the sin. The Pope, tearful and trembling, admitted his guilt, whereupon the saint replaced him as celebrant at the altar. Later, after calling on the Pope to confess, Antidius gave him absolution and departed. Such is the substance of the legend responsible for the Sanctoral miniature whose air-borne comic-strip figures encourage the imagination of an informed observer to anticipate the successful finale. The Northern painter's talent for narrative is amply demonstrated in this unusual composition.[8] The dynamic rendering of St. Antidius stands in marked contrast to the stereotyped iconic figures of Ferreolus and Ferrucius, who, as Besançon's patron saints, enjoyed greater prominence throughout the city. Thus within the Missal's programme of illustration Antidius' distinctive treatment carries an implied emphasis which merits consideration. This is discussed below.

The second miniature, *The Meeting of the Magi*, (Plate 5), by the Provençal painter, introduces the Mass for the Epiphany, and shows the artist departing from the traditional image for that feast, namely *The Adoration of the Magi*.

---

[6] See H.L. Kessler, "On the State of Medieval Art History," *The Art Bulletin* LXX no. 2 (1988): 166–87; see especially 181–82 for discussion of the role of the patron.

[7] For St. Antidius see *Biblioteca Sanctorum* vol. 1, 56–57. The miniature is situated above the Introit for the Ordinary Mass for a martyr-bishop. See also U. Chevalier, *Repertoire des Sources Historiques du Moyen Age* (New York: repr. 1960) vol. I, 267. St. Antidius' legendary exploits are recorded in *Vie de St. Antide*, Troyes, Bibl. Mun. ms. 1 248 (10–11th century), cited in *Histoire de Besançon des origines à la fin du xviᵉ siècle*, ed. C. Fohlen (Paris: 1964) 233, n. 1. For the legend illustrated in the Missal see S. Baring-Gould, *The Lives of the Saints* (Edinburgh: 1914) vol. 6, 352ff.

[8] The originality lies in the configuration of St. Antidius and the devil, not in the energetic rendering of the demon *per se*, since such creatures abound in medieval art (for example, in scenes depicting Hell or the conflict with St. Michael).

READING MEDIEVAL IMAGES 131

Three equestrians appear in the mid-ground. Their facial expressions and posture are peaceable: two are associated with shadowy figures, and all three have lances behind them. The central figure on horseback is accompanied by a negroid youth, who stands to the front of the picture glancing up at his master. A hound, sketched in, streaks off to the right. The background is cut short by trees and two bulbous hillocks, one with a steep zig-zag path. The Provençal Master displays his impressionistic technique, using thinly applied pallid washes of paint, short flecks for grass, and shadows suggested by thin hastily drawn long lines; but his penchant for creating naturalistic landscapes with long vistas—a hall-mark of his style (already discussed in relation to the *Stoning of Stephen* and *St. Thomas*)—is not apparent in this composition. Little attention has been paid to pictorial recession or atmospheric perspective in plotting this particular background. Nevertheless he has created a convincing composition in a coherent pictorial space within which the three cavalcades are strategically placed for their moment of recognition which is the climax of the legend. Indeed, the originality of the compositional setting suggests that the artist was not aware of any traditional visual model.

This surmise finds support in the apparent rarity of the theme in earlier art.[9] In panel painting of the late fourteenth and early fifteenth century *The Meeting of the Magi* does not seem to have been treated as a separate theme. Cavalcades with retinues of horsemen and exotic animals appear in the background of some representations of *The Adoration of the Magi,* and could be construed as generalized references to the Magi's Meeting. But it is more likely that these subsidiary elements describe a later event—the journey of the Magi to Jerusalem—a pictorial theme with a long history.[10] In a group of paintings of *The Adoration* stemming from fourteenth and fifteenth century Italy, the horsemen in the background are actually converging, and it has been assumed that the event portrayed is the *Meeting of the Three Kings*, a legend recounted in a late medieval chronicle. However, in these Italian paintings the retinues contain unbridled animals fighting one another, and agitated grooms ready to intervene with drawn swords. Such warlike motifs, as Sterling has argued, refer to a quite different medieval tradition which held that the Three Kings were mortal enemies until they met under the guidance of the star, whereas in the original written account of *The Meeting* it was explicitly stated that they had no prior acquaintance.[11]

---

[9] V. Leroquais, for example, has no examples of the theme in his survey of late fourteenth and fifteenth century French Missals; see *Les Sacramentaires et les Missels Manuscrits des Bibliothèques publiques de France* (Paris: 1924) vols. II and III. It is not included, for example, in the extensive Magi Cycle on the Virgin Portal of Amiens Cathedral. For this see Marcia R. Rickard, "The Iconography of the Virgin Portal of Amiens," *Gesta* XXII.2 (1983): 147–157, 148 ff. In fact, G. Schiller, *Iconography of Christian Art* (London: 1973) vol. 1, 113ff., points out that the legend was unknown in the West until the second half of the fourteenth century. See also E. Panofsky, *Early Netherlandish Painting* (Cambridge, Mass.: 1953) 393 n. 1.

[10] See Schiller 98–99.

[11] C. Sterling, "Fighting Animals in the Adoration of the Magi," *Bulletin of Cleveland Museum of Art* LXI (1974): 350–359. Sterling discusses this assumption held, *inter alia,* by Panofsky (see note 9). For the written account of *The Meeting* see note 15.

132   VERA F. VINES

Thus for an unequivocal interpretation of the legend of *The Meeting* the cavalcades must appear to converge towards a destination point, and they should also appear peaceable. These requirements are met in a subsidiary scene in a panel painting of the *The Adoration of the Magi* by the Netherlandish artist Jacques Daret painted in 1434 (Figures 59, 60).[12] The painter has set the events in a Flemish landscape. Behind the stable in the foreground a cavalry procession gallops towards an inn where a larger group of horsemen is already assembled (Figure 60). In the far distance two or three horsemen are also converging. The group at the inn does not look warlike, although several soldiers are in armour. Some have their backs turned to the oncoming procession; all are waiting upon the other travellers, and a meeting between the first two cavalcades is imminent. Thus Daret's version acknowledges the temporal dimensions of the narrative and, in this one respect, it has an affinity with the Missal illustration.

During the fifteenth century *The Meeting* was sometimes included in the borders of manuscripts as a subsidiary motif to the main *Adoration* image. However, the only well-known earlier illustration which treats *The Meeting* as a main theme occurs in the *Très Riches Heures* of the Duc de Berry dated before 1416 (Figure 58).[13] Here three processions are set in a rocky mountainscape. The riders, all splendidly robed and mounted on magnificent steeds, with pennants flying and exotic animals in train, make their way towards a wayside shrine. It is, however, not certain who will be the first to arrive, for the three retinues appear to converge simultaneously towards the Gothic wayside shrine above which the guiding star is already shining. In fact, the earlier moment of climax (when, according to the legend, the fog lifts to reveal the star to the three assembled Magi) has been subsumed into the temporal flow of the story. For the *Meeting* was inserted to face the *Adoration of the Magi* in the Duke's prayer-book, forming a diptych (fols. 51 ᵛ–52) to introduce the Hour of Sext. The viewer, confronted by succeeding episodes of the Magi story, is thus encouraged to recall and imagine the earlier happenings—the Magi's separate journeys and their fog-bound meeting before the star was revealed. It is precisely this earlier moment of meeting which the Provençal artist has chosen to portray, in simple terms without recourse to a wayside shrine. Thus the version in the Besançon Missal has little in common compositionally or functionally with the

---

[12] This is now in the Gemäldegalerie, Staatliche Museen Preussischer Kulturbesitz, Berlin. Daret's *Adoration* with its subsidiary motif has been discussed in my doctoral dissertation "The Arras Altarpiece of J. Daret. A reassessment of the Artist on the Basis of his only Documented Work," diss., U. of Melbourne, 1981, 142–45. Daret's imagery has no sense of warlike intent attributed to the processing Magi in the Bosch late fifteenth century "Prado *Epiphany*". For this see L.B. Philip, "The Prado Epiphany by Jerome Bosch," *Art Bulletin* XXXV (1953): 267–93; see 284–85.

[13] M. Meiss, *French Painting in the Time of Jean de Berry. The Limbourgs and their Contemporaries.* (London: 1974): 156–57 and notes 332–33. The following analysis is based on the discussions by Meiss and Panofsky (see note 9 above). Subsidiary images occur, for example, in Vienna Nat. Bibl. cod. 1840, f. 65 (see Pächt-Thoss, *Die Illuminierten Handschriften der Österreichischen National Bibliothek Französische Schule* 1 (Tafeln), Abb. 146; The Wharncliffe Hours (f. 40ᵛ) (see M. Manion, *The Wharncliffe Hours* (London: 1981), Plate 22). See also Roger S. Wieck, *Time Sanctified. The Books of Hours in Medieval Art and Life.* Exhibition Catalogue. (Baltimore: 1988), nos. 43, 46, 49 and 53.

READING MEDIEVAL IMAGES   133

Limbourg *Meeting of the Magi*.[14] Moreover, unlike the *Très Riches Heures*, the Missal contains no depiction of the *Adoration of the Magi* and on this account the artist's choice of *The Meeting* to illustrate the Epiphany assumes added interest.

To shed light on the Provençal artist's compositional vocabulary we need to turn to the literary source of this legend. In about 1364 a Westphalian Carmelite prior, John of Hildesheim, wrote *The Three Kings of Cologne*. Claiming to have compiled his chronicle from various Eastern, biblical, apocryphal and traditional sources, the author interfused plausible narrative with strange topographical details and fanciful miracles.[15] His compilation was inspired by the widespread importance of the cult of the Magi whose relics had been carried to Cologne in 1164. The popularity of the "Three Kings of Cologne" was such that the Chronicle was soon widely disseminated. It was translated into German in 1389 and there were several English versions by about 1400. The author narrates the Kings' Meeting carefully, locating it precisely in a "biblical" landscape, and commenting also on the adverse weather conditions. Since his prolix descriptions (which in previous discussions have been abbreviated) are important in the present context, they are reported in full.[16]

> When the three kings, each with his own company had come within two miles of Jerusalem, a great fog and dark cloud covered all the earth and they lost the star, as Isaiah had prophesied: *Surge illuminare Ierusalem quia venit lumen tuum et gloria domina super te orta est: quia ecce tenebre operient terram et caligo populos;* that is to say: "Jerusalem, arise and take light for thy light is come and the Joy of God is sprung upon thee: for lo darkness shall cover the earth and a cloud the people" (Is. 60: 1–2). When these three kings were near Jerusalem, Melchior king of Nubia and Araby, with his people, halted in the fog beside the mount of Calvary. On this hill there was a highway, and to this highway were three highways meeting together. After Melchior, next to him a little under this cloud, came Balthazar king of Godolia and of Saba with his

---

[14] The Limbourg diptych exemplifies the pictorial narrative convention which Ringbom (following earlier scholars) calls "cyclic narrative" (see note 1). Some fifteenth century French depictions of *The Meeting* have been described as *The Journey of the Magi*: see Walters MS 223, f. 62 ᵛ; *Time Sanctified* no. 46, p. 82, Pl. 22; Great Book of Hours of Henry VIII, Pierpont Morgan Library, Heinemann Collection, H.8, f. 10 ᵛ (see *Renaissance Painting in Manuscripts. Treasures from the British Library* ed. T. Kren (New York: 1984) 178, Figure 23 g.); *The Journey* (placed above *The Adoration*) occurs in the *Tilliot Hours* (c. 1500), B.L. Yates Thompson MS 5, f. 48 ᵛ (see Kren 176, Figure 23 c.) Comparisons are instructive. Compositionally the two themes can be distinguished in terms of processional arrangements, and the figurations of the kings and their gestures. *The Meeting* in the Besançon Missal does not resemble any of the other versions in its compositional format.

[15] C. Horstmann, ed., *The Three Kings of Cologne*, Early English Text Society LXXXV (London: 1886) Introduction and 52–58. For a recent study of the text see S. Christern in the catalogue from the exhibition *Achthundert Jahre Verehrung der Heiligen Drei Könige in Köln, 1164–1964* (Cologne: 1963) 180–204.

[16] The rendering given here closely paraphrases the Middle English text of *The Three Kings*, 52–58. It should be noted that the account makes no mention of a wayside shrine at the foot of the Mount of Calvary—see the discussion above of the disparities between the Limbourg and Besançon depictions of the episode.

134   VERA F. VINES

folk who stopped beside the mount of Olives in a little town called
Galilee, which town is frequently mentioned in the Gospels and not to be
confused with the province of Galilee which is three days journey from
Jerusalem. When these two kings came and abode in these places in the
cloud and in darkness, the fog began to lift but the star was still hid. So
when the two Kings saw that they were near the city of Jerusalem they
did not know each other but took their way towards the city with all their
folk. When they came to this highway, beside the mount of Calvary
where the three highways met, then came Jaspar king of Tarsus with all
his host, and all three met, kissing each other in great joy and reverence
although they had not known each other before, relating the reason for
their coming. They then rode forth together and at sunrise came to
Jerusalem with such numbers of men and beasts that they could not all be
lodged within the city but for the most part they lay without the city all
about as Isaiah had prophesied: *Fortitudo gencium venerit tibi inundacio
camelorum operiet te dromedarij Madian et Effa; omnes de Saba venient
aurum et thus deferentes et laudem domino annunciantes et cetera.* That
is to say: ''the strength of folk cometh to thee (that is to say to the city of
Jerusalem) great plenty of camels shall hail thee and dromedaries of
Madian and Epha shall come to thee all men shall come from Saba bring-
ing gold and incense and showing praising to God'' (Is. 60: 5–6). After-
wards when the three kings had come to Jerusalem, Herod was in the city
and so they asked of the people about the child that was born, as the
evangelist said in his Gospel...

If we return now to the miniature in the Besançon Missal, we see that the artist
was familiar with John of Hildesheim's account, for his composition fits the literary
source closely. The sequence of events and the descriptive details of the legend are
clearly conveyed within the small dimensions of the miniature. The two landmarks
distinguished in the chronicle—the Mount of Calvary and the Mount of Olives—are
shown as two bulbous outcrops, on one of which is the 'single highway', a zig-zag
line. Melchior, identified by his negroid page as the king of Nubia, has arrived first
for his horse is almost stationary, and, inclining his head, he accepts a greeting
already extended by Balthazar on the left. The equestrian on the right is Jaspar, the
third king to arrive at the junction of the highways, still in the act of doffing his
crown—and the other two seem as yet unaware of his presence. The lines drawn
behind the kings signify lances of the assembled retinues—the 'folk', or 'company'
of the English text—while the hound on the move represents the 'numbers of
beasts'. The Magi do not look upwards because, although the fog has begun to lift,
the star is still hidden. Their journey to Jerusalem has yet to happen, for the artist
has selected the moment when the three independent cavalcades have just converged
before the Mount of Calvary—the instant of recognition, immediately *before* the
kings saw the star and kissed each other ''in great joy and reverence...''. Thus the
artist has succeeded in conveying the temporal dimension of the narrative by

READING MEDIEVAL IMAGES

suggesting an ongoing sequence of events within the framework of a single composition.

* * * * *

The question arises: Given the widespread popularity of the Adoration theme, why was *The Meeting* substituted to illustrate the Epiphany in Charles de Neufchâtel's Missal? On the most general level, this could be construed as a register of the importance placed by the people of Besançon on narrative legends about the Three Kings, whose relics had been carried long before through nearby Burgundy en route to Cologne. There was an abbey in the city dedicated to the Three Kings in which the Neufchâtel seigneurial family had a chapel where Mass was said daily for the Archbishop's uncle Thibaud. Evidently there was family loyalty to the cult.[17] In addition, it is on record that during the Middle Ages and beyond, the Three Kings were honoured in Besançon's Cathedral of St. Stephen by a liturgical drama during the Epiphany Mass.[18] It is recounted that, after the Epistle, three clerics retired to the sacristy to put on 'royal' capes and gold crowns. Then, led by chanting choristers with candles and censors, they processed along the aisles of the nave, following a luminous star which moved overhead, suspended from the vaults. Next, the 'Three Kings' mounted the rood screen and each intoned one section of the Gospel. They then pointed to the star, proclaiming "Ecce stellam quam vidimus", and proceeding across the choir they laid their gifts at the feet of the celebrant and presented him with their crowns, which he placed upon the altar.

This interlude, intended to enrich the liturgy, thus presented the succeeding episodes of the Magi's journey and their homage, anticipating the Gospel (St. Matthew 2: 1–12) which was to proclaim the Manifestation of Christ to the Gentiles. Thematically, therefore, *The Meeting of the Three Kings* would have been a fitting accompaniment to the liturgical drama being presented before the congregation. It was thus a highly appropriate choice to illustrate the Epiphany Mass in a Missal which was to be used in the cathedral.

This image is appropriate for another reason. The legend of the Meeting of the Magi, signified by its illustration above the Introit, becomes a visual gloss or commentary, interacting with the biblical readings for the Epiphany. For, as the English version makes plain, the chronicler had appropriated sentences from Isaiah's

---

[17] This is referred to in *Histoire de la Seigneurie du Neufchâtel-Bourgogne*, L'abbé Loyé ed. (Montbeliard: 1890): 197ff.

[18] L'abbé Guibard, *Cérémonies qui se pratiquaient au Moyen Age dans nos deux cathédrals de S. Jean et de S. Etienne*, Annales franc-comtoises, *Revue religieuse, historique et littéraire*, tome XII, Nov. 1869, 330–342. There is a note to the effect that the material was gathered from a manuscript written in 1646 by the Canon d'Orval, apostolic protonotary entitled *Etat de l'Eglise de Besançon*. The Besançon drama was one of many associated with the popular theme of the Magi. The miniaturist could have been familiar with descriptive details of *The Meeting* in association with Besançon Epiphany pagentry. R. Hatfield, in "The Compagnia de Magi," *Journal of the Warburg and Courtauld Institute* 33 (1970): 107–61, discusses the pageantry and the devotional practices associated with the Magi for which an important lay confraternity in Florence was responsible, and which attest to the widespread popularity of the cult. See also the discussion in Sterling (note 11).

136 VERA F. VINES

prophecy of Christ's coming in order to flesh out the Magi's own story. Thus the biblical quotation, "For lo darkness shall cover the earth and a cloud the people", was used to describe the legendary circumstances of the Three Kings' Meeting. Isaiah's camels and dromedaries and the men from Saba became the Three Kings' men and beasts, said to be too numerous to lodge in the city.

These two miniatures—*The Legend of St. Antidius* and *The Meeting of the Magi*—gain further significance if the manuscript commission is set into the broader context of Charles de Neufchâtel's achievements as Archbishop of Besançon.

When the Missal was commissioned, Charles was a young man, recently installed as archbishop who, some months earlier in July 1463, had made a solemn entry into his cathedral city. The *Adventus Ceremony* of welcome, originally codified in monastic centres for medieval kings, had by the fifteenth century also been accorded to other dignitaries, who were received at the city gates with traditional ritual, and often with extravagant displays in the manner of the *joyeuses entrées* of the French kings and the Duke of Burgundy.[19] Some prelates, remembering that one prototype for the *Adventus Ceremony* was Christ's entry into Jerusalem, had eschewed pomp and had even ridden on a donkey.[20] But Charles was received with pomp as the prince-archbishop who was to be temporal ruler of Besançon, arriving with a huge escort of horsemen, said to number eight hundred—the élite of the Franche-Comté nobility.[21] At the city gate consecrated for solemn entries, he would have been greeted by town and clerical dignitaries before entering his domain.

It should be said that such emphasis on temporal power, the hallmark of authority, denotes only one aspect of Charles de Neufchâtel's character. Set aside for the Church at an early age, well educated, versed in Latin, philosophy and theology, he actively promoted liturgical reform. He saw the need for a single text of the Sanctoral which retained local feasts, and also revised books of prayers for his diocese. He compiled a catechism, and annotated Missals and Breviaries were printed under his direction for distribution to his clergy—many of whom were ignorant of the nature of their religious duties.[22] As aids to devotion, he published

---

[19] See E.H. Kantorowicz, "The King's Advent and the Enigmatic Panels in the Doors of Santa Sabina," *Art Bulletin* 26 (1944): 207–31. In this detailed historical analysis see especially 208–11, 216–17.

[20] Kantorowicz 217, note 66. In a near-contemporary Burgundian description of the Congress of Arras the chronicler notes that when news came of the impending arrival of the Cardinal of Cyprus the vested bishop and abbot and the governor of the town with attendants went on horseback to the gate of St. Michael consecrated for solemn entries. The abbot presented the cardinal with a cross to kiss, which the cardinal did, while still on horseback. Then everybody processed to the cathedral. The Cardinal Alberti, however, arrived unheralded—a matter for concern to the abbot. This account highlights the different approaches of prelates to "solemn entries". See A. de la Taverne, *Journal de la Paix d'Arras (1435)*, A. Boussat ed. (Arras: 1936) 6–8.

[21] See *Histoire de la Seigneurie* 174–95. Charles, in fact, owed his benefice to the influence of his family. His father, Jean II de Neufchâtel-Montaigu, who occupied important positions in the Burgundian court, had taken possession of the archbishopric for Charles in May 1463. Charles' ceremonial entry took place on 11 July 1463. He was not installed as archbishop until 23 May 1464. (See, however, *Histoire de Besançon*, 515–516, which dates his personal temporal rule after 1466.)

[22] See *Histoire de Besançon*, 490–491, 503–527. See also *Histoire des Diocèses de France, VI: Les Diocèses de Besançon et de S. Claude*, under the direction of Maurice Rey (Paris: 1977) 79–82. I am indebted to B. de Vregille, S.J., Institut des Sources Chrétiennes, Lyon, for detailed information on

READING MEDIEVAL IMAGES

various tracts, for example on the prayer of St. Bernard, on the joys of Paradise, and on the torments of Hell. Other devotional texts printed under his direction included several *Specula* and the poem *Viri venerabiles sacerdotes Dei...*,[23] popular since the thirteenth century, which exalted the dignity of the priesthood.

The formidable list of publications, which continued unabated during the period of the Archbishop's long exile,[24] attests to a prelate of stature, concerned with the administration of his diocese and with technical considerations of ceremonial, as well as with questions of liturgical reform. Also clear is the Archbishop's deeply felt pastoral concern for his clergy and his wish to improve their calibre through education and spiritual exercises.

Such concerns are highlighted not only by the stress laid on teaching manuals and devotional literature, but also by his use of an apocryphal tale when reminding his canons of their obligation to recite the Divine Office. He enlivened his exhortation by citing a terrible and horrible history of an archbishop of Magdeburg who was neglectful of his duties. It is quite possible, therefore, that another apocryphal tale—the legend of S. Antidius whose mission was to reform the Pope—would have been understood by Charles de Neufchâtel as a metaphor for his own reforming zeal. Under these circumstances the dynamic interpretation of St. Antidius astride a devil would have spoken to the archbishop more powerfully and directly than, for example, the iconic figures of Ferreolus and Ferrucius.[25] Could the *Meeting of the Magi* also have been of personal moment to Charles in his role as prince-archbishop? To answer this question we need to turn to the Introit for the Epiphany which begins "Ecce advenit dominator Dominus: et regnum in manu ejus, et potestas, et imperium".

This is an adaptation of the prophecy of Malachai 3: 1. So, too, is the verse "Ecce mitto angelum meum, qui praeparabit viam tuam ante faciem meam" used since the tenth century for the Entrance verse in the consecration service for a prince, and sung while he was conducted to the altar of the cathedral.[26] There are indeed strong links between the liturgy for the Feast of the Epiphany and the consecration procession for a prince. Thus, it is quite possible that the equestrians in the Missal miniature above the Introit would have triggered Charles' memory to recall the

---

Charles de Neufchâtel's activities as liturgical reformer and educator. To Charles' credit were printed synodial statutes and liturgical and devotional books; see Manion, Vines and de Hamel for details.

[23] These appeared with the Besançon printed edition of the *Statuta* in 1488.

[24] The Neufchâtel family, loyal to the Duke of Burgundy, lost favour after the Battle of Nancy when Louis XI overran the region and devastated the countryside. In 1480 Charles pleaded with the city to capitulate, which so angered the nobility still loyal to the Burgundian cause that de Neufchâtel was declared a traitor and forced to flee. Louis XI gave him the bishopric of Bayeux where he lived until his death in 1498. However he remained Archbishop of Besançon, leaving the administration of the diocese to an auxiliary bishop. Charles' publications stem from this period of exile.

[25] Marrow's remarks on "artistic meaning" and "image-and-viewer relationships" are relevant here; see Marrow 161–67, 169. Also relevant are some ideas expressed in a recent article on a Byzantine manuscript; see R.B. Nelson, "The Discourse of Icons Then and Now," *Art Bulletin* 12 no. 2 (1989): 144–57, especially 150ff.

[26] See Kantorowicz 217, notes 67 and 69. See also H. Hendrickx, *The Infancy Narratives* (Manila: 1975) 66.

138   VERA F. VINES

ceremonial and pomp of the meeting at the city gate, prior to his installation as
Archbishop of Besançon. But, as we have seen, the prelate also had his less worldly
side, striving as he did over the years for the betterment of his clergy, and his personal spiritual life was doubtless shaped by the writings of the great medieval mystics and contemplatives who so widely influenced contemporary affective devotional
practice. Paradoxically, then, we may suppose that Charles, in tune with the religious thinking of his age, also interpreted *The Meeting* as a metaphor for his own
spiritual aspirations. Through this narrative image he could "journey" to Beth-
lehem, to "worship" at the crib, and "experience" the Epiphany.[27]

---

[27] The sense of being physically and emotionally involved was a continuing theme in late medieval
devotional literature; for example, St. Bridget's vision relates empathetic responses to her "actual"
presence at Christ's Nativity (see Schiller 78–79). Ludolph of Saxony enjoined the Christian soul to
"go" each day between the Nativity and the Purification to adore Christ "in the stable". See Ludolph
le Chartreux, *La Grande Vie de Ihesus Christ*, trans. Dom. Marie Prospera Augustin (Paris: 1863):
I.230ff. M. Bodenstadt enlarges upon Ludolph's widespread influence on fifteenth century mystics and
preachers; see *The Vita Christi of Ludolphus the Carthusian* (Washington: 1944) Introduction. See
also James H. Marrow's discussion of the practices of emotional and physical devotional exercises during the later Middle Ages in *Passion Iconography in Northern European Art of the Late Middle Ages
and Early Renaissance* (Courtrai: 1979) 10–28, and "Symbol and Meaning" 165ff. (see note 2 above).

Figure 52 St. Thomas the Apostle. Missal, Auckland, Public Library MSS G. 138–39, vol. 1, f. 174^v; 305×225 mm.

Figure 53 The Stoning of St. Stephen. Missal, Auckland, Public Library MSS G. 138–39, vol. 1, f. 15^v; 305×225 mm.

Figure 54 The Transfiguration. Missal, Auckland, Public Library MSS G. 138–39, vol. 2, f. 197; 318×238 mm.

Figure 55 The Conversion of St. Paul. Missal, Auckland, Public Library MSS G. 138–39, vol. 1, f. 184^v; 305×225 mm.

Figure 56 Saints Ferreolus and Ferrucius. Missal, Auckland, Public Library MSS G. 138–39, vol. 2, f. 155^v; 318×238 mm.

Figure 57 St. Antidius. Missal, Auckland, Public Library MSS G. 138–39, vol. 2, f. 157; 318×238 mm.

Figure 58 Meeting of the Magi. *Très Riches Heures*, Chantilly, Musée Condé f. 51^v; 290×210 mm.

Figure 59 Jacques Daret, Adoration of the Magi. Berlin, Dahlem Staatliche Museum; 570×520 mm.

Figure 60 Jacques Daret, Adoration of the Magi. Detail. Berlin, Dahlem Staatliche Museum; 570×520 mm.

IX

Editing the *Exeter Book* :
A Progress Report

Bernard J. Muir

For the past two years I have been working on a new edition of Exeter Cathedral Library MS 3501, better known as the *Exeter Book*, and in July-August 1988 spent four weeks conducting a thorough examination of the manuscript *in situ*.[1] Since an optimistic estimated completion date for the new edition is approximately three years from now, it seems advisable to offer a summary of some of my observations and conclusions at this point rather than withholding information which may be of use to others and of advantage to the progress of *Exeter Book* studies. Apart from some introductory remarks, this paper is a discussion of the *Table* below, a database summarizing a large amount of information about the *Exeter Book*, which can be manipulated in various ways.[2]

In the *Preface* to the 1936 edition of the *Exeter Book*, Dobbie writes, "The text has been based on the admirably clear facsimile edition of the Exeter Book published in 1933, with the introductory chapters by Max Förster, R.W. Chambers, and Robin Flower".[3] Like Dobbie and many other editors since his time, I too believed that the facsimile was of such excellent quality that there would probably be little to be gained from an extended examination of the manuscript itself, but went to Exeter in the hope of discovering some unturned stone which might lead to new

---

[1] I should like to thank John Stirling, Librarian of Exeter University, for granting me permission to consult the manuscript on a daily basis and for allowing ultra-violet photographs to be made of some of the manuscript's folios, and also Peter Thomas, Assistant Librarian of Exeter Cathedral, for being most helpful and offering assistance whenever it was needed.

[2] For example, it might be desirable to compare punctuation patterns, correction techniques and the distribution of special letter forms in arguing the number of scribes involved in copying the manuscript.

[3] G.F. Krapp, E. van K. Dobbie, eds., *The Exeter Book*, Anglo-Saxon Poetic Records III (New York: Columbia U.P., 1936; henceforth *ASPR III*). Krapp and Dobbie indicate in their notes to *Christ* (p. 247) that, though they did not consult the manuscript itself, they have used Ker's readings for the first folio, obtained using ultra-violet photography.

150   BERNARD J. MUIR

developments in *Exeter Book* studies (perhaps that which *ða wyrhtan iu wiðwurpon to weorce*).[4] I was not prepared for what I found: there are over four hundred scribal alterations in the manuscript that are not discussed by Krapp and Dobbie (or by any other editor so far as I am aware) because they *are not visible* in the facsimile. There are, in addition, a substantial number of alterations to letters which *are* visible on close examination of even the facsimile that have also gone unnoticed, and consequently have never been assessed or annotated.

Robin Flower refers to the script of the *Exeter Book* as "the noblest of Anglo-Saxon hands", and few would argue that it is not.[5] The fact that hundreds of corrections have been made in the course of the copying of the manuscript should not diminish our estimation of the skill of the scribe, but suggest, if anything, that he was a most conscientious craftsman. In the majority of cases, the original reading of a corrected word cannot be recovered, and thus the presence of these alterations does not affect past readings and interpretations of the poems. However, there are many changes to the text which seem to have been made in an attempt either to alter its dialect or to update its orthography, and a comprehensive analysis of these may provide new data about the transmission and reception of poetic texts in the tenth century. This is a large undertaking, and will have to be carried out as the edition progresses; however, a small number of representative corrections are discussed below, some with reference to the accompanying figures. An analysis of the types of corrections in the *Exeter Book* and of the technique used to make them will reveal a great deal about how one particularly careful scribe worked, and perhaps more about the working habits of Anglo-Saxon scribes in general.

Great strides have been made in our understanding and appreciation of Old English texts in the past fifty years, and new editions of the major manuscript collections are long overdue. This is particularly true of the *Exeter Book*, since it has rightly been the subject of a massive amount of critical writing, which has not yet been brought to bear on the collection as a whole. Of course, many fine editions have been made of individual poems, but the tendency to treat the texts individually has drawn attention away from the collection as an anthology. The near total absence of critical literature dealing with the manuscript as an anthology seems, at least, to indicate this.

One critic currently studying the manuscript in its entirety is Patrick Conner, who, however, has forwarded the proposition that the *Exeter Book* as we know it today is a compilation of three booklets.[6] Scholars who in recent years have found Kevin Kiernan's theories concerning the evolution of *Beowulf* and its manuscript unsettling may well find this theory equally disturbing. However, Conner's arguments are well formulated and deserve attention, though my primary concern in this paper is not to discuss exhaustively the merits of his thesis. In presenting my

---

[4] "the workmen of old cast aside from the workplace" (*Advent Lyrics* 2b–3a).

[5] "The Script of the *Exeter Book*," *The Exeter Book of Old English Poetry*, eds. R.W Chambers, Max Förster and Robin Flower (London: Percy Lund, Humphries and Co., 1933) 83.

[6] "The Structure of the Exeter Book Codex", *Scriptorium*, XL (1986), 233–42; this is a reworking of a paper delivered to the *International Society of Anglo-Saxonists* at Cambridge in 1985.

EDITING THE *EXETER BOOK* 151

statistical analysis of the *Exeter Book*, of necessity I make reference to Conner's work repeatedly, and sometimes suggest other possible interpretations of the data.

Conner states, in dealing with the codicology of the manuscript, that "divisions among the booklets are supported by the intersection of several kinds of evidence" (p. 234), which he subsequently lists as, i) the presence of soiled first folios; ii) the use of different grades of limp parchment, each restricted to one of the three booklets; iii) the different techniques used in each booklet for adding auxiliary rulings; iv) the different treatment of the decorative initials in each booklet; v) the presence and disposition of drypoint etchings in the manuscript; vi) the use of various ligatures; and vii) the distribution of special letter forms.

I have not duplicated all of Conner's research, but often our purposes cross, and at times we have come up with conflicting data: for example, he observes that "there are no drypoints in the first booklet" (p. 237), but I found three incised etchings on f. 24 ^{v} (Figure 61) and some crude attempts at making capitals in the margin of f. 47 ^{v}; I have not checked his figures for the distribution of ligatures and of the various forms of the letter *y*, but I note in passing that, whereas in his *Table 4* he lists 47 occurrences of the *oc* form of the letter *a* (distributed 19–29–9 in the three hypothetical booklets), I find 79 occurrences (distributed 28–39–12).

Perhaps a few words about the format of the new edition would not be amiss before discussing the database. Most of the data presented in the Introduction to *ASPR III* in tabular form is included, but is relegated to the apparatus at the bottom of the page so that it is more accessible to the reader. (How many times has any of us paused while reading a poem to see where the accents fall and to consider the possible significance of their distribution?) There will be an annotated diplomatic transcript of the manuscript on fiche included in the edition, recording data of interest perhaps more to palaeographers and lexicographers than to literary critics.[7] This will allow those without access to the limited edition 1933 facsimile to have a graphic representation of the appearance of the manuscript with annotations detailing the condition of its damaged sections.

The edition includes indices of biblical allusions and of patristic and other sources for the texts (so far as these are known), and an appendix containing a small number of Latin liturgical texts which have inspired (parts of) some of the poems. The textual annotations found at the end of *ASPR III* have been edited and extended to include editorial work of the past fifty years. The texts are treated conservatively, allowing many forms previously emended to conform to a hypothetical classical form of Old English to stand as evidence for the state of the language in the third quarter of the tenth century; this is particularly important in light of the extent to which the scribe (and / or a nearly contemporary corrector) made significant linguistic alterations to the text.

---

[7] For example, the distribution of small capitals, or the physical state of the manuscript (where drypoints occur, or where the manuscript has sustained damage).

152 BERNARD J. MUIR

The Database (see *Table*)

It should be borne in mind when making calculations from the following data that a considerable amount of text has been lost from the manuscript. By the time the first foliation was done in the sixteenth century there were ten single folios missing, and perhaps three (or more) complete gatherings. Of course, the beginning of the manuscript has been lost, and there may have been more texts following the riddle which ends at the bottom of folio 130 ᵛ (see below). The table includes a considerable amount of data already available elsewhere, but puts it into a unique configuration which allows readers to use it easily in conjunction with the data tabulated by Conner.

Discussion of the database

The folio numbers of the manuscript appear down the left hand side of the page (with recto and verso treated individually). A group of two *Xs* in this column (corresponding to the recto and verso) indicates the position of a lost folio. Each column across the page is labelled at the top to identify the type of data it contains. This data has been organized into six sections: codicological data (*Columns 1–11*), distribution of large and medium sized initials (*12–13*), methods of correcting the texts (*14–16*), presence of Latin or runic writing (*17–18*), use of punctuation (*19–22*), and distribution of specific letter forms (*23–28*). A series of dashes runs across the chart where a folio is missing. Where appropriate in the following analysis, the columns are labelled either *logical* (with T(rue) or F(alse) values) or *numeric* (with the value in a numeric field recording the quantity or number of occurrences of a specified type of data on each folio). Subtotals for the three hypothetical booklets are given before the overall totals at the end of the table, and a solid line appears before folios 53 ʳ and 98 ʳ in the table to mark the booklet boundaries.

Gathering Preparation, Collation and Text Layout

There are 17 extant gatherings, the first 16 of which are regularly composed of 8 folios (giving 16 pages), though some gatherings contain singletons (2, 6, 15, 16); the seventeenth may have had as few as six folios or as many as ten, but the uniformity of the first 16 suggests that the last one also had 8 folios, in which case three folios have been lost (one before the present f. 126 and two after f. 130). However, if gathering seventeen was originally in final position, then the scribe may have needed only six folios to finish copying his exemplar (*Riddle 95* finishes at the very end of the verso of f. 130), in which case, the only loss would be of a single folio at the end of the manuscript.

I agree with Conner's observation that the text of *Partridge* has been lost after one and a half lines, and that the text beginning on the top of the present f. 98 ʳ is the end of a different poem whose beginning has been lost.[8] In addition to the gathering

---

[8] Conner designates this fragment *Homiletic Fragment III* (p. 234). It might also be noted that it would be exceptional for a *Physiologus* poem to contain dialogue, as does the text beginning at the top

EDITING THE *EXETER BOOK*   153

lost here, Pope argues—rightly, I believe—that another is wanting, that which contained the ending of *Guthlac* and the beginning of *Azarias*.[9]

In summary, at present the *Exeter Book* contains 123 folios. One folio has been lost before folio 8, and 12 more single folios thoughout the text (or 10, if the 17th gathering had only 6 folios). Two gatherings (probably of the usual 8 folios) have also been lost. Thus the manuscript would have comprised 152 (or 150) folios when it was described as *an mycel Englisc boc be gehwilcum þingum on leoðwisan geworht* in the Leofric donation list in the eleventh century.[10]

Column 1 lists the numbers of the extant gatherings. [According to Conner's thesis, Booklet 1 comprises gatherings 1–6 (written last), Booklet 2 gatherings 7–12 (written first), and Booklet 3 gatherings 13–17 (written second).]

Column 2 indicates the number of each folio's conjugate.

Column 3 (logical) indicates which folios are singletons. [There are no singletons in Conner's second booklet.]

Column 4 (logical) indicates which side of the folio is the hair side of the parchment. With some of the poorly prepared, darker sheets of parchment it is sometimes difficult to establish by appearance alone which is the hair side; in some such instances, the texture of the surface can be of help in determining this. It will be seen that the scribe has not always been careful to match hair and flesh sides in a regular pattern; of course, this is impossible in gatherings containing singletons. [From the data in *Columns 1–4* the complete collation of the manuscript can be determined.]

Column 5 (numerical) shows how many lines of text normally appear in a gathering (sometimes lines are left blank—see *Columns 7* and *8*); and *Column 6* (logical) indicates where the prickmarks or rulings equal the number of lines of text.

Twenty-two lines per page is the norm, though gatherings 1 and 6 have 23, and gathering 11 has 21 throughout. Gathering 12 is ruled for 22 lines of text, but the scribe has written just 21 lines on its first five folios (91^r–93^r) before reverting to 22 (though he spread them out over the total area of the writing grid). He may have done this so that the first page of the gathering matched the last of the previous one (90^v). He reverted to the proper 22 lines at the top of a verso (93^v) where the shift would not be quite so obvious.

Column 7 (numeric) shows where blank lines have been left between texts or sections of poems (but not at the bottom of a folio), and *Column 8* (numeric)

_____
of 98^r.

[9] "Palaeography and Poetry: some solved and unsolved problems of the Exeter Book," *Medieval Scribes, Manuscripts and Libraries: Essays presented to N.R. Ker*, eds. M.B. Parkes and A.G. Watson (London: Scolar Press, 1978) 40. Of course, it is possible to argue that *two* gatherings are missing at this point, depending on how much of each poem is thought to be wanting.

[10] "one great English book on various subjects composed in verse." The most recent edition and study of the inventory of books left to Exeter Cathedral by Leofric is by Michael Lapidge, "Surviving booklists from Anglo-Saxon England," *Learning and Literature in Anglo-Saxon England*, eds. M. Lapidge and H. Gneuss (Cambridge: Cambridge U. P., 1985) 64–69; the most detailed description of the complete donation is the one by Förster, "The Donations of Leofric to Exeter," in the 1933 facsimile, pp. 10–32.

154 BERNARD J. MUIR

indicates where lines have been left blank at the bottom of a folio. [No lines have been left blank at the end of a folio in Conner's third booklet.]

Column 9 (numeric) indicates where text wrap marks appear.[11] In all but one case, these resemble a reversed *s*-shaped scroll placed before the designated text; on f. 125 ᵛ (line 17) before *gierwed* a double forward-sloping slash is used (//). [Wrap marks appear in all three hypothetical booklets.]

Column 10 (logical) indicates folios on which there are traces of goldleaf. The presence of these traces in a manuscript lacking illumination indicates that at some stage after the *Exeter Book* was copied, and probably when its texts could no longer be understood, it became a repository for sheets of goldleaf used to decorate other manuscripts produced in the scriptorium. The high number of folios on which traces can still be found today (90) indicates that the scriptorium was well-equipped and well-endowed in its heyday.

Column 11 (logical) indicates where drypoint etchings occur, usually in the left or right margins, but in one instance in the centre of the bottom margin (f. 123 ʳ). Förster notes only decorative etchings (p. 60), and thus does not include the series of diagonal slashes on f. 59 ᵛ which Conner lists as the first drawing in the manuscript (p. 237). The drypoints on folios 24 ᵛ and 47 ᵛ were not noticed by Conner (or Förster), who argues that the absence of drypoints from the first hypothetical booklet serves to differentiate it from the second and third—an argument no longer valid. [He also observes that the unique orientation of the only drypoint in the third booklet—it is upsidedown—serves to differentiate it from the second.]

Another previously unnoticed drypoint is found on folio 96 ʳ. I had suspected its presence when in Exeter, but all that could be seen with the naked eye and an ultra-violet lamp were faint curving lines in the lower right hand margin, which I thought might be part of another robed figure. Figure 63 (an ultra-violet photograph) shows that this is indeed the case. The head of the figure is opposite lines 13–14, and his feet touch the bottom of the folio. Unlike the gowned figure on 87 ᵛ which seems to be stepping forward (Figure 64), this figure appears to be standing still. Although details are very hard to discern, the robe of the figure on 96 ʳ seems to have more elaborate folds than that of the figure on 87 ᵛ. In addition to the full length figure, a small, long-haired, disembodied head can be seen below the last word on the page (*sellend*). A hand is holding up a tilted drinking vessel in front of the head. It is possible that the rest of the body was also drawn originally, but if so, it is no longer visible.

Figure 61 shows the three etchings on f. 24 ᵛ. This style of vine and tendril patterning is unique in the manuscript. On f. 47 ᵛ etchings appear in the top and left margins. These are quite faint, but appear to be letter forms executed in a rather crude style (perhaps including *eth* and *wynn* among the more recognizable shapes),

---

[11] These text wrap marks are placed before text that could not be fitted in at the end of a line; the scribe writes the text at the end of the preceding or following line, and places the symbol before it, indicating that the designated text is not part of the line in which it appears. Wrap marks in the shape of animals and grotesques are common in elaborate Gospel books (such as *The Book of Kells*). Irish scribes called them 'turn-in-the-path' (*cor fa casan*) or 'head-under-the-wing' (*ceann fa eitil*).

EDITING THE *EXETER BOOK* 155

quite unlike anything found elsewhere in the manuscript. Those in the left margin start approximately opposite the third line of text and finish opposite the eleventh. There are two in the top margin over the first word of line one of the text, most closely resembling an *O* and a *P*. As is the case with the diagonal slashes, these etchings have no artistic merit and should not be considered ornamentation in the manuscript.

The previously noted drypoints are:

1 - a series of diagonal slashes down the left margin of f. 59 ^{v};
2 - a foliate rosette in the left margin of f. 64 ^{v} opposite lines 16–22 (Figure 65);
3 - the head and wings of an angel in the right margin of f. 78 ^{r} opposite lines 1–4 (Figure 66);
4 - two large initial *eths* in the right margin of f. 80 ^{r} opposite lines 5–7 and 14–17;
5 - a full-length robed figure holding a scroll or book in its left hand in the left margin of f. 87 ^{v} opposite lines 1–8 (Figure 64);
6 - two ornate initial *Ps* (one above the other) above two right hands extending from sleeves with fingers pointing downwards in the left margin of f. 95 ^{v} opposite lines 1–14 (Figure 62);
7 - a rider on horseback (upsidedown) in the centre of the bottom margin of f. 123 ^{r} (which did not come out clearly in the u-v photograph).

On folio 112 ^{r} there are 2 sets of ribbon-like lines incised across lines 6–7 and 8–14, and on the verso a group of intersecting incised strokes opposite lines 3–8 in the left margin. There are also very faint curving lines suggesting the presence of drypoints in the margins of two other folios (106 ^{r} and 121 ^{v}), but the technology either to verify their presence or to recover them is not available at this time. Förster thinks that the drypoints were added later, but Conner is right in observing that in several instances the writing goes over the drawings, and that they must therefore have been executed before the text was copied (p. 237).

It should also be noted that in seven instances the scribe has pressed hard enough when making the drypoint to leave an impression of the etching on the folio beneath it.[12] This means that—for whatever reason—the scribe made these etchings after the gatherings were in a state of final preparation awaiting the copying of the text—even the upsidedown horseman.[13]

---

[12] Folios 59 ^{v}, 64 ^{v}, 78 ^{r}, 80 ^{r}, 87 ^{v}, and 95 ^{v}; on a few occasions the impression is found on two or three underlying folios.

[13] It seems unlikely, for example, that he was whiling away the time while someone prepared ink for him, since the drawings appear so frequently. Moreover, it is possible that they were not all made by the same person, since they are executed with varying degrees of skill—for example, the initials on 95 ^{v} are far superior to those on 80 ^{r}. As there are no drawings incorporated in the text proper, it cannot even be ascertained if the drypoints are by the scribe who copied the text. In short, a great deal of analysis of the style and disposition of the drypoints remains to be done.

156 BERNARD J. MUIR

Initials

Columns 12–13 chart where large and medium size initials occur respectively. Uppercase and lowercase forms are used to indicate the shape of the initial as it appears in the manuscript. It was found upon measuring all the initials in the manuscript that the scribe seems to have had a notional size for a large or a medium size initial—30 and 15 mm. respectively. In the database, therefore, large initials are those which are 30 mm. or larger, and medium are from 15–29 mm. This is perhaps awkwardly arbitrary in that a 29 mm. initial is very close to being *large*, but there are not many examples such as this.[14] The scribe seems to have tried consciously to have some sort of initial on nearly every opening, as if for aesthetic effect, but it is not immediately apparent that there is a rationale behind the choice between a large and medium initial.[15] [There are twice as many medium initials as large ones, but they do not alternate in a predictable fashion, there being a high concentration of initials at the beginning of the riddles.]

Conner states that the decorative initials of the hypothetical first booklet are executed more competently than those of the second and third, "a judgment which cannot be readily demonstrated in the facsimile, but...can be seen in a good light at Exeter" (pp. 235–36), but a comparison of sample initials from each booklet failed to convince me of this. Compare, for example, the following initials: f. 15 [r] *wynn*, f. 70 [v] *thorn* and f. 117 [r] *wynn*; f. 41 [v] *I* and f. 107 [v] *I*; and, f. 87 [r] *F* and f. 98 [r] *h*. Admittedly, the scribe has added the crossbar to an uppercase *eth* in an unusual manner on one occasion (f. 58 [v]), but this is most easily explained as an oversight, and does not suggest immediately that he may have been unused to drawing *eths* if his "copying tasks were dominated by Latin texts" (Conner, p. 236); in fact, it is observed below that the scribe does his best work when copying vernacular texts.

Corrections

The scribe corrects the manuscript in several ways: he underpoints letters to be ignored (expunction—*Column 16*, numeric); he adds superscript or subscript letters, with or without an insertion sign (*Columns 14 and 15* respectively—numeric);[16] he alters a letter by scraping bits away and adding strokes to change it into another letter; and, he carefully scrapes away one or more letters and enters the new reading.

---

[14] The size of every initial is listed in the edition. For purposes of clarification and consistency, initials smaller than fifteen mm. but larger than a normal size capital are called *large capitals* in the edition.

[15] There is further evidence of the scribe's concern for aesthetics at the end of *Christ II* (folios 31 [v]–32 [r]) where—knowing from his exemplar exactly how much text remained to be copied—he began to space out his text so that it would end near the bottom of a folio, allowing him to start the next major poem (*Christ III*) at the top of a new folio and opening; despite his efforts, he still finished three and a half lines short of the end of f. 32 [r].

[16] With the exception of two ys on f. 43 [v], all the subscript alterations to the texts (11 in number) are identical: a slightly smaller *g* has been added just below the line of writing—these all appear to be in the principal scribe's hand. The disposition of the two exceptional letters—they are a considerable distance below the line of writing—suggests that they were added by a different person.

EDITING THE *EXETER BOOK*

Most examples of the last type of correction have never been documented, as noted above (over 400 of them). The scribe makes this sort of correction so skilfully that they are often detectable only when the manuscript is held up at different angles to a strong light source. Even then they are not always visible, and must be detected by passing the hand lightly over the surface of the text and *feeling* for the slight abrasiveness left by the scraping.

Expunction is the least common method of correction (if superscript and subscript corrections are taken together), though it is used throughout the manuscript. [Subscript additions are the only type of correction not found in all three of Conner's booklets, there being none in the third.] The second most common method of altering a reading is by scraping away from and adding bits to an existing letter; although these alterations are visible in the manuscript, many have not been noted.

The corrections described here illustrate different types of alterations made by the scribe; the same techniques of correcting appear uniformly throughout the manuscript. Photographs of two folios on which a number of alterations have been made are reproduced as Figures 67 and 68.

17 ^v   The scribe has made five corrections on this folio, only one of which is noted in *ASPR III*: *hiw* (.2): *i* is altered from a letter that had a descender; *snyttru* (.5–6): *n* is written over an erased letter; *sumum* (.13): -*u(m)* added above; *sped* (.13): *wynn* is altered to *s* by scraping away part of its diagonal stroke; *bryttað* (.19–20): final *ð* is altered from *t*; and *ængum* (.20): *n* is written over a *g* (which is still partly visible in the facsimile). (Figure 67)

60 ^v   Three of the four alterations to the text of this folio are noted in *ASPR III* (because they are *visible* in the facsimile): *eastan* (.6): first *a* has an unerased descender; *sceawiaþ* (.8): original final *n* altered to *þ*; *onmearm stane* (.12): *e* of *mearm* expuncted, and the *r* erased (though still visible)—these changes were made after the text had been copied; *sidwegum* (.14): there is an expunction sign in the loop of the *g*. (Figure 68)

63 ^r.5   *gefremmaþ*: *þ* is altered from *n* by erasing 2 elements and adding an ascender and a descender; the same adjustment is made at 64 ^r.19 to *siþiaþ*.

89 ^v.2   *torhtre*: the scribe first made a descender, then changed his mind and made an *o* by scraping away the descender; note the flat side of the *o*.

94 ^v.19   *grorn*: 1st *r* is altered from *n*; the scribe traced over the first minim and extended it below the line.

101 ^r.8   *hrofum*: *h* is altererd from *r*, and *r* from *f* (it seems).

105 ^v.2   *seomað*: *ð* is altered from *d* by adding a crossbar. The crossbar is not visible in the facsimile so that *ASPR III* records the manuscript reading as *seo mad* and emends the text unnecessarily. The scribe made six other adjustments to the text on this folio, none of which is noted in *ASPR III*.

105 ^v.22   *firenaþ*: *a* is altered from either *u* or *n*, *þ* is altered from *wynn*, and a letter has been scraped away at the end of the word.

158 BERNARD J. MUIR

107 ʳ.4 *wæt: w* is altered from *þ* by scraping away the ascender.

107 ᵛ.7 *onfindeð: ð* is altered from *t*; the upward stroke of *ð* is crossed by the remnant of the horizontal top stroke of the *t*, and then the crossbar was added.

109 ᵛ.21 *tidum: i* is altered; *d* has been altered from an *l* by adding a loop to it, so that it now has a vertical ascender (which is exceptional).

115 ʳ.1 *þa: a* is altered from *e* by scraping away the tongue of the *e* and adding a tail to the *a*. This is a common type of adjustment; there are three examples of it on f. 119 alone: 119 ʳ.8 *earfoþum* (*o < e*); 119 ʳ.16 *wynna* (*a < e*); and 119 ᵛ.4 *gode* (*o < e*).

116 ᵛ.10 *byman: y* altered from *i*. This is a very common adjustment, at times made during the course of the copying, and at others being made after the text was copied out (the implications of this are explored in the edition).

118 ʳ.12 *(nu) þu: þ* altered from *wynn* by adding an ascender. *firen: r* altered from *n*; the serif of the foot of the first minim of the *n* is visible on the descender of the *r*.

124 ᵛ.16 *swa: f* altered to *s* during the course of copying the word. The scribe sometimes confuses these two letters, but usually corrects himself; see, for example, 105 ʳ.17 *swist*, 104 ᵛ.1 *swift*, 125 ᵛ.1 *swiftre* and 121 ʳ.3 *lyste*.

Latin

Column 17 (logical) indicates which folios contain text in Latin. There are a few standard abbreviations (e.g. *scs* for *sanctus* and *am* for *amen*), and sometimes one or more whole verses are in Latin (e.g. in the macaronic ending of the *Phoenix*). One text, *Riddle 90*, is completely in Latin. With the exclusion of literary considerations,[17] there appears to be nothing remarkable about the use and distribution of Latin words in the manuscript.

Runes

Runes appear throughout the codex (*Column 18*—numeric). They are used twice in the runic signature of Cyn(e)wulf, in *Christ II* (797–807) and in *Juliana* (704–708). In the latter part of the manuscript they appear most often in riddles, at times being used within a text to spell out its solution (e.g. *Riddle 19*, f. 105 ʳ) and at others being written in the space between texts to offer a clue to the solution for the following riddle (e.g. on fols. 102 ᵛ, 103 ʳ, and 105 ʳ). In *The Ruin* (f. 124 ʳ), the *m* rune is used for the word *mon* in the compound *mondreama* and the *w* rune is used for -*wynn* in *Riddle 91* (f. 129 ᵛ). Less frequently a rune appears for no apparent reason (e.g. after the fifth stanza of *Deor* on f. 101 ᵛ). The large, poorly-formed runes incised in the right margin of f. 125 ʳ (opposite *Riddle 64*) are impossible to date with any certainty.

---

[17] For example, why does the *Phoenix* poet use a macaronic ending? Is it to do with a spirit of experimentation with literary forms evident elsewhere in the manuscript? Etcetera.

EDITING THE *EXETER BOOK*

Punctuation and its function

The most common punctuation mark in the *Exeter Book* is the point (or fullstop) in a raised position, approximately half the height of a minuscule letter above the line of writing.[18] The point standing on the line of writing appears only 10 times (*Column 22*—numeric) [and not at all in Conner's second and third booklets]. The raised point is used sparingly (less than five times per folio side) on approximately one quarter of the folios in the manuscript [distributed almost equally in the hypothetical booklets (*Column 21*—logical)].[19]

On several occasions (usually in lists and catalogues, or passages with a high density of rhetorical figures), the raised point has been used at the end of a number of consecutive verses; this is tabulated in *Column 20* (logical). The number of times points occur within a verse is so small as to appear insignificant or aberrant, and they are much more common at the end of a *b* verse than after an *a* verse. Although the spacing between words and particles throughout the manuscript at first appears unpredictable (as it does in the other poetic codices), close study of the patterns of division is beginning to suggest there may be some discernible principles at work; these will be outlined in detail in the edition. For the moment, suffice it to say that on only ten occasions in the whole corpus of poems are words joined together where the caesura occurs, indicating that the scribe was aware of the principles of versification and understood precisely what he was writing (*Column 19*—logical).[20]

The only other punctuation in the manuscript is the combination of symbols used to mark the end of poems (and sections of longer poems); the scribe often uses several of these at a time or repeats the same combination two or more times. Common combinations are: the point with a diagonal slash above or after it (.′); a colon followed by a 'seven' (:7); a colon followed by either an undulating or a straight dash (:~ or :—); and a 'seven' with an 'umlaut' above it (7).[21]

Special Letter Forms

The use of three special letter forms is charted in the database. The curved, 'upside-down' type *r* (*Column 23*—numeric) is used 6 times, always at the end of a line

---

[18] The dot which appears frequently at the end of the long tail of final *a* where the writing instrument leaves the parchment is not regarded in the edition as a deliberate attempt by the scribe to punctuate without wasting movement. When he wishes to place a point after an *a*, he does so very clearly, as can be seen at f. 85 ʳ.4 and .16 (in *Widsith*).

[19] Although I thought at times that I could distinguish between points with different elevations, the lack of any perceivable consistency or rationale in the use of such a system led me to abandon further investigation of this possibility.

[20] In order to make any sort of statement about word spacing, an arbitrary decision had to be made as to how great a space had to be present before two words or particles became separate entities. After reading the whole manuscript letter by letter, I decided that the minimal distance would be 2 mm., which is the figure upon which statements regarding word spacing are based in this paper. Of course, I did not measure the space between every letter in the manuscript, relying after a period on my visual judgment.

[21] For examples of these, see fols. 20 ᵛ, 35 ʳ, 65 ᵛ, 96 ᵛ, 100 ᵛ and 127 ʳ.

160   BERNARD J. MUIR

[never in Conner's first booklet]. The *oc* form of the letter *a* is used 79 times in the manuscript: the general impression given in reading the manuscript is that the scribe reserved the *oc* form of *a* for special occasions, since he often uses it in proper names (×37, *Column 24*—numeric) and Latin words (×13, *Column 25*—numeric), but he uses it quite frequently in less significant Old English words (×29, *Columns 26–27*—numeric), especially *ac* when it begins a new sentence or clause (×11, *Column 27*). The *hooked e* is used on 15 occasions (*Column 28*—numeric), and is not confined to any one section of the manuscript.[22]

Summary

Most of the observations made in this conclusion are relevant—in one way or another—to a consideration of Conner's 'booklet' theory. As Conner observes, different grades of parchment occur throughout the manuscript, but I am less willing than he to derive any conclusion from this fact. Both thick, heavy parchment and a much thinner, fine grade parchment are found, usually mixed together in gatherings (although the whole eleventh gathering is comprised of limp vellum). Conner argues that three different grades of limp vellum have been used, each confined to a single booklet (p. 234). This is a very fine distinction to make, and I should be hesitant to make much of it if other data suggest that one scribe can be seen working in a consistent manner throughout the whole codex. It is perhaps worth noting that defective parchment has been used in nearly every gathering,[23] which suggests to me that a large quantity of high grade parchment was not set aside for the copying of the manuscript because it was to contain texts that were in the vernacular, not Latin, and because it was not a liturgical book; that is, it is the sort of compilation in which an assortment of parchments might be expected to be found.

It has also been shown that the scribe demonstrates consistent work habits throughout the codex—in punctuating it, in his use of large and medium size initials, in his technique of correcting the text,[24] and in his use of special letter forms (among other things). He demonstrates by his observation of the caesura that he understands the principles of Anglo-Saxon verse, and is most likely a native speaker (which makes it unlikely that he would have had trouble executing large initial *eths*). He has copied the *Exeter Book* with much greater care and concern than he exhibited in copying the two Latin codices attributed to him, Bodley 319 and Lambeth Palace 149.[25]

---

[22] On several occasions after the text was copied out, the scribe (or a corrector) has altered an *æ* to an *e* by scraping away parts of the letter; these and other linguistic matters will have to wait to be dealt with comprehensively in the full edition.

[23] Folios 13, 28, 31, 40, 43, 44, 56, 66, 78, 80, 106, 110, 112, 113, 114, 116 and 127 had defects before they were used.

[24] As a matter of both codicological and literary interest, it is noteworthy that the scribe generally has a lower error rate in shorter poems: this could be either because it is easier to maintain attention during the copying of a shorter poem, or because some of the shorter poems were popular, and perhaps familiar to him (for example, *The Wanderer* and *The Gifts of Men* are almost error free).

[25] Kenneth Sisam first brought the relationship between Lambeth 149 and the *Exeter Book* to Flower's attention ("The Script of the Exeter Book," in the 1933 facsimile, p. 85), and Neil Ker was

EDITING THE *EXETER BOOK* 161

There are many other, more minute types of evidence which suggest that one scribe copied the manuscript, probably as a single codex.[26] If the distribution, style and subject matter of the texts suggest that groups of poems originated at different times (as Conner suggests, in a preliminary fashion on pp. 240–42), there is nothing implicit in this paper which argues that the scribe did not have as his exemplar two, three or more smaller booklets of poems. I find, however, that my study of the codicological data to date does not induce me to support the theory that the codex known today as the *Exeter Book* is a composite manuscript consisting of three booklets written at different times by the same scribe.

---

the first to establish the connection with Bodley 319 (in his review of the facsimile edition, *Medium Ævum* 2 (1933): 230–31). I intend to present a detailed analysis of the relationship between these manuscripts in a separate study in the near future.

[26] These will all have a place in the new edition. They include, for example, observations about how he uses blank spaces to demarcate one text from another and how he squeezes in parts of words at the bottom of folios (which he does in nine instances throughout the manuscript).

TABLE

Key to column identification							
1	gathering	2	conjugate	3	singleton	4	hair
5	no. of lines	6	ll. = prickings	7	blank ll.	8	endblanks
9	wrap mark	10	goldleaf	11	drypoints	12	lg initial
13	med initial	14	expunction	15	subscript	16	superscript
17	Latin text	18	runes	19	caesura	20	verse-pointing
21	sparse pointing	22	low pointing	23	curved *r*	24	*a* (names)
25	*a* (non-O.E.)	26	*a* (O.E.)	27	*a* (in *ac*)	28	hooked *e*

	1	2	3	4	5	6	7	8	9	10	11	12	13	14	15	16	17	18	19	20	21	22	23	24	25	26	27	28
X	1	14		-	23	-	-	-	-	-	-	-	-	-	-	-	-	-	-	-	-	-	-	-	-	-	-	-
X	↓			-	↓	-	-	-	-	-	-	-	-	-	-	-	-	-	-	-	-	-	-	-	-	-	-	-
8ʳ		13				T																						1
8ᵛ				T		T											T							1				
9ʳ		12		T		T	1					E				1	T									1		1
9ᵛ						T																						
10ʳ		11		T		T	1						E								T							
10ᵛ						T																			1	1		
11ʳ		10				T									1				T		T							
11ᵛ				T		T							E								T							
12ʳ		9				T															T							
12ᵛ				T		T									1				T									
13ʳ		8		T		T	1						E								T							
13ᵛ						T															T	T						
14ʳ		-				T	2			T		N									T							
14ᵛ		-				T				T										T								
15ʳ	2	21		T	22	T	1					W								T	T							
15ᵛ	↓				↓	T				T						3				T								
X		-	T	-		-	-	-	-	-	-	-	-	-	-	-	-	-	-	-	-	-	-	-	-	-	-	-
X		-	T	-		-	-	-	-	-	-	-	-	-	-	-	-	-	-	-	-	-	-	-	-	-	-	-
16ʳ		20				T										1												
16ᵛ				T		T	1			T		δ																

	17'	17'	18'	18'	19'	19'	20'	20'	21'	21'	22'	22'	23'	23'	24'	24'	25'	25'	26'	26'	27'	27'	28'	28'	29'	29'	30'	30'	31'	31'	32'	32'	33'	33'	34'	34'	35'	35'	36'	36'	37'	37'	X	X
28																																					1						1	· ·
27																					1		1																		1		· ·
26																			1	1					1			1															· ·
25																																											· ·
24													2		2																												· ·
23																																											· ·
22												6			1																				3								· ·
21					1		1		1		1 1		1		1		1 1 1													1													· ·
20	1	1																																									· ·
19																																									1		· ·
18						7																																					· ·
17																																											· ·
16	1	1			2		1											1					2		1			1		1		1											· ·
15	1																		1																								· ·
14					1										1				1				1					1															· ·
13		D		N																	N		N		S						M		G		8								· ·
12						8		S		4		4															S																· ·
11															1																												· ·
10	1		1					1		1		1		1 1		1 1		1		1						1 1									1		1						· ·
9											1						1		1								1																· ·
8																									3								·										· ·
7									2		1												1										1										· ·
6	1	1	1	1	1 1	1	1	1	1	1	1	1	1	1	1	1	1	1	1	1	1	1	1	1	1	1	1	1	1	1	1	1	1	1	1	1	1	1	1	1	1	1	· ·
5											22→																22→																22→
4	1			1	1		1			1 1			1 1		1		1		1 1		1 1		1			1 1		1			1 1		· ·
3				1 1																																						· ·
2	18	17		·	·	16	15	29		28		27		26		25		24		23		22		37		36		35		34		33		32		31		30			44			
1								3→															4→																			5→		

	43	42	41	40	39	38		52	50			49	48	46			45	60	59	58	57	56	55	54
28	1					1			1															
27		1				1 1												1		1				
26																								
25																								
24					2 2 2		4											4		4 1				
23																								
22																								
21		1		1	1	1 1 1 1 1 1 1				1							1			1 1 1 1 1 1				
20																								
19																								
18																								
17																		1						
16					1												1		1 1			1	1	
15				2	1				1								1					1		
14		1				1	2				1							1		1				
13		G		D		O	b O		b	D										D		D		
12	h		1		D		W									h	B	h					A	
11						1																	1	
10	1	1	1	1 1	1	1											1 1		1 1 1 1 1			1		
9	1			1													1							
8																								
7		1	1		2	1		1			1 1							1			1 1			
6	1 1 1 1 1 1 1 1 1 1 1 1 1 1 1 1 1 1 1 1 1 1 1 1																	1 1 1 1 1 1 1 1 1							
5						23 →												22 →						
4	1	1	1 1	1	1	1 1	1 1	1		1 1	1		1				1	1	1	1 1		1	1	
3						1 1			1 1															
2	43	42	41	40	39	38		52	50			49	48	46			45	60	59	58	57	56	55	54
1						6 →												7 →						

	60'	60"	61'	61"	62'	62"	63'	63"	64'	64"	65'	65"	66'	67'	67"	68'	68"	69'	69"	X'	X"	70'	70"	71'	71"	72'	72"	73'	73"	X'	X"	74'	74"	75'	75"	76'	76"	77'	77"	78'	78"	79'	79"
1	8 →																	9 →														10 →											
2	53		68		67		66		65		64		63	62		61		74				73		72		71		70				69		82		81		80		79		78	
3																																											
5	22 →													22 →																		22 →											

	80'	80'	81'	81'	82'	82'	83'	83'	84'	85'	85'	86'	86'	87'	87'	88'	88'	89'	89'	90'	90'	91'	91'	92'	92'	93'	93'	94'	94'	95'	95'	96'	96'	97'	X	X		98'	98'	99'	99'	100'	100'
1			11 →																	12 →																		13 →					
2	77		76		75		90		89	88		87		86		85		84		83		·	·	97		96		95		94		93		92		91		105		104		103	
3																																											
4	⊢	⊢		⊢	⊢		⊢	⊢		⊢	⊢		⊢	⊢		⊢	⊢		⊢	⊢		⊢	⊢		⊢	⊢		⊢										⊢		⊢	⊢	
5				21 →															21 →					22 →														22 →				
6	⊢	⊢	⊢	⊢	⊢	⊢	⊢	⊢	⊢	⊢	⊢	⊢	⊢	⊢	⊢	⊢	⊢					⊢	⊢	⊢	⊢	⊢	⊢	⊢										⊢	⊢	⊢	⊢	⊢
7					1		1			1		1															1		1									2					
8																																											
9																																											
10	⊢	⊢	⊢	⊢			⊢	⊢	⊢		⊢			⊢	⊢		⊢		⊢					⊢				⊢										⊢		⊢	⊢	
11	⊢									⊢												⊢	⊢																			
12		m		h		W				F			F		F		R		W		M																	h				W	
13	D																			M		N		H		·	·											BWW				L	
14							⊢	⊢																			1			1	·	·											
15																					1					1		·	·														
16	1			1			1				1									1		·	·								1												
17																				⊢		·	·																				
18																																						1					
19			⊢																																								
20			⊢				⊢	⊢	⊢	⊢	⊢	⊢								⊢		·	·																				
21	⊢	⊢		⊢		⊢		⊢					⊢		⊢	⊢				⊢	⊢				·	·															⊢		
22																										·	·																
23				⊢	⊢			⊢		⊢														·	·							⊢										
24							⊢																																				
25																						·	·																				
26	1		1	1															1		1		·	·																			
27			1				1															·	·																				
28	1						1														1		·	·																			

	1	2	3	4	5	6	7	8	9	10	11	12	13	14	15	16	17	18	19	20	21	22	23	24	25	26	27	28
101'		102		T		T				T		h	Im			1		1			T							
101''		101		T		T				T		1	hJ			1		2	T		T							
102'		100				T				T			F								T							
102''		99		T		T				T			II								T							
103'		98		T		T				T			h					19										
103''			22 →										IIII								T							
104'													·					·			·							·
104''													·					6			·							·
105'				T		T			1			1	AE			1	T		T		T					1		
105''		111		T		T				T		1	II				T				T							
X													m								T							
106'		110				T						1	BI															
106''		109		T		T							−															
107'		108				T			1				IW															
107''		107		T		T							Im															
108'		106		T		T							IIG															
108''							1						E															1
109'						T																						
109''						T																						
110'			15 →										·	·														
110''						T			·			·	·								·							
111'				T		T			1			W	−								T							
111''		117		T		T			2				IWM								T							
X													IIW															
112'			T			T						II	IIh															
112''		116	T	T		T						1	IIb	1					T		T							
113'		115		T		T							δ	1							T							
113''		113				T						W																
114'				T		T							Λ															
114''		112		T		T							·	·							·							·
115'				T		T							·	·							·							·
119'			16 →										O	1							T							
119''				T		T															T							

	1	2	3	4	5	6	7	8	9	10	11	12	13	14	15	16	17	18	19	20	21	22	23	24	25	26	27	28
120'		-	T			T																		5				
120''		-	T	T		T																						
121'		125		T		T																						
121''						T							W								T							
122'		123				T							SG								T							
122''				T		T							II														1	
123'		122		T		T			1		T	h									T							
123''						T							OW					5										1
124'		-	T	T		T												1			T						1	
124''		-	T			T							OI								T							
125'		121				T			1			I	OI					18										
125''				T		T			1				WW															
X		119		T		.	.	.	.	.	.	.	.	.	.	.	.	.	.	.	.	.	.	.	.	.	.	.
X						.	.	.	.	.	.	.	.	.	.	.	.	.	.	.	.	.	.	.	.	.	.	.
X	17	-		-	22	.	.	.	.	.	.	.	.	.	.	.	.	.	.	.	.	.	.	.	.	.	.	.
X	↓	-		-	↓	.	.	.	.	.	.	.	.	.	.	.	.	.	.	.	.	.	.	.	.	.	.	.
126'		-		T		T			2				III								T							
126''		-				T							I								T							
127'		130				T						I						4			T							
127''				T		T						F	IA								T							
128'		129		T		T															T							
128''						T							NW															
129'		128				T			1			I	I														1	1
129''				T		T							m				T	1								3		
130'		127		T		T						F	I										T					
130''						T							I								T							
X		-				.	.	.	.	.	.	.	.	.	.	.	.	.	.	.	.	.	.	.	.	.	.	.
X		-		T		.	.	.	.	.	.	.	.	.	.	.	.	.	.	.	.	.	.	.	.	.	.	.
X		-				.	.	.	.	.	.	.	.	.	.	.	.	.	.	.	.	.	.	.	.	.	.	.
X		-				.	.	.	.	.	.	.	.	.	.	.	.	.	.	.	.	.	.	.	.	.	.	.
I	6		4				20	3	6	27	2	13	18	17	9	10	2	7	3	5	29	10		16		6	6	7
II	6						17	2	1	51	6	20	12	15	4	14	3	8	4	14	31		4	16	13	6	4	6
III	5		4				3		9	12	1	18	72	4		3	3	58	3		29		2	5	3	3	1	3
Total	17		8				40	5	16	90	9	51	102	36	13	27	8	73	10	19	89	10	6	37	16	15	11	16

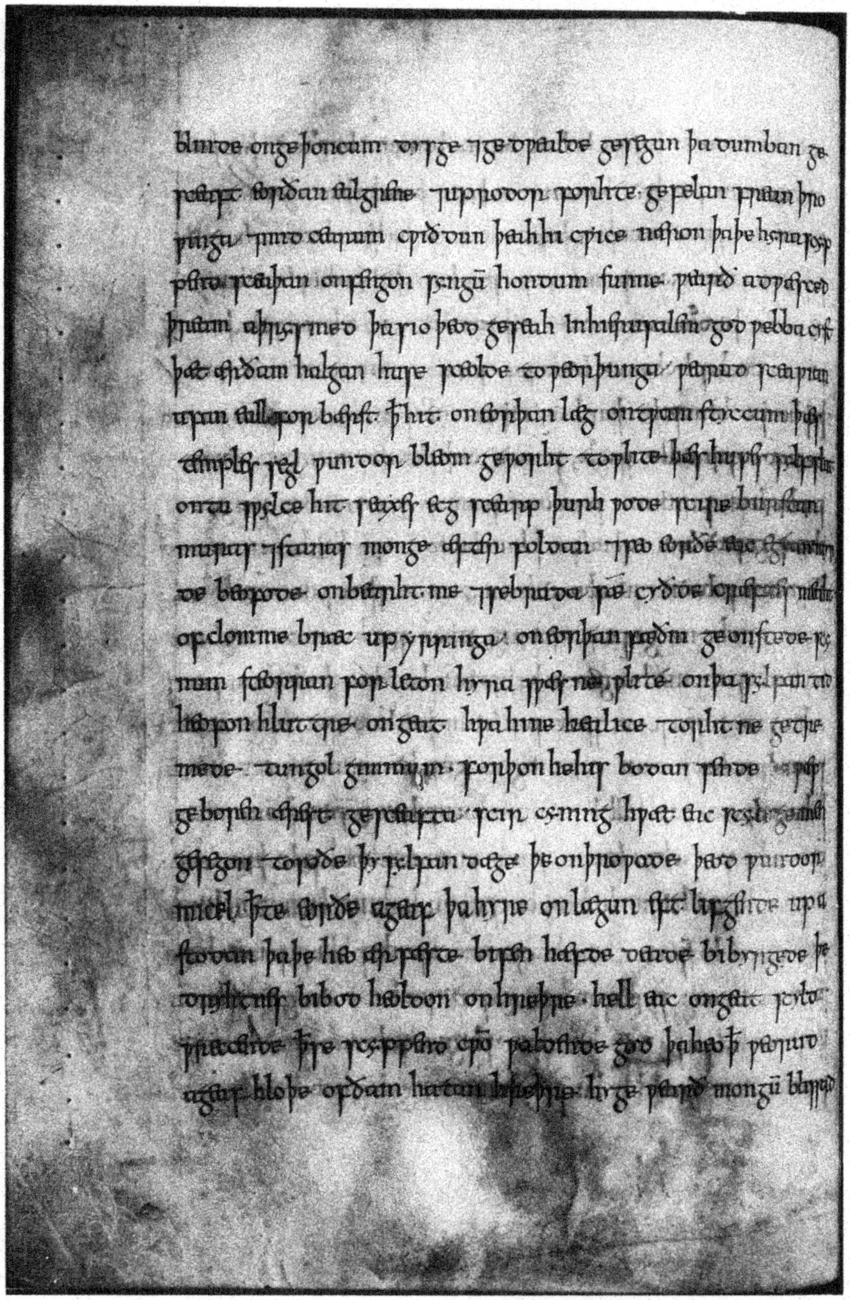

EDITING THE *EXETER BOOK*

Figure 61 Foliate and vine and tendril patterning (incised) in the left margin (half way down and at the foot of the page); Exeter, Cathedral Library MS 3501, f. 24 ᵛ; 310–320×218–225 mm [however, the leaves of the *Exeter Book* are not uniform in size].

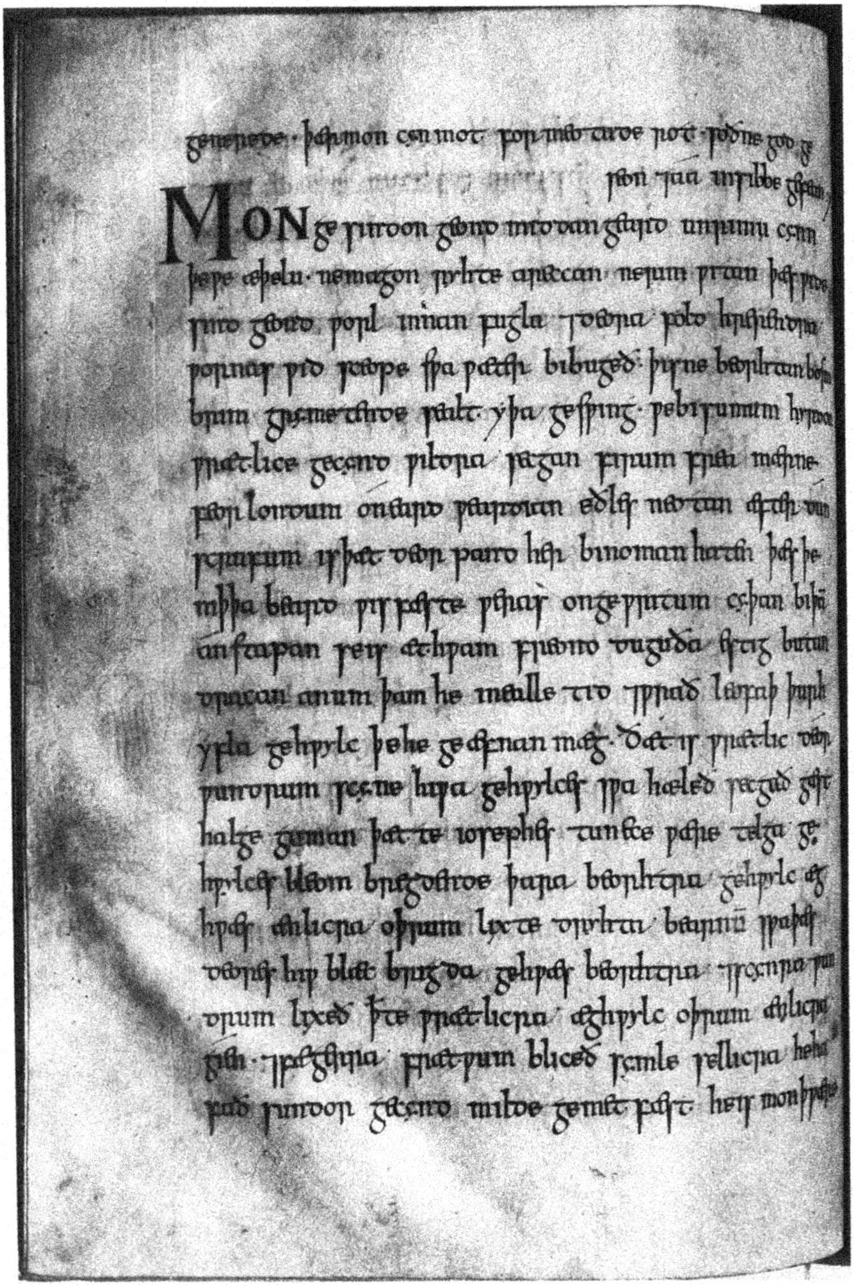

Figure 62 Two decorated initial Ps and two sleeved hands pointing downwards in the upper half of the left margin. Exeter, Cathedral Library MS 3501, f. 95 ^{v}; 310–320×218–225 mm.

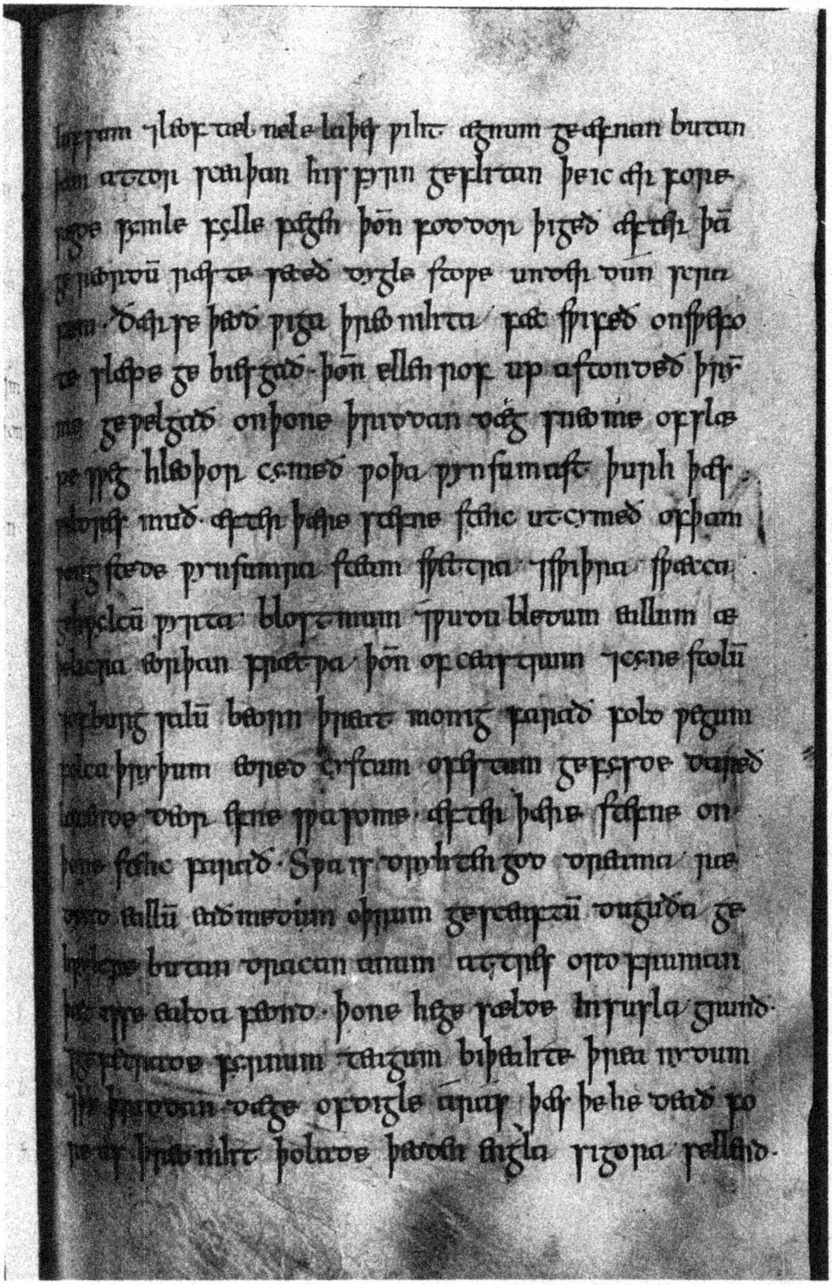

EDITING THE *EXETER BOOK*

Figure 63 A standing robed figure in the lower half of the right margin (scarcely visible in the ultra-violet original—its feet rest on the bottom of the page), and a small head (below *sellend* in the last line). Exeter, Cathedral Library MS 3501, f. 96 ʳ; 310–320×218–225 mm.

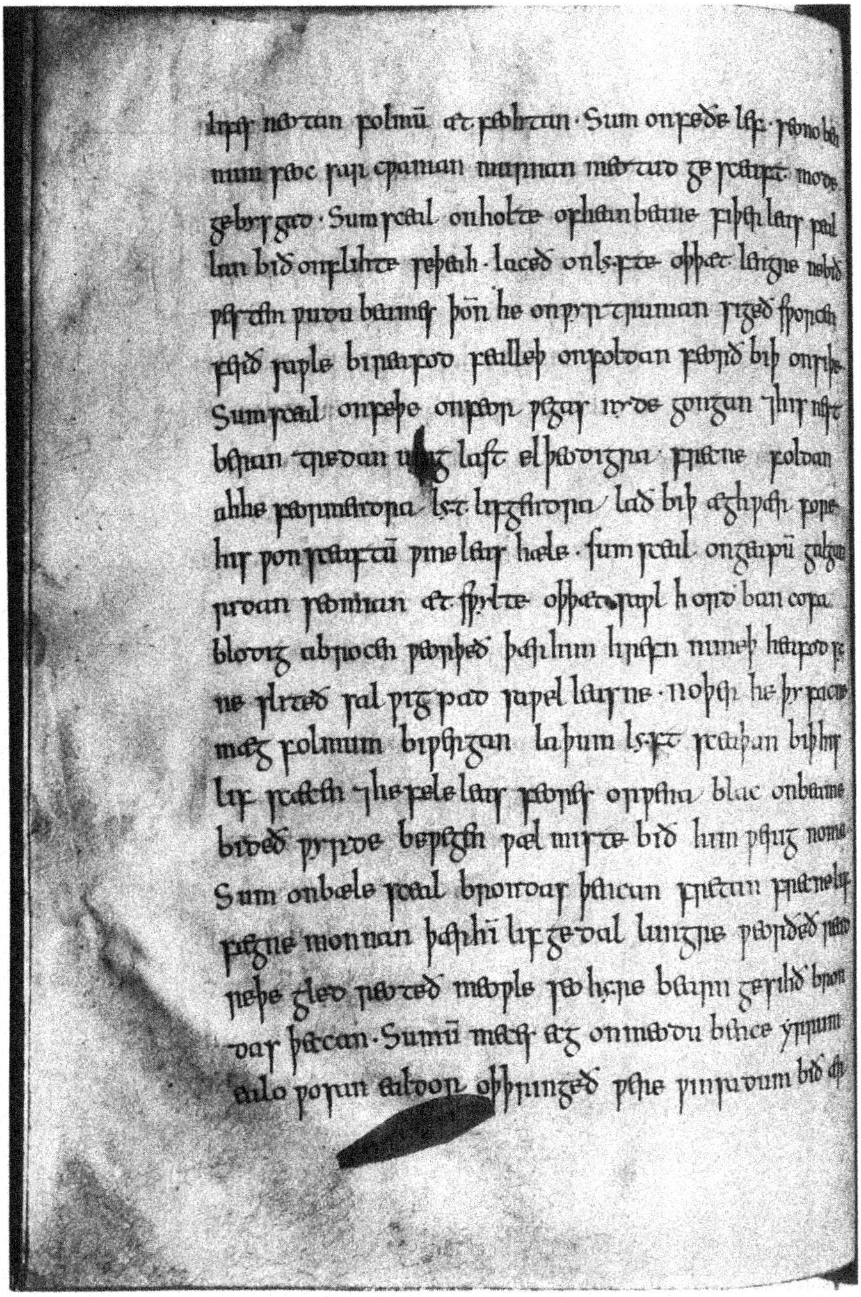

Figure 64 A standing robed figure holding a book in the upper half of the left margin. Exeter, Cathedral Library MS 3501, f. 87 ^v; 310–320×218–225 mm.

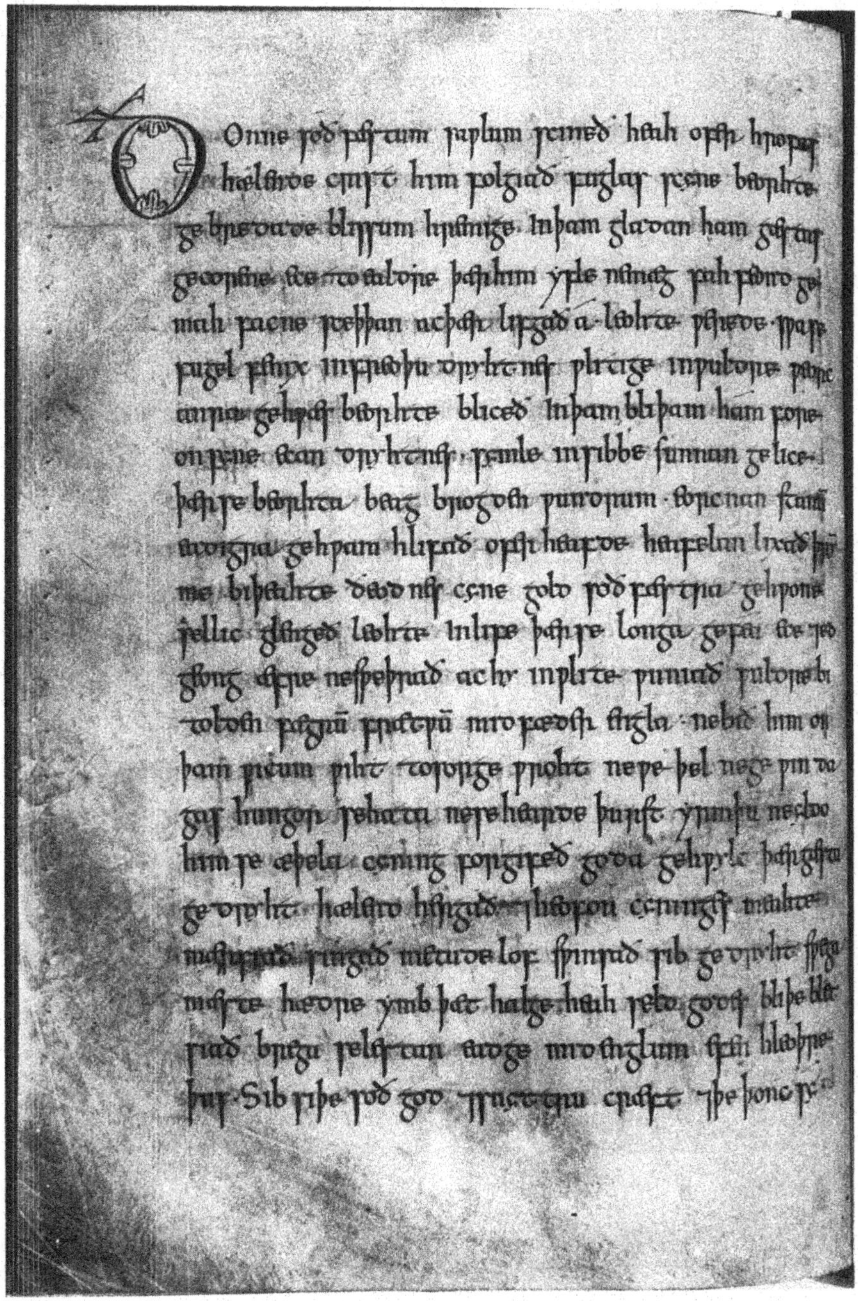

EDITING THE *EXETER BOOK* 173

Figure 65 A foliate rosette in the lower portion of the left margin. Exeter, Cathedral Library MS 3501, f. 64 ᵛ; 310–320×218–225 mm.

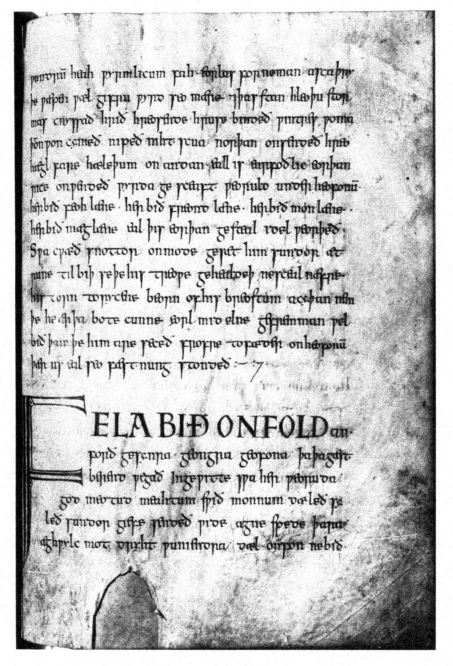

Figure 66 Head and wings of an angel in the upper portion of the right margin. Exeter, Cathedral Library MS 3501, f. 78ʳ; 310–320×218–225 mm.

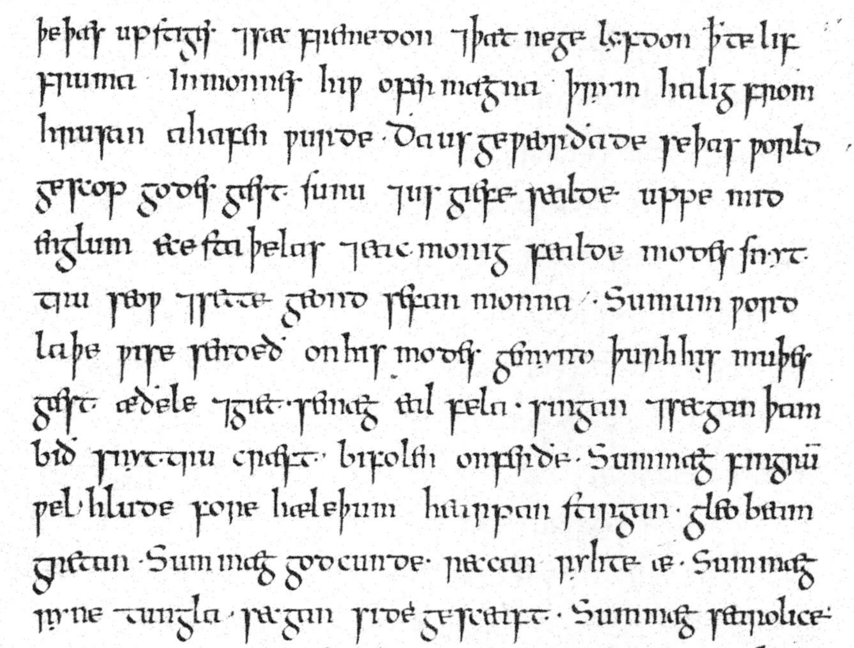

Figure 67 Corrections discussed in the paper. Exeter, Cathedral Library MS 3501, f. 17 ᵛ; 310–320×218–225 mm.

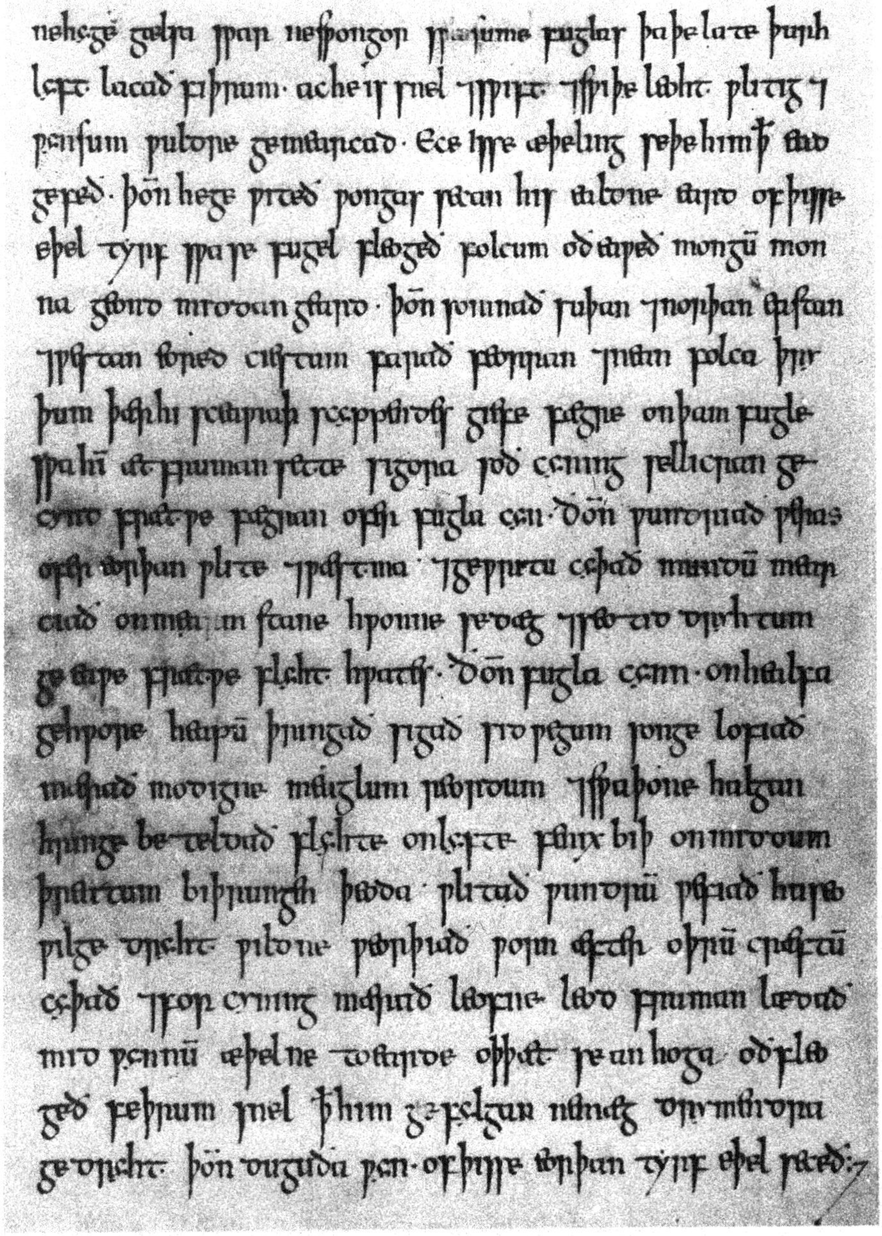

Figure 68 Corrections discussed in the paper. Exeter, Cathedral Library MS 3501, f. 60 ᵛ; 310–320×218–225 mm.

X

Art and Devotion: The Prayer-books of Jean de Berry

Margaret M. Manion

Members of the royal family and their close kin played an important part in the development of devotional practices in Medieval Europe. Not only did they sponsor large church building programmes, endow monastic and clerical foundations and help to furnish them with appropriate works of art, but they were also responsible for harnessing the clerical and artistic energies required for conducting religious services in their own households and in the churches which they frequented.

From an early age they themselves spent a considerable time each day in private and public prayer, being expected to set an example in this respect to their subjects.[1] The role of their chaplains and confessors was consequently wide-ranging and influential. As well as being responsible for the celebration of the liturgy these clerics assisted in the education of the children of the household and they could also be called upon to compile the texts for the family prayer-books, books which helped to fashion the devotional lives of their owners.[2]

An examination, from this perspective, of the extant prayer-books of Jean, Duke of Berry, third son of Jean le Bon, King of France (1350–1364), serves to complement earlier studies which have tended to focus on either the contribution which these books make to our knowledge of individual illuminators and related

---

[1] F. Lehoux, *Jean de France, duc de Berri*, 4 vols. (Paris: 1966) provides a wealth of information on the Duke's attendance at religious services. For further examples see C.A.J. Armstrong, "The Piety of Cicely, Duchess of York: A Study in Late Medieval Culture," *For Hilaire Belloc*, ed. Douglas Woodruff (London: 1942), and S.J. Bell, "Medieval Women Book Owners: Arbiters of Lay Piety and Ambassadors of Culture," in *Signs: Journal of Women in Culture and Society* 7.4 (1982): 742–767.

[2] See Lehoux, vol.1, 35–36 for the chaplains' role in the education of princes. For the involvement of the Dominican Guillaume de Valan, confessor to Philippe le Hardi, in the compilation of Philippe's *Grandes Heures* see P. de Winter, *La Bibliothèque de Philippe le Hardi, duc de Bourgogne (1364–1404)* (Paris: 1985) 187.

178   MARGARET M. MANION

ateliers, or on the significance of the Duke as artistic patron and dedicated bibliophile.[3] Even more fundamental for an appreciation of these works, is the fact that they were primarily designed for devotional use. As such they bear the marks of long-established family customs. Not only do they elucidate the interaction between the development of official liturgical practice and more personal religious expression, but their artistic dynamic is dependent to a very large extent on the integration of text and imagery, while the relationship between clerical adviser or text-compiler and artist-illuminator was of critical importance in their production.

This is a large subject. Only a few facets of the rich material in the Duke's prayer-books are discussed here to demonstrate the value of studying such works with reference to their devotional purpose.

Among the oldest of the known extant Books of Hours recorded in the Duke's inventories is the *Petites Heures* (215×145mm), now Paris, BN ms lat. 18014, which seems to have been designed and written in the early 1370s. Its illumination was begun at this time by Jean le Noir; but it was interrupted around 1375, perhaps by the death of the artist, and completed in a second campaign under the direction of Jacquemart d'Hesdin c. 1385–1390.[4]

In addition to the elements usually to be found in a Book of Hours—the Hours of the Virgin, Penitential Psalms, Litany, Office of the Dead, etc.—the *Petites Heures* contains a substantial group of more distinctive prayers and Offices, many of which also occur in the *Très Belles Heures*, which was probably designed and written about the same time although its illumination spans some forty years.[5] The Duke's inventory indicates that the model for these particular texts was available in a Book of Hours that had belonged to King Jean le Bon, father of Jean and Philippe, and from which the king had learnt to read as a child.[6] Through it or another like it

---

[3] See especially M. Meiss, *French Painting in the Time of Jean de Berry. The Late XIV Century and the Patronage of the Duke*, 2 vols. (New York: 2nd ed., 1969–74).

[4] For the *Petites Heures* see V. Leroquais, *Les Livres d'heures manuscrits de la Bibliothèque nationale*, vol. 2 (Paris:1927), 175–187; Meiss, I, 155–193; F. Avril, *Les Fastes du Gothique. Le Siècle de Charles V* (Paris:1982), 343–344; and F. Avril, L. Dunlop and B. Yapp, *Les Petites Heures de Jean, duc de Berry*, 2 vols., Introduction and Facsimile of BN ms lat. 18014 (Paris:1989) [the French version of the Commentary has been used in this paper].

[5] The Master of the 'Parement de Narbonne' began the illumination of the *Très Belles Heures de Notre Dame de Jean de Berry* (here called the *Très Belles Heures*), at the time the book was written, and it was continued by the Baptism and Holy Ghost Masters c. 1404, after which the book was split up and the completed section given by the Duke to the keeper of his inventory, Robinet d'Estampes (BN ms n.a. lat. 3093). Two paintings were executed by the Limbourg Brothers c. 1412. The illumination of the second section was not finished until c. 1422, by which time it had found its way to the Dutch court. Flemish or Dutch artists carried out the decorative programme on what now goes by the name *The Turin-Milan Hours*. One part of this second section was destroyed by fire in 1904. Despite the extended and interrupted nature of the book's decoration, the original integrated plan for text and illumination was adhered to throughout. See P. Durrieu, *Les Heures de Turin* (Paris:1902; rev. ed. by A. Chalelet, 1967); G. Hulin de Loo, *Les Heures de Milan* (Brussels:1911); P. Durrieu, *Les Très Belles Heures de Notre Dame du Duc de Berry* (Paris: 1922). For more recent discussion of dates and attributions, see also Meiss, I, 107–133; Avril, *Les Fastes du Gothique...*, 339–341; and the *Commentary to the Facsimile..., passim*.

[6] This book did not come into the Duke's possession until 1407 when his nephew, Louis II d'Anjou, gave it to him as a present, but it was probably well known to Jean de Berry from his childhood. See Meiss, I, 48 note 152 and 388 note 9, and his citation of the inventory of 1413, note 968; and Avril, *Commentary to the Facsimile...* 65–67, 83–84.

THE PRAYER-BOOKS OF JEAN DE BERRY   179

the devotions practised by an earlier generation of the royal family were handed down to their children.

The importance of fostering a regular life of prayer is explicitly stated in a series of precepts entitled *L'Estimeur du Monde*, which occur in the *Petites Heures* after the Calendar (fols. 8–15). Written in French, they comment on the Scriptural text *Non solo pane vivit homo, sed in omni verbo quod procedit de ore Dei* ("Man does not live by bread alone but on every word that proceeds from the mouth of God" [Matt. 4: 4]). The author states that while these teachings are important for all Christians they are specifically directed to the children of kings, princes and noble lords. In this context he makes reference to the model Christian king Saint Louis, whose mother ensured that he was instructed from early childhood by prudent men, good clerics and wise religious; and the saint's own *Enseignements* given before his death to his eldest son follow on folios 15^v–20^v.[7] *L'Estimeur du Monde* survives only in the *Petites Heures*, but the description of Jean le Bon's lost Hours shows that it also appeared there.[8] Both the precepts and their illumination are worth exploring in detail as they establish the context for the prayers which they preface.

After a general introduction which emphasises the need to nourish the spiritual and intellectual part of man, since it is this which distinguishes him from the beasts, the precepts address the training of young princes and nobles in regular morning and evening prayer, in daily attendance at Mass and in the recitation of the Hours. They also state how rulers should conduct themselves in church. Recourse to prayer and participation in the ceremonies and Offices of the Church are presented as a pervasive and consistent part of a prince's daily schedule.

The three miniatures which accompany the precepts indicate their Dominican authorship. On folio 8 (Figure 69) a prefatory scene shows a friar in Dominican habit directing the attention of the prince who kneels before him to the heavenly zone above, where God is surrounded by music-making angels. The friar appears again as teacher on folio 9^v (Figure 70). Here, he counsels the prince to live by the word of God, the soul's true nourishment; he must not follow those who think only of material food and who like Nebuchadnezzar are fit only to dwell with the beasts.[9] The friar's gestures contrast Christ, the bread of angels above, with Nebuchadnezzar, naked except for his crown, who feeds with the beasts below. That these teachings are directed both to the younger generation and to their parents is made clear in the allusion in the text and the final illustration to the punishment meted out to the High Priest Eli for neglecting to correct the godless behaviour of his sons Hophni and Phineas (fols. 11^v–12).[10]

The same precise and somewhat recondite use of Scriptural exempla and typology appears also in the Calendar of the *Petites Heures* (Figure 71), long recognized as deriving from that designed for the *Belleville Breviary* of Dominican Use

---

[7] For the *Enseignements* see D. O'Connell, *The Teachings of Saint Louis* (Chapel Hill: 1972), and Avril, *Commentary to the Facsimile...* 227–230.

[8] Avril, *Commentary to the Facsimile...* 65–66.

[9] Dan. 4: 24–26; 32–34.

[10] Meiss, II, Figure 88.

MARGARET M. MANION

(1323–1326).[11] In the upper and lower margins of its pages, the theme of the passage of time explicit in the Calendar text itself, is elaborated to embrace Salvation History. Below, in the *bas-de-page,* pairs of prophets and apostles enact the transition from the Old to the New Dispensation. Each apostle makes a literal gesture of revelation as he draws aside the cloak of his Old Testament predecessor to disclose the book which he holds. The prophets, for their part, assist in the transition from one era to another by dismantling, stone by stone, the edifice which symbolises the Synagogue to make way for the Church. By December the structure which appeared impressively solid at the beginning of the year is in ruins.

Scrolls linked to the figures elaborate these themes of transmission, revelation and transformation. Appropriate verses from the works of the prophets are changed into an article of faith from the Creed traditionally assigned to a particular apostle. In the upper margin, the scheme is further developed. Mary, through whom the human race gains access to Paradise, stands above the gates leading to the New Jerusalem. Her pennant for each month displays a representation of an article from the Creed. These pennants were originally designed to parallel the verses on the scrolls of the apostles below. At her feet appears Saint Paul, the apostle "born out of due time". January depicts his conversion while subsequent months show him addressing the audiences of his Epistles—the Romans, Corinthians, Galatians, etc. Citations from these writings provide in their turn an explication of the scenes on the Virgin's pennants.[12]

Although the *Belleville Breviary* was not commissioned for a member of the royal family it seems to have come into the possession of Philippe VI de Valois shortly after 1343 and is listed in the inventory of Charles V in 1380. The detailed decorative programme of both the Calendar and of the liturgical divisions of the Psalter is explained in a contemporary French commentary attached to the Breviary. The intent of the imagery must have been understood early in royal circles since the Calendar was adopted independently of the commentary for several of their family prayer-books.[13] It did not, however, become a "workshop pattern" for indiscriminate use outside this milieu.

---

[11] For the *Belleville Breviary* (BN mss lat. 10483–10484), see V. Leroquais, *Les Breviaires Manuscrits des bibliothèques publiques de France,* Vol. 3 (Paris:1934), 198–210; K. Morand, *Jean Pucelle* (Oxford: 1962), 9–12, 43–45; and Avril, *Les Fastes du Gothique...* 293–296.

[12] Avril has shown how this very detailed and elaborate interweaving of visual and textual commentaries has become somewhat confused in the *Petites Heures* where the order of prophets and apostles in the lower margin and the verses on their scrolls differ from those in the *Belleville Breviary,* although the images on the pennants held by the Virgin still follow the Breviary order. Thus the two fail to match. He suggests that this may be because in a lost intermediary model the scrolls had not contained identifying verses and the cleric involved in the design of the Calendar for the *Petites Heures* had turned to an alternative system disseminated through the thirteenth century *Speculum Theologie* by the Franciscan Jean de Metz. He had failed to see, however, that the upper register was altered accordingly (Avril, *Commentary to the Facsimile...* 208–222). The main message is nevertheless clear, and even such inconsistencies reveal continuing clerical and artistic interaction.

[13] See E. Panofsky, *Early Netherlandish Painting* (Cambridge, Mass.: 1953) Part I, 373 note 2; Meiss I, 135–136; and Avril, *Commentary on the Facsimile...* 208–209, n. 4.

THE PRAYER-BOOKS OF JEAN DE BERRY 181

The Dominicans were a powerful influence in medieval Paris. They were closely associated with the University and hence with book production, and they also had strong links with royalty, providing chaplains and confessors not only for the king's household but also for other members of the Valois and related houses, including the Duke of Berry.[14] Works such as the *Belleville Breviary* suggest that Jean Pucelle, the leading Parisian illuminator of the early fourteenth century, worked extremely closely with them to produce the detailed and highly organised visual programmes used to decorate and elucidate the texts destined for prayerful use in royal and noble establishments. Under Pucelle and his immediate followers, foremost of whom was Jean le Noir, miniature, historiated initial and marginal scenes especially those of the *bas-de-page,* were often integrated into a visual commentary of typological or theological significance. The love of drolleries and whimsicality for their own sake, however, was never completely abandoned.[15]

The Duke, in due course, was to acquire several books by Pucelle, including the *Belleville Breviary,* but the illuminators responsible for the *Petites Heures* and the *Très Belles Heures* were already inheritors of the Pucelle tradition. In both works the pictorial programme integrates miniature, initial and *bas-de-page.* In the *Petites Heures* this system marks such major divisions as the Hours of the Passion and the Penitential Psalms, while the introduction to the Hours of the Virgin is dramatically signalled as the heart of the book by the use of an architectural frame to enclose the miniature of the Annunciation together with the opening words of the text and an historiated initial of the Duke at prayer (Figure 72). This frame is comprised of Gothic niches peopled with the twelve apostles, the prophet Jeremiah, and an image of the Man of Sorrows flanked by the Virgin and Child and John the Baptist. Placed under the Annunciation and the surmounting image of the Man of Sorrows, the prophet announces the great theme of Salvation History. This encompasses the foreshadowings of the Old Testament, the redemptive life and death of Christ and the witness of the Apostolic Church. Such is the comprehensive nature of the context established for the recitation of the Hours of the Virgin. The theme of the prophets as a type or foreshadowing of apostolic leadership in the New Dispensation is presented in a variety of ways in works of art commissioned by the Duke and it was an important element in contemporary Christian teaching.[16]

In the *Très Belles Heures,* the integration of miniature, initial and *bas-de-page* into one consistent and informative unit, of substantial theological or Scriptural complexity, dominates the visual organisation of the whole book (Figure 73). This extensive programme was clearly planned *in toto* from the outset, and it was carefully followed in the long-drawn out decoration of the work.

---

[14] For the close association of the Dominicans with the French Royal House and for their involvement in book production in Paris, see R. Branner, *Manuscript Painting in Paris during the Reign of Saint Louis* (Berkeley: 1977) and W.A. Hinnebusch O.P., *The History of the Dominican Order* vol. 1 (New York: 1966).

[15] In addition to the *Petites Heures* and the *Très Belles Heures,* examples of this integrated system appear in The Missal of St. Denis (Avril, *Les Fastes du Gothique* note 273), The Breviary of Charles V (Avril note 287), and The Bible of Jean de Sy (Avril, note 280).

[16] See Meiss I, 135–140 and 385 (notes 1–20).

182 MARGARET M. MANION

The privileged nature of the Hours of the Virgin in Books of Hours has long been acknowledged. Both the focus of the most elaborate decoration on this section and the fact that the Book of Hours takes its popular name from this source are clear indications of its importance. Instructions such as those we have mentioned in the *Petites Heures*, prescribe the daily recitation of this Office; and the devotion could be performed in a variety of ways. The Hours could be recited in private or with one's chaplain and family. Sometimes the female and male members joined together; at other times they prayed separately. On special feasts, these prayer gatherings could include a larger and more varied representation of the household. Other Offices in Books of Hours were also regularly recited, either on particular days of the week, on feast days or during the appropriate liturgical season. The Hours in honour of the Passion or of the Cross and the Vigils or Office of the Dead, held an especially favoured place in devotional life, a fact which is underlined by the degree of illumination which their texts proportionately attract over the life of the Book of Hours. Devotions such as the Penitential Psalms and the Litanies were also suitable for particular occasions or to foster an appropriate affective frame of mind. Together with time-honoured prayers to the Virgin and a host of suffrages in honour of the saints or more personal prayers directed towards particular needs or cults, they could be incorporated into domestic prayer services or be recited privately.[17]

The wealth of such material and the demand for Books of Hours confirm that communal and private prayer formed a substantial part of daily life; but where, one may ask, did attendance at Mass fit in this devotional schema? It is here that the Duke of Berry's prayer-books are particularly informative. The precepts in the *Petites Heures,* we have said, exhort the princely leader to attend Mass daily. In fact noble men and women often heard more than one Mass a day. The liturgy might be performed at the start of the day in the presence of the head of the house virtually for his or her private devotion. Later, especially on major feast days and Sundays, a more public service would be held in which musicians and choir played an important part.

The private Mass was viewed as a sacred ritual which when attended with appropriate spiritual dispositions brought its own blessings. It was not necessary to participate in the liturgy with the priest; one might simply recite favourite prayers during its celebration. These could include the Hours of the Virgin or various offices. Many other prayers and devotions in Books of Hours were also considered suitable for recitation at Mass, for example those in honour of the Body of Christ and of the Cross, those commemorating particular saints and those for special needs. For since the Mass was interpreted as the sacred re-enactment of Christ's redemptive sacrifice, calls for rescue or help were rightly made in its context. Moreover, the Mystical Union of the faithful in the community of the Church was often interpreted as an extension of specific family and clan ties; thus local or favourite saints were

---

[17] For the variety of devotions in Books of Hours and some examples of their use see J. Harthan, *Books of Hours* (London: 1982): especially 32-33; and also R.S. Wieck, *Time Sanctified. The Book of Hours in Medieval Art and Life* (New York: 1988).

THE PRAYER-BOOKS OF JEAN DE BERRY

viewed as special advocates. Honouring them at Mass guaranteed their support in life's daily challenges and conflicts.[18]

An understanding of the importance of this personal and localising element in medieval spirituality helps to clarify the relationship of the Book of Hours to the Mass. Often, too, among its pages there are specific prayers to be said at those points of the Mass which engage a personal act of faith or commitment—at the elevation of the Host, for example, or before or after Communion.

The *Petites Heures* and the *Très Belles Heures,* however, contain more detailed sequences of prayers in French and Latin, for recitation at Mass. These seem to have been designed explicitly for the use of the royal family and appear also in the contemporary *Grandes Heures de Philippe le Hardi,* Fitzwilliam Museum, MS 3–1954.[19] In both the *Petites Heures* and the *Très Belles Heures,* they are accompanied by a detailed series of miniatures; but since the decoration of this section of the *Très Belles Heures* was not completed until the fifteenth century, it is best to concentrate on the *Petites Heures* to demonstrate how text and illumination reinforce one another and would have assisted the Duke to enter into the liturgical celebration.

A unity of place is established for the pictorial sequence by the use of a similar setting of curtained recess set against a patterned background for each scene (Figures 74 and 75). This also indicates a relatively private space for prayer. Constant actors throughout the series are the priest at a simple altar table and the prince who kneels at a draped *prie-dieu* with prayer-book open before him. The celebrant is normally accompanied by one assistant, and the cast is expanded to include cantors, additional acolytes or clerical attendants where appropriate, as at the Introit, the chanting of the Gospel and the distribution of Holy Communion. In the Communion scene the prince is accompanied by male and female members of his family. The miniatures, therefore, do not represent a specific occasion, but rather provide an imaginative reference to the context in which these prayers are to be recited, a context which had a considerable range of daily application. But these images communicate something more. If we follow them with the text, we find that they explicate the Mass in a complementary way to the prayers. The rubrics indicate how the prayers are to be recited in between, as it were, the major actions of the liturgical celebration while the pictures, for the most part, register the actions themselves.

Thus, the chanting of the Introit and of the Gospel, the Offertory donation, the Elevation of the Host, the Kiss of Peace and the distribution of Communion are the visual signposts for the lay participant who makes his way through the ritual by reciting a series of prayers which take their inspiration from the ordinary of the Mass and are interwoven with it. Some of the sections common to the priest and the choir such as the *Sanctus* and *Agnus Dei,* or familiar to the laity because of their being recited aloud by the celebrant like the *Pater Noster* and the prayer *Libera nos*

---

[18] See J. Bossy, "The Mass as a Social Institution 1200–1700," *Past and Present* 100 (1983): 29–61.

[19] See F. Wormald and P.M. Giles, *A Descriptive Catalogue of the Additional Illuminated Manuscripts in the Fitzwilliam Museum,* (Cambridge: 1982) vol. 2, 479–499, Figures 40–41, Plate 11; and Avril, *Commentary to the Facsimile... 76–78, 86–87.*

quaesumus...which follows it, or the *Domine non sum dignus* are prescribed to be said (silently) with the priest. Latin prayers in honour of the Body of Christ are also designated for silent recital, while a series of prayers in the vernacular expand the sentiments appropriate for particular parts of the Mass. Provision is made for including the names of one's choice at the commemoration of the living and of the dead, and in the prayers before Communion the aid of the angels and saints is invoked with special reference to Saint John the Baptist and Saints Peter and Paul.

The kneeling prince who figures prominently in all the miniatures clearly is to be identified with the lay user of the book—the Duke himself. The artist responsible for this series of miniatures in the *Petites Heures* has been identified as a collaborator of Jacquemart d'Hesdin—the Pseudo-Jacquemart, who was involved in the second campaign (c. 1385–1390).[20] The interrelated text and image sequence, nevertheless, reveals the same precise theological and devotional articulation as that which characterises the Calendar and Psalter of the *Belleville Breviary*. Like the Calendar, the Mass prayers and miniatures formed a unit which was copied or adapted for more than one member of the royal family. The close nexus between text and illumination and their explicit devotional function suggest the guiding hand of a cleric concerned with the education of the royal family in an affective and quasi-liturgical appreciation of the Mass.

Following the text of the Ordinary of the Mass and of the Proper—that is, Introit, Gradual and Communion verses, Epistle and Gospel readings and the prayers of Collect and Post Communion—implies a liturgical awareness on the part of the laity which transcends purely private devotion. In the Middle Ages and indeed until the liturgical reforms of the Church Council, Vatican II (1963–65), both ways of sharing in the Mass were acceptable. Liturgical involvement, however, required more specialised knowledge, and was dependent, to a large degree, on the availabilty of the texts of the Propers, as well as those of the Ordinary or unvarying setting of the Mass—the *Kyrie, Gloria, Credo, Agnus Dei*, etc. Full liturgical participation, moreover, was usually associated with the celebration of solemn or High Mass in a public church or chapel, with many of the texts being sung by the choir and the chief celebrant being assisted by deacons as well as acolytes.

Books for members of the laity containing only the texts for liturgical participation in the Mass—lay Missals—are rare before printing. Many Books of Hours, however, contain one or more votive Masses, often in honour of the Virgin. In Italian Books of Hours votive Masses of the Virgin become standard practice from the late fourteenth century, and this section is regularly signalled by major illumination.

It is understandable that appropriate texts would be provided for French royalty and related nobility of this period to enable them to participate meaningfully in the religious ceremonies which were such an important part of their regular schedule. The words of the chronicler from the reign of Charles VI, for example, provide a contemporary affirmation of the Duke of Berry's commitment to attendance at such

---

[20] See Avril, *Commentary to the Facsimile...* 315–321.

THE PRAYER-BOOKS OF JEAN DE BERRY   185

liturgies:

> Animated always by an ardent devotion to the service of God, he maintained in his home many chaplains who day and night sang the praises of God and celebrated mass, and he took care to compliment them whenever the service lasted longer or was more elaborate than usual.[21]

Nor is it surprising that the selection of Masses appended to Books of Hours for the use of members of the French royal family was based on those whose importance was often highlighted by rubrication or decoration in Parisian Missals made for the use of clerics. Since Pucelle and le Noir were experienced in the illumination of such works, they and their followers had precedents to turn to for their execution of Mass texts for lay patrons.[22]

Three of the prayer-books commissioned by the Duke of Berry contain substantial sequences of illuminated Mass texts which seem to take their origins from a royal family tradition.[23]

The *Très Belles Heures* has a series of Masses for the major feasts of the Church's Temporal Cycle: Advent, Christmas, Epiphany, the Purification, Holy Week, Easter, Ascension, Pentecost, Trinity Sunday and Corpus Christi, together with a selection from the Sanctoral: St. John the Baptist, St. Peter, the Assumption, the Nativity of the Virgin, St. Michael, the Angels, St. Hilary, All Saints, All Souls, votive Masses of the Holy Cross and of the Virgin, the Vigil of St. Andrew and the feast of St. Andrew. All the Masses, from both the Temporal and Sanctoral cycles, are arranged in sequence so that the whole selection covers chronologically the Church's year and all are illuminated.[24]

A very similar series appears in the *Grandes Heures de Philippe le Hardi*. This book also contains votive Masses for each day of the week, that are specifically associated with a royal chapel.[25] The latter group feature as well in the additions made for Charles V to *The Hours of Blanche of Savoy*.[26] In both these manuscripts the master in charge of the illumination seems to have been Jean le Noir.

The hierarchical grading in liturgical terms of feasts in the Church's Calendar had long been translated into decorative language in many clerical Missals. Particularly important Masses were often singled out by the use of introductory historiated initials or small miniatures. Full-page illuminations were normally confined to the

---

[21] M.L. Bellaguet, ed., *Chronique du religieux de Saint-Denys, contenant le règne de Charles VI, de 1380 à 1422* vol. VI (Paris: 1852) 32, quoted (and translated) in Meiss I, 39.

[22] Products from their workshop include the Missal of Montier-en-Mer, now Paris, Bibliothèque Mazarine ms 41, c. 1330–1335, the Missal for the Use of Saint-Vaast d'Arras, BN ms Nouv. Acq. lat. 3180, c. 1330–1340, the Missal of Paris, Lyon, Bibliothèque de la Ville, ms 5122, c. 1345–1350, and the Missal of Saint-Denis, Victoria and Albert Museum, MS 1346–1891, c. 1350. See *Les Fastes du Gothique*... 296–297, 297, 321–322.

[23] Meiss (I, 109) is incorrect when he says that a sequence of Masses also appears in the *Petites Heures*.

[24] For reproductions see Meiss II, Figures 39–50.

[25] Wormald and Giles 483.

[26] Wieck 178.

opening pages of the solemn Canon Prayer, the most common subject being a Crucifixion, often paired with a page depicting the *Maiestas* theme.[27]

Once the Missal texts were appropriated for lay use the relationship between text and decoration was susceptible to much greater variation, since the lay user was not constrained to read at a regulated pace. Thus in the *Très Belles Heures* the decoration for each of the pages introducing the Masses is of the same format as those for the other sections of the book, and these as we have already observed contain a considerably detailed programme which integrates miniature, historiated initial and *bas-de-page* (Figure 76).[28]

The two Books of Hours illuminated for the Duke of Berry in the early fifteenth century by the Limbourg Brothers also contain Masses. Those of the *Belles Heures* c. 1409 have a series from the Temporal for Christmas, Easter, Ascension, Pentecost, Trinity Sunday and Corpus Christi together with the Mass for the Exaltation of the Cross and a votive Mass of the Virgin (fols. 195–209). The sequence continues after a set of miniatures in honour of St. John the Baptist illustrating extracts from the text of the *Golden Legend*, with Masses for the feasts of the Baptist, Saints Peter and Paul, All Saints and All Souls, which also serves as a votive Mass for the Dead (fols. 212ᵛ–221).[29]

The visual presentation of the introductory pages of these Masses varies considerably. The first group on fols. 195–209 follows the format of a small miniature above the Introit, with the text divided into two columns and decorated initials and rubrics clearly signalling particular prayers and the abbreviated texts for the Ordinary of the Mass—the *Kyrie eleison, Gloria, Agnus Dei*, etc.[30] The Masses that follow the excerpts from the *Golden Legend*, on the other hand, are introduced by compositions that harmonise with the decoration of the Legend (Figures 77 and 78). Large miniatures with dramatic scenes of the Baptist's martyrdom, the death of Simon Magus, and the beheading of St. Paul, dominate the pages and visually continue the story of the saints. Indeed the Introit for the Mass of Saints Peter and Paul is extended over two pages (f. 215–215ᵛ) with a large miniature heading the four lines of text on each. The Mass for All Saints (f. 218) is presented as the climax of the combined Sanctoral section with the Virgin in rich blue holding the Christ Child as the radiant centre around which are grouped the assembly of saints, while God the Father and the Holy Spirit hover above. The Mass for All Souls (f. 221) has a more

---

[27] For numerous examples see V. Leroquais, *Les sacramentaires et les missels manuscrits des bibliothèques publiques de France*, 3 vols. and Plates (Paris: 1924)

[28] This is not to say that elaborate illustrative programmes are absent from clerical Missals. Several of the contributors to this volume are currently researching the range and variety of fourteenth- and fifteenth-century Missal illumination, and the articles by V. Condon and V. Vines discuss examples of very distinctive programmes. Works such as the Missal of Saint Denis also demonstrate the application of related miniature and border unit to this genre. Nevertheless, research to date points to a greater freedom in manipulating the relationship of text to illustration in books not destined for use by the celebrant and which comprised both personal and liturgical prayer.

[29] See M. Meiss and E.H. Beatson, *Les Belles Heures de Jean Duc de Berry* (London: 1974) and Meiss, *French Painting in the Time of Jean de Berry. The Limbourgs and their Contemporaries* 2 vols. (London: 1974) 102–142.

[30] See Meiss and Beatson for facsimile reproduction of these folios.

THE PRAYER-BOOKS OF JEAN DE BERRY   187

subdued colour scheme, and in place of the drama of martyrdom, an oblique view is provided of the interior of a chapel where mourners follow the service of the dead from their open books. Before them is set a draped coffin under the burning candles of a *chapelle ardente*. This scene is modelled on a familiar pattern often used for the Vigils of the Dead and its size, once again, affects the format of the opening words of the Introit so that the page forms part of a visual sequence both with the preceding miniatures and with that of the concluding prayer for a safe journey.

It is often observed that the *Très Riches Heures* is an exceptional work and that it should not be interpreted as a typical Book of Hours. Nevertheless, it must not be forgotten that its lavish and splendid decoration is based on a compilation of texts which are no less devotional than those of the Duke's older prayer-books. Many aspects reveal the contribution of his chaplains or theological advisers with whom the Limbourgs must have worked as closely as did Jean Pucelle and Jean le Noir with their predecessors at the royal court.[31]

I single out here the extensive Mass cycle whose decoration was planned and begun by the Limbourg Brothers c. 1411–1416, when the book was written, but which was not completed until c. 1485–89. By that time the work had passed into the possession of Charles I of Savoy, who employed Jean Colombe to finish it.

The series of Masses from the Temporal includes as well as those in the *Belles Heures* a Lenten sequence, which comprises the first four Sundays in Lent, Passion Sunday and Palm Sunday. The Masses drawn from the Sanctoral, in addition to those in the *Belles Heures,* are for the feasts of the Assumption, St. Michael, the Vigil of Saint Andrew and possibly the Purification. The series for the Sundays in Lent does not appear in earlier extant books of the Duke or his close family. They do feature, however, in a Franciscan Missal-Hours of Lombard work, BN ms lat. 757, which has been dated c. 1390. This book belongs to a group of North Italian Missal-Hours produced around the turn of the century.[32] Both the Duke and the Limbourgs had close associations with this region, and the selection of Masses for the *Très Riches Heures* may well have been influenced from this quarter.[33]

In the *Très Riches Heures* the small-sized miniature at the head of the Introit is maintained for some Masses, but the majority are introduced by large-scale compositions, with four lines of the Introit text being presented in the same way as the opening words of the Book's Offices and other major sections (Figure 79). The Limbourgs also characteristically vary the shape of the frames of their miniatures and the designs of the border decoration, so that the pages are presented as individual pictorial units as well as part of a sequence.[34]

---

[31] See J. Longon and R. Cazelles, *Les Très Riches Heures de Duc de Berry* (London: 1969) and Meiss, *The Limbourgs and their Contemporaries* I, 143–224.

[32] See Leroquais, *Livres d' heures* vol. I, 1–7, VIII-XIII; and F. Avril, in the *Catalogue Dix Siècles d'Enluminure Italienne (VIᵉ-XVIᵉ siècle)* (Paris: Bibliothèque Nationale, 1984) no. 83.

[33] The unusual illustrations of the Litany of the Saints in the *Très Riches Heures* for example have a precedent in BN ms lat. 757.

[34] See Longon and Cazelles, *Les Très Riches Heures,* for facsimile reproductions which show the range and variety of shapes, frames and borders.

188 MARGARET M. MANION

Themes chosen to illustrate the Masses in the *Très Riches Heures* are relatively varied. As well as drawing their inspiration from the feast, they sometimes allude specifically to the Gospel for the day. This is the case with several of the Lenten Sunday Masses. Jean Colombe presumably followed the general designs of his predecessors and in some places actually completed pages begun by them. Three of his Mass compositions (fols. 164, 184 and 201), however, enclose both miniature and text in substantial architectural frames characteristic of the late fifteenth century, and here the words of the Introit are presented as though on a placard which draws attention to the visual drama rather than vice versa (Figure 80).[35]

The depiction of High Mass for Christmas Day which introduces the series in the *Très Riches Heures* (f. 157ᵛ; Plate 7) is the work of both the Limbourgs and Jean Colombe. The Limbourgs were responsible for the design of the border which expresses the theme of worship in the kneeling figures of shepherds, who are each assigned their particular space for prayer, within circles created by curving gold and coloured acanthus branches. The Limbourgs also designed the architecture with its soaring walls of figured stained glass and columns bearing gilded statues. We can presume, therefore, that the enactment of the liturgy painted by Jean Colombe is true to the original plan. It communicates in vivid fashion the variety of participation in the ceremony. At the altar the chief celebrant is attended by deacons dressed in matching gold vestments and acolytes in white surplices; on the right, the choir grouped around a large Gradual sings vigorously. Nearby lie smaller volumes for the reading of the Epistle and the chanting of the Gospel. Two women pray from books in the foreground; perhaps they recite the Hours. Behind them the congregation extends into the body of the church beyond the choir screen. The Duke—in Colombe's composition Charles of Savoy—has his own curtained recess close to the altar on the right. His gold cloak matches that of the celebrants and he kneels at a *prie-dieu* draped in matching blue and gold on which he may rest the book he uses to follow the liturgy.

The Duke of Berry and his fellow patrons delighted in richly illuminated prayer-books. These were never, however, planned as purely collector's items. Both their texts and decoration were executed as an aid to public and personal prayer, and collaboration with informed clergy as well as an understanding of the book's purpose was essential for even the most innovative of artists involved in their production.

---

[35] This placard device, which had been in use since the time of Jean Fouquet, is employed by Colombe in several other compositions in the *Très Riches Heures*; see Longon and Cazelles, *Les Très Riches Heures*, for reproductions.

Figure 69 Dominican Friar Instructing Young Prince. *Petites Heures,* Paris, BN ms lat. 18014, f. 8; 215×145 mm.

Figure 70 Dominican Friar contrasting Christ as Bread of Angels with Nebuchadnezzar among the beasts. *Petites Heures*, Paris, BN ms lat. 18014, f. 9^v; 215×145 mm.

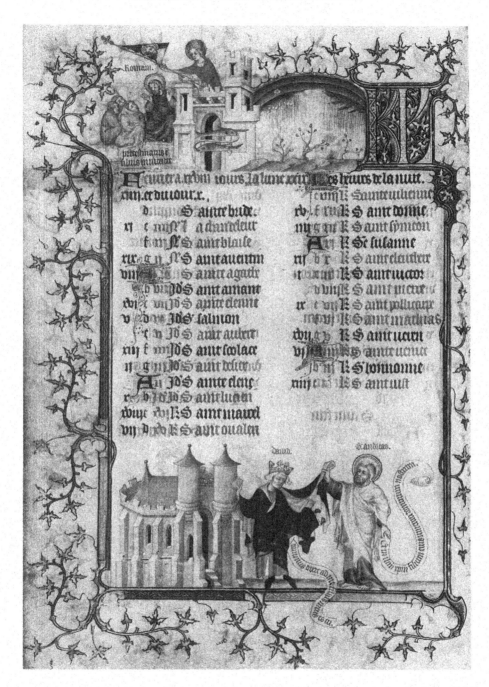

Figure 71 Calendar for the month of February. *Petites Heures*, Paris, BN ms lat. 18014, f. 1ᵛ; 215×145 mm.

Figure 72 The Annunciation. *Petites Heures,* Paris, BN ms lat. 18014, f. 22; 215×145 mm.

Figure 73 The Baptism of Christ. *Très Belles Heures*, Paris, BN Nouv. Acq. lat. 3093, p. 162; 279×199 mm.

Figure 74 The Elevation of the Host. *Petites Heures*, Paris, BN ms lat. 18014, f. 172; 215×145 mm.

Figure 75 Prince kissing the Paten. *Petites Heures*, Paris, BN ms lat. 18014, f. 173^v; 215×145 mm.

Figure 76 The Annunciation. *Très Belles Heures* (Milan Hours), Turin, Museo Civico, f. I[v]; 284×205 mm.

Figure 77 The Martyrdom of St. John the Baptist. *Belles Heures,* The Metropolitan Museum of Art, The Cloisters, f. 212; 238×170 mm.

Figure 78 Salome with the Head of the Baptist. *Belles Heures,* The Metropolitan Museum of Art, The Cloisters, f. 212^v; 238×170 mm.

Figure 79 The Feeding of the Five Thousand. *Très Riches Heures*, Chantilly, Musée Condé ms 65, f. 168ᵛ; 290×210 mm.

Figure 80 The Ascension. *Très Riches Heures,* Chantilly, Musée Condé ms 65, f. 184; 290×210 mm.

XI

Et Verbum Caro Factum Est:
The Prayer-book of
Michelino da Besozzo

Katherine McDonald

The small richly illuminated manuscript in the Pierpont Morgan Library, (MS M. 944) which goes by the name of *The Prayer Book of Michelino da Besozzo* was probably produced in Pavia or Milan during the first decade of the fifteenth century.[1] The quality of its full page miniatures and the distinctive character of its naturalistic flower-borders have long been acknowledged by art historians.[2] Very little attention however has been paid to the text which comprises forty-seven Latin prayers for the major liturgical feasts and selected saints' days arranged according to the Church Year.[3] Yet a knowledge of the content of these prayers and of the devotional tradition from which they stem is important to appreciate the evocative and expressive qualities of the accompanying illumination.

---

[1] Vellum; the Latin use of Milan 170 x 120 mm; trimmed; 95 Leaves I^4, II^8, III^9, IV^8, V^9, VI^7, VII^9, VII^6, IX^5, X^4, XI^7, XII^8, XIII^8, XIV^3; 47 prayers; 22 full-page miniatures (with 25 missing); 1 historiated initial and 46 decorated letters; rounded Gothic script in brown ink; one-line gold and blue rubrics; 15 lines of text per page; ruling: 33 [64] 23×53 [95] 22, in faint brown ink; ruling unit: 6.8 mm; illuminated by Michelino da Besozzo, (c.1370–c.1450).

[2] See P. Toesca, *La Pittura e la miniatura nella Lombardia dai piu antichi monumenti alla meta del Quattrocento* (Milan: 1912; repr. Turin: 1966; O. Pächt, "Early Italian Nature Studies and the Early Calendar Landscape", *Journal of the Warburg and Courtauld Institutes* 13 (1950): 13–47; R. Schilling, "Ein Gebetbuch des Michelino da Besozzo", *Munchner Jahrbuch der bildenden Kunst* 3rd series, 8 (1957): 65-80; and L. Castelfranchi-Vegas, "Il Libro d'Ore Bodmer di Michelino da Besozzo e i rapporti tra miniature francese e miniature lombarda agli inizi del Quattrocento", *Etudes d'art français offertes à Charles Sterling*, ed. A. Chatelet and N. Reynaud (Paris: 1975) 91–103.

[3] I should like to acknowledge the kindness of Edward Storman, S.J. and John Moore, S.J., of the Jesuit Theological College, Parkville for their assistance with the translations of the Latin prayers and for sharing their knowledge of the liturgy with me.

202   KATHERINE MCDONALD

Although a study of the prayer-book as a whole is impeded by the fact that twenty-five of the original forty-seven miniatures have been excised by later owners and that with them also has been lost those sections of the text which were written on the reverse of the painted page, enough remains to establish the book's basic structure. Each of the prayers begins on the recto of the folio and is introduced by a full-page miniature on the facing verso. All have the same format being introduced by a short Versicle and Response, often Scriptural in origin, which is followed by the word "Oremus".[4] This liturgical and formulaic setting, however, is in strong contrast to the tone of the prayers themselves. Written in the first person and often charged with intense emotion they belong to the tradition of the *Libelli Precum*, collections of prayers for private devotion which became widespread in Europe from the ninth century, and which played an important part in the development of medieval spirituality.[5]

Several of the prayers in MS M. 944 are North Italian and Augustinian in character, and while some may be traced back several centuries, the inclusion of more recent feasts such as that of St. Nicholas of Tolentino, who died in 1305, and of the Trinity, indicates that the text was probably compiled no later than the third decade of the fourteenth century.[6] Whether or not this compilation is unique is yet to be established and the authorship and origins of many of the specific texts have also to be determined. I have, however, identified several excerpts or adaptations for the prayers of St. Anselm (1033–1109), native of Aosta in Northern Italy, who became abbot of the Norman abbey of Bec and later Archbishop of Canterbury. In his busy life, Anselm found time to write long meditative compositions for his friends, and in a letter to the Countess Mathilda of Tuscany, the recipient of some of these, he

---

[4] In the following list incomplete prayers are asterisked and those lacking a miniature are followed by a double dagger: *The Nativity* (fols. 3–4ᵛ); *The Circumcision* (fols. 5–6);‡ *The Adoration of the Magi* (fols. 7–8); *Anthony Abbot* (f. 9–9ᵛ); *St. Agnes* (fols. 10–11);‡ *The Purification of the Virgin* (fols. 12–14); *St. Blaise* (f. 15–15ᵛ);* *The Annunciation* (fols. 17–19); Holy Thursday (*The Washing of the Feet*; f. 20–20ᵛ); Good Friday (fols. 22-24);‡ Holy Saturday (*The Entombment*; f. 25–25ᵛ); *The Resurrection* (f. 27–28ᵛ); *St. George* (f. 29–30);‡ *SS. Philip and James* (fols. 31–32ᵛ); *The Finding of the Cross* (fols. 34–35); *The Ascension* (f. 36–36ᵛ);* *Pentecost* (fols. 37–39);‡ *The Holy Trinity* (fols. 40–41ᵛ); *Corpus Christi* (42–43ᵛ);‡ *St. Anthony of Padua* (f. 44–44ᵛ);‡* *St. John the Baptist* (fols. 45–46);‡ *St. Peter* (fols. 47–48ᵛ);‡ *St. Paul* (fols. 50–51ᵛ); *The Visitation* (f. 53–53ᵛ); *St. Mary Magdalene* (fols. 54–55ᵛ);‡ *St. James, Apostle* (f. 57–57ᵛ);* *St. Christopher* (f. 58–58ᵛ);‡ *The Assumption* (fols. 59–60ᵛ);‡ *St. Louis of Toulouse* (fols. 61–61ᵛ);‡* *St. Louis, King of France* (f. 62–62ᵛ);‡* *St. Augustine* (fols. 63–64ᵛ); *The Nativity of the Virgin* (fols. 65–66ᵛ);‡ *St. Nicholas of Tolentino* (fols. 67–68ᵛ);‡* *The Exaltation of the Cross* (fols. 70–71ᵛ);‡* *St. Francis* (fol. 72–73);‡ *St. Gall* (fols. 74–75); *St. Luke* (fols. 76–77ᵛ); *All Saints* (fols. 78–80);‡ *St. Martin* (f. 81–81ᵛ);* *The Presentation of the Virgin* (fols. 82–83);‡ *St. Katherine* (f. 84–84ᵛ): *St. Ambrose* (fols. 85–86ᵛ);‡ *The Immaculate Conception* (fols. 87–88ᵛ);‡ *St. Lucy* (f. 90–90ᵛ); *St. John the Evangelist* (fols. 91–92ᵛ);‡ *St. Monica* (fols. 93–94);‡

[5] See J.A. Jungmann, *Christian Prayer Through the Centuries* (New York: 1967) 92–95; for a more detailed analysis and bibliography see P. Salmon, *Analecta Liturgica: Extraits des manuscripts liturgiques de la Bibliothèque Vaticane* (Rome: 1974).

[6] Cecilia O'Brien, Department of Fine Arts, The University of Melbourne, first alerted to me the Augustinian nature of the prayer-book reflected in the prayers to St. Augustine, St. Monica and other saints revered by the Augustinian order. She also drew my attention to the number of works executed by Michelino da Besozzo for Augustinian patrons and pointed me in the direction of the *Libelli precum*.

THE PRAYER-BOOK OF MICHELINO DA BESOZZO

counselled that "they should not be read cursorily or quickly but little by little, with attention and deep meditation. It is not intended that the reader should feel impelled to read the whole, but only as much as will stir up the affections to prayer".[7]

The practice of *lectio divina* or the prayerful reading of the Scriptures and spiritual classics was an integral part of monastic life and both the texts and accompanying illumination in Michelino's prayer-book preserve and foster this tradition. Anselm's own compositions are adapted or shortened to fit the overall shape of the book. The prayer to St. Mary Magdalen (fols. 54–55), for example, comprises the first two sections of Anselm's long text (with the omission of a passage that refers to the reader as male).[8] It is given an introductory Versicle and Response and a more definitively concluding sentence. The prayers in honour of Saints Peter, Paul and Monica contain more fragmentary excerpts.[9]

The intense personal emotion that characterises these devotions finds a sympathetic counterpart in the illumination. Michelino's all too human types with their wistful, sometimes wizened faces and hunched, delicate bodies seem familiar with life's hardships, while the individualized flower borders, which frame both miniature and text on the double-page openings for each prayer, echo and expand the sentiments generated by the words and images. It is precisely this relationship on which I wish to focus here by examining in detail some extracts from the prayers in the context of their illumination.

A splendid border of huge gold-studded blooms delicately modelled in ultramarine blue visually dominates the opening pages for the feast of The Purification of the Virgin (fols. 12–14; Plate 4). In the miniature Mary's robe takes up the hue, while its silky green lining conforms to the rhythm of the border's leaves. In her blue garment, amongst blue flowers, Mary appears as the loveliest flower of all, which is how the opening words of the prayer address her:

> Flower of virgins, glory of heaven and earth, holy and ineffable Virgin Mary, Mother of our Saviour, most holy in body, most chaste in behaviour, most beautiful Virgin of all virgins, never defiled in heart or mouth, wholly beautiful, wholly without stain! Inviolate Virgin, Virgin inviolate in body and mind, you owe nothing to the law, because you are

---

[7] See B. Ward, S.L.G., *The Prayers and Meditations of St. Anselm with the Proslogion* (London: 1973). Ward discusses the general influence of the liturgy and of Carolingian works on St. Anselm's prayers and cautions that they are "only the ground on which his genius worked" (p. 43). She accepts the nineteen prayers distinguished by Dom. A. Wilmart as the genuine work of St. Anselm (see *Auteurs spirituels et textes dévots du moyen âge latin* (Paris: 1932) 162–201, and his introduction to Odo Castel's French translation, *Les meditations et prières de S. Anselme* (Paris: 1923) XI. See also a critical edition of the prayers, *Meditations and Prayers*, Vol. 3, *Letters*, Vols. 3-5 *Proslogion*, Vol. 2, ed. F. Schmitt).

[8] Ward 201, "Most blessed Lady, I who am the most evil and sinful of men do not recall your sins as a reproach, but call upon the boundless mercy by which they were blotted out..."

[9] A part of St. Anselm's prayer to *St. Peter* (several lines from the eighth paragraph) recurs in the prayer to *St. Monica* (fols. 93–94); two-thirds of the first paragraph and most of paragraph eight of St. Anselm's prayer to *St. Paul* has been used in the prayer-book for the devotion to that Saint (f. 50–51ᵛ); the first seven lines of text which open the prayer to *St. Peter* by St. Anselm occur in the prayer to St. Peter (f. 47–48ᵛ) in the prayer-book.

not tainted with any deviation.

The temple setting of the Purification, clearly expressed in the miniature through the architectural frame and the altar table, is developed as the contemplative focus of the prayer by means of repetition:

...To the Temple you carried with you to be purified him who, born God and man, added to you the glory of integrity, O Mother undefiled. To the Temple you carried with you to be purified him who knowing our sins— for to him all things are laid bare and open—daily cleanses us from our most secret failings through repentance and confession; and, from those of others, through the spirit of continence, he spares his servants. To the Temple you carried with you to be purified him whose blood, on the Cross of his passion, washing us from the original taint, daily also, on the altar of the cross, through the most Holy Mysteries cleanses us, repentant and having confessed, from our personal sins.

The prayer for The Washing of the Feet (fols. 20–20^v; Figure 81) imaginatively absorbs the reader into the solemn rite traditionally enacted within the celebration of the Eucharist on Maundy Thursday. In developing the theme of adoration and wonder at the Saviour's humility, it plays on the image of the kneeling Christ, the pivot also of Michelino's painting:

I adore the divine mysteries and your highest actions, Jesus Christ, when I contemplate such signal manifestation of your most profound humility, as your great majesty bends over the feet of the apostles and God genuflects before men...

The word "genuflects" or "kneeling" conjures up both the greatness of God who is to be worshipped and the paradox of his performing, in the person of Christ, such lowly service for the apostles—a paradox which is driven home in the prayer by a series of contrasts which underline the difference between God and sinful man:

Holiness genuflects before sinners, Justice before the unjust, Creator before the creature, Sun before the stars, Light before the darkness...

The poetry of the prayer expands beyond the immediate event of the Washing of the Feet only to return to it with greater intensity and to the image of Christ presented in the miniature:

...and you bend over washing, King of Kings, Lord of all Lords. There can be no greater humility in any creature. I also contemplate you, Lamb of God, Highest Priest and the true Pontiff who today handed over to your disciples your flesh, a most pure Host, and your Blood to be eaten and drunk at this noble supper...

Within such an evocative context details of the painting are also suggestive beyond their immediate meaning. The striking vermilion red of the floor, for example, an unusual colour in the manuscript, aligned with the chalice-like basin of water, visually echoes the allusion to Christ's blood and the rite of Holy Communion.

The depiction of *The Entombment* and its border (fols. 24^v–25; Figure 82) takes on added poignancy as the accompaniment to a prayer which not only dwells on Christ's Burial but in which the suppliant also asks for a safe passage to eternity.

THE PRAYER-BOOK OF MICHELINO DA BESOZZO   205

It is as though the reader witnesses their death as well as Christ's:
My flesh shall rest in hope. And you will not suffer corruption.
Let us pray.
Lord Jesus Christ who suffered yourself to rest in the grave so that you might bring us out of our graves and restore us to health with the glory of your resurrection, hear my supplications and grant that at the end of this frail life there may be quiet sleep for me in my tomb as you ordain and that on the day of judgement with all the saints there may be a joyful resurrection. Bind me to yourself completely, Lord, totally possess me so that you permit no part of me to be absent from you, but live solely in me and make me come to live in you alone who is the true God of glory. Amen.

The shape of Christ's body swathed in filmy raiment is reflected in the horizontal pods of the border which, coffin-like enclose bulging peas, while the black centres of the blue flowers vertically positioned above each border pod seem to be lifted heavenwards in the hope of "joyful resurrection".

Another striking example of the power of the image to bring alive the sacred Word occurs on the opening pages for the feast of The Ascension (fols. 35^v–36; Figure 83). Michelino heightens the viewer's awareness of the spatial zone immediately in front of the surface of the page by projecting Christ—and one of the trumpets—into the upper border, so that he appears to hover outside the miniature, while his diagonal elevation is echoed by the inclined placement of the lilac border blossoms. Their tubular forms join the trumpets in heralding the Saviour's departure from this earth for heaven. Exultantly, the prayer emphasises the same upward movement of body and spirit:
God ascends with jubilation.
Alleluia.
And the Lord with voice of the trumpet.
Alleluia.
Let us pray
May my prayer ascend to you, Christ, may the prayer of my mouth, God, enter into your sight, may my pleading reach you Lord who today as a conqueror ascends above all the heavens and who, having conquered the power of death, bore away the spoils of the human race, from whence you came...

The sense of weightlessness created by the border flowers, by Christ and by the disciples—whose feet seem to be unwillingly anchored to the ground—is further accentuated by the burnished gold roots at the bottom of the page which, as Eisler aptly puts it "appear to have pulled themselves from the sheltering earth permitting the illuminated page and its prayer to rise".[10]

Prayer and miniature for the feast of St. Katherine (fols. 83^v–84; Figure 84) demonstrate how the conventional iconic image of the standing saint is also used by

---

[10] C. Eisler, *The Prayer Book of Michelino da Besozzo* (New York: 1981) 17.

Michelino to reinforce the thrust of the devotional text which here reads:

Pray for us Blessed Katherine that we may be made worthy of the promises of Christ.

Let us pray.

O God you wrought wonderful things for a member of the fragile sex your devoted spouse, the Virgin most blessed Katherine. Glowing like a most beautiful star and armed with the arrows of faith, she triumphed over the wisdom of the world and overcame by your strength, torments which would have shaken marble foundations, I beg thee, through her intercession, to be saved from the world and from those fears which we should not fear. Guard me and all those who trust in your goodness. Her body was bathed from head to foot with a marvellous liquid and was wonderfully placed on Mt. Sinai by your angels, may I with them enjoy perpetual happiness, through the prayers of your martyr, Katherine, you who live and reign forever and ever. Amen.

Dressed in a sumptuous green garment and blue cloak lined with tiny ermine tufts—dress which befits a princess, Katherine's hair hangs in short ragged locks that betray the "torments which would shake marble foundations". She stands upon a mound of seemingly arid ground, an allusion to Mt. Sinai. Surprisingly, it sprouts leaves and small white flowers as though nourished by the heavenly fluid referred to in the prayer, while the angels responsible for translating the saint's body to the holy mountain are shown presenting her with a jewelled crown and the palm of martyrdom.

The use of matching flower borders and tapestry-like backdrops for the images of a series of standing saints in the Sanctoral is more than a linking device. It helps thrust the figures forward so that they assume a more life-like appearance. As they turn slightly in their voluminous gowns, with their attributes of gold and silver, these holy ones give the impression of crossing from the world of the spirit into the one which we inhabit, and of clothing the words of the prayers with flesh and blood—"et verbum caro factum est". This for the contemplative reader was an essential element of the book's dynamic, and one which the artist has intimately understood.

Figure 81 The Washing of the Apostles' Feet. Prayer-book, New York, Pierpont Morgan Library MS M. 944, fols. 19^v–20; 170×120 mm.

Figure 82 The Entombment. Prayer-book, New York, Pierpont Morgan Library MS M. 944, fols. 24^v–25; 170×120 mm.

Figure 83 The Ascension. Prayer-book, New York, Pierpont Morgan Library MS M. 944, fols. 35^v–36; 170×120 mm.

Figure 84 St. Katherine. Prayer-book, New York, Pierpont Morgan Library MS M. 944, fols. 83^v–84; 170×120 mm.

General Index

[*Note: **et passim** following a page reference indicates that that entry occurs frequently in the article cited. Any subsequent numeric references are to other articles following that one in the collection. Italicised entries refer to literary works, pictorial and monumental works of art, or foreign phrases.*]

Aaron...97, n. 16
Abbot (Portrait of an)...61
Abraham...25; 81, n. 51; 94
Adam...26; 79; 81; 127, n. 2
Adoration of the Magi,
    The...130 –133; 202, n. 4
Advent...25 *et passim*; 77–78; 79,
    n. 40; 81, n. 50; 99; 185
Advent Lyrics...150, n. 4
Adventus Ceremony...136
Agnus Dei...184; 186
Alberti...73
Alberti, Cardinal...136, n. 20
Albertian...8
Albertini...72, n. 4
Albigensians...2, n. 5 and n. 6
All Saints...77 *et passim*; 185–186;
    202...n. 4
Amalekite...59
Amiens Cathedral (Virgin Portal)...131, n. 9
Angôuleme...93, n. 8
Annunciation...28; 48; 51; 181
Annunciation, The...26–28; 59– 62;
    202, n. 4
Antiphon...27–31
Antiphonal...29
Antonine...6, n. 19
Apocalypse...30, n. 16
Apocalyptic Woman (or Virgin)...112;
    115

Apollo...71
Apollo at Corinth...94; 98
Araby...133
Architecture...73
Aristotle...73
Ark of the Covenant...96–97
Arras, Congress of...136, n. 20
Ascension...27 and n. 8; 30, n. 16;
    31–32; 81; 185–186; 205
Ascension, The...202, n. 4
Aspiciens a longe...78
Assumption...2, n. 6; 77; 115; 116 and
    n. 22; 185; 187
Astronomy...73
Attavante...76–78
Augustinian...2, n. 8; 202 *et passim*
Augustus, Emperor...116, n. 22
Azarias...153
Azarias...99

Balthazar...133
banderole...44; 113–114
Baptism...39 and n. 17; 31–32
Baptism Master...178, n. 5
Bartholomew of Trent...2, n. 4 and
    n. 7
bas-de-page...29–30; 180 –181; 186
Bec...202
Bedford, Duke of...27, n. 6; 30
Bedford Hours...31, n. 24

212 MEDIEVAL TEXTS AND IMAGES

Bedford (Master, Workshop or Style)
...4; 12; 27 *et passim*
Belles Heures...115
Belleville Breviary...25; 29–30; 96,
n. 12; 100; 179–180
Belvedere...72; 80
Benedictine...92
Benediction...76, n. 24
Beowulf...150
Besançon Missal...128 *et passim*
Bible...47; 96; 98; 101
Bible historiale...9; 99, n. 22; 100
Bible of Jean de Sy, The...181, n. 15
biography...73
Bladelin Altarpiece...117, n. 26
Blanche de France...28, n. 12; 29
Blessing God the Father...78, n. 31
Blois...93, n. 8
Book of Hours...6; 9; 26–28; 30; 43;
52 and n. 51; 57; 62; 96, n. 12;
101; 111 *et passim;* 178 *et Pas-
sim*
Boqueteaux (Style / Master)...4; 6;
9–12
Borgia...73, n. 9
Borromeo, Carlo...76, n. 24
Bosch, Jerome...132, n. 12
Boucicaut (Hours, Master or Work–
shop)...4; 12–13; 61, n. 15; 113,
n. 14; 115–116
Bourges...93, n. 8
Bramante...73; 79
Breviary...5– 6; 25; 27–32; 76; 77,
n. 29; 78; 79, n. 40; 80 and n. 44;
81, n. 50; 96, n. 12; 136; 180
Breviary of Charles V, The...181, n. 15
Brive...93, n. 8
Brussels Hours (of Jean, Duc de Berry)
...116
Burgundy, Duke of...7, n. 26; 136;
137, n. 24
Burning Bush...81, n.51
Bylling Bible...97, n. 15; 99, n. 22; 100

Calendar...5; 25; 57, n. 1; 59; 83; 91;
128; 179–180; 184; 185
Calvary...133
Canon...77–79; 81–82; 128; 186
Carolingian...202, n. 7
Caxton...1, n. 1; 78, n. 36
Centurion...46 *et passim*
Chaldeans...98
chapelle ardente...187
Chapter...27; 29; 32–33
Charles I...31, n. 22; 187–188
Charles II...31, n. 22
Charles V...5; 11; 28, n. 9; 29; 180;
185
Charles VI...184
Charles d'Anjou...12
Châteauroux Breviary...27; 31–33
Châtillon...93, n. 8
Children of Israel...98–99
Christ...149, n. 3; 156, n. 15; 158
Christ (Child)...111 *et passim*; 186; (in
Majesty)...5; 25; 29–33; 77;
(showing his wounds) 25; 43; 45;
76; 77, n. 27; 81; (of the Second
Coming) 81; (in Judgment) 32;
(of the Ascension) 81
Christ offered the Sop...61
Christmas...185–186; 188
Cicero...74
Circumcision...27
Circumcision, The...202, n. 4
Cité des Dames...7–8
Cleres Femmes...12
Clock Chamber...60
Collect...92 *et passim*; 184
Colombe, Jean...12; 187–188
Common of an Apostle...80, n. 46
Common of the Saints...78; 93
Communion of the Mass...183–184;
204
Communion of Saints...79
Compline...33, n. 26; 97
Confiteor...79, n. 39

GENERAL INDEX

Confrérie de la Passion et Resurrection...26, n. 4
Conversion of St. Paul...129
Corinthians...180
Coronation...72, n. 28
Coronation of the Virgin...1, n. 6; 5–6; 60–61; 77–78
Corpus Christi...26, n. 2; 27; 30, n. 16; 76, n. 24; 96; 185–186
Corvinus, Matthias...77, n. 27 *et passim*
Cosmography...73
Counter-Reformation...75; 76, n. 24
Court of Heaven...60; 77
Coventry (Play Cycle)...see Ludus Coventriae
Creator Mundi (Trinity)...28; 31
Creed (or *Credo*)...180; 184
Crocus, King of the Vandals...130
Cross...25; 43–44; 46
Crucifixion...7; 43 *et passim*; 186
Crucifixion...60 *et passim*
Cynewulf...158

da Besozzo, Michelino...201 *et passim*
da Montefeltro, Frederico...72
Daniel...59
Dante...74; 83, n. 58
Daret, Jacques...132–133
d'Armagnac, Jacques, Duc de Nemours ...5, n. 17; 6
d'Auxy, Jean, Chamberlain to Philippe le Bon...4; 13
David...25–26; 29; 32; 79; 96–97; 116, n. 22
David and Nathan...60–62
Death of Saul...59
de Beauvais, Vincent...9
de Bourgogne, Jeanne...3; 8
de Brézé...92–93
de Bruges, Louis, Seigneur de la Gruthuyse...4; 11
de Carvajal, Bernadino...81, n. 51

December...180
de Chasteigner...92–93
de Châtillon, Elizabeth...92
de Châtillon, Madeleine-Angelique-Marie...92
de Chourses, Antoine, Seigneur de Maigne...4, n. 14; 11
de Cleves, Philippe...4, n. 14; 12
de Coëtivy, Catherine...4, n. 14; 11
Decretals...72 *et passim*
de Croy, Charles...4; 11
Dedication of a Church...27
de Gaucourt, Raoul, Chamberlain to Charles VII...12
de Grassis, Paris...76, n. 24; 82 and n. 57
de Maillé (Mailly), Jean...2, n. 4 and n. 7; 3, n. 10; 92–93
de Medici, Cosimo...73
de Neufchâtel, Charles...128 *et passim*
de Neufchâtel, Jean II...136, n. 21
Deor...158
de Parthenay...92
de Pisan, Christine...7, n. 26
de Poitiers, Aymer...12
Deposition...112
de Rochechouart...92–93
de Saluces, Amadée...114
d'Espinques, Evrard (and Workshop of)...4–5; 11
d'Estampes, Robinet...178, n. 5
d'Estes, Isabella...72; 83, n. 64
de Sully...92
de Thouars...92
De Trinitate (St. Augustine's)...30, n. 20
de Valan, Guillaume
de Vignay, Jean...1 *et passim*
devil...98; 130; 137
de Vivonne, Isabeau...92–93
de Voragine, Jacobus...1 *et passim*
d'Hesdin, Jacquemart...178; 184
Dio Cassius...83

214   MEDIEVAL TEXTS AND IMAGES

Disciple offering his Heart to Sapientia...62
Disciple shutting out Sapientia...62
Disputa...72 *et passim*
Dixit Dominus (Trinity)...25; 28; 31–32; 78 *et passim*
Domine non sum dignus...184
Dominican...2; 82–83; 177, n. 2; 179–181
Douce, Francis...91
dove...29–30; 96
drolleries...181
drypoint etchings...151 *et passim*
du Mas, Jean, Seigneur de l'Isle...4–7; 11

Easter...27 and n. 8; 30 –31; 48, n. 34; 185–186
Ecclesia...2, n. 6
Elevation of the Host...183
Eli...179
Ember (Friday etc.)...95; 98–99
Enseignements (of St. Louis)...179
Entombment, The...202, n. 4; 204
Ephesus...98
Epilogus in gesta sanctorum...2, n. 4
Epiphany...27; 30, n. 16 and n. 19; 114 and n. 16–17; 130; 133; 137; 185
Epistle...79, n. 39; 92 *et passim*; 180; 184; 188
Esdras...97–98
Eucharist...204
Evangelistry...77, n. 29; 81, n. 50
Eve...26; 79
Exaltation of the Cross...186
Exeter Book...149 *et passim*
Exodus...28, n. 9
Ezechiel...26

Fall of Man...74 and n. 14
Fiesole Library...73
Fifteen Joys of the Virgin...111, and n. 1; 115; 117

Finding of the Cross, The...202, n. 4
Fitzalan, William, Earl of Arundel...12
Flaying of Marsyas...74 and n. 14
Fleures des histoires...7–9
Fontenay-le-Comte...93, n. 8
Forty Hours...76, n. 24
Foucault, F.J....92–93
Fouquet, Jean...116; 188, n. 35
Fra Angelico...74; 83, n. 57
Fra Bartolomeo...77
Franche Comté...136
Franciscan...80, n. 44; 91–93; 101; 180; 187
Françoise de Luxembourg...4, n. 14; 12
Frederick II...2, n. 5
frontispiece...112

Gabriel...25–26; 48; 59
Galatians...180
Galilee...134
Genesis...28, n. 9
Geneva...99, n. 21
Gerson, Jean...112, n. 8
Ghent (altarpiece)...78, n. 34
Gifts of Men...160, n. 24
Gloria...184; 186
Godolia...133
Golden Age...83
Golden Legend...77, n. 29; 78 and n. 36 and n. 40; 80; 186; see also *Légende dorée*
Good Friday...27, n. 8
Good Shepherd...100
Gospel...30; 43 *et passim*; 57, n. 1; 92–95; 101 *et passim*; 135; 183–184; 188
Gospel Books...96, n. 12; 100, n. 25–26; 101, n. 28–29; 154, n. 11
Gradual...29; 184; 188
Grandes Chroniques de France...9–10
Grandes Heures de Duc de Berry...6

GENERAL INDEX

Grandes Heures de Philippe le Hardi...6; 177, n. 2; 183; 185
Great Book of Hours of Henry VIII...133, n. 14
Gréban, Arnoul...26–27
Gregory III...80
Guthlac...153

Haymo of Faversham...80, n. 44
Hell...97, n. 16; 130, n. 8
Herod...47, n. 27; 134
Hérolt, Johannes (called Discipulus) ...116, n. 25
Heures de Jeanne de Navarre...28
Histoire Ancienne jusquà César...9
Holkham Bible...100, n. 24
Holy Ghost Master...178, n. 5
Holy Saturday...98, n. 18
Holy Spirit...31–32; 95–98; 186
Holy Trinity, The...202, n. 4
Holy Week...92; 98; 185
Homiletic Fragment III...152, n. 8
Hophni...179
Horloge de Sapience...45, n. 13; 57 *et passim*
Host...76; 79; 81–82; 95, n. 11
Hours of Blanche of Savoy...185
Hours of Etienne Chevalier...116
Hours of Isabella Stuart...113 and n. 15; 115
Hours of Jeanne d'Évreux...100
Hours of Joanna of Castile...116
Hours of the Cross...46, n. 16; 49 and n. 41; 57, n. 1; 182
Hours of the Holy Spirit...32, n. 25; 57, n. 1; 187
Hours of the Passion...181–182
Hours of the Virgin...6; 26; 49, n. 41; 57, n. 1; 111, n. 2; 178; 181

icon...47–49; 129–130; 137
Imperial History...73
Incarnation...2, n. 6; 26; 29–32; 53; 117

Introit...29; 92–97; 130, n. 7; 135; 137; 183–184; 186–187
Invention...128
Invitatory...27; 32
Isaiah...25–26; 29; 32; 133; 135

Jacob...25; 96–97 (Ladder)
James, Thomas...77, n. 27
January...59; 180
Jaspar...134
Jean de France, Dauphin...31, n. 22
Jean de Metz...180
Jean, Duc de Berry...6; 7, n. 26; 115–116; 132; 177 *et passim*
Jean le Bon (King of France)...177; 179
Jean le Noir...178; 181; 185; 187
Jean sans Peur...27, n. 8; 30, n. 19; 32
Jeremiah...26; 28; 181
Jeremiah...28, n. 9
Jerusalem...98; 116, n. 22; 131; 133; 180
Jesse (Tree of)...25–26
Joel...98
John, Prior of Hildesheim...133–134
Judas...98
Judas Maccabeus...81, n. 51
Judgement of Solomon...74
Juliana...158
Julius II...71 *et passim*
Jurisprudence...73–74
Just Judges...78, n. 34
Justice...75; 78, n. 34; 82
Justinian...74

Kiss of Peace...183
Klosterneuburg Altarpiece...44, n. 7
Kyrie...184; 186

Labours of the Month...59
Lamb...78; 79, n. 39; 204
Lamentation...111, n. 2; 112
Languedoc...2, n. 5

216 MEDIEVAL TEXTS AND IMAGES

Last Judgement...51; 77
Lateran...81, n. 51
Lauds...33
Law...74, n. 14
Lechery and Chastity...61
Lectionary...5
Legend of St. Antidius...136
Legenda aurea...see *Légende dorée*
Légende dorée...1 *et passim*; see also
    Golden Legend
Lent...92; 98, n. 18; 187
Leo X...77, n. 27
Leofric, Bishop of Exeter...153 and
    n. 10
Le Somme de Roi...96, n. 12
Lesson...27–28; 30; 80; 82; 92–95; 97
    et passim
L'Estimeur du Monde...179
libelli...9; 202
Liberal Arts...72
Libera nos quaesumus...184
Liberation (St. Peter's)...81, n. 51
Libra...59
Liedet, Loyset...4; 13
Limbo...26
Limbourg, Hermann...133
Limbourg Brothers...115; 178, n. 5;
    186–188
Litany...178; 182
Liturgical Year...2; 28; 32; 92–93; 96;
    128; 201
London Hours...58 *et passim*
Longinus...47, n. 27
Losien, Jacques...13
Louis II d'Anjou...178, n. 6
Louis XI, King of France...137, n. 24;
    179
Louis de Guyenne, Dauphin...31
Louis le Bâtard de Bourbon...4; 12
Louis, Dauphin...31, n. 22
Lucan Master (Follower of the)...11
Ludolph of Saxony...138, n. 27
Ludus Coventriae...33

Lyon...101

Madian...134
Magdeburg...137
Magus...114
Maiestas Domini...77 *et passim*; 186
Maître du 'Polycratique'...5; 12
Maître François (and Chief Associate
    of)...4–8; 11; 26; 45; 58; 62
Malachi...25; 33; 137
Man of Sorrows...181
mandorla...29
Mansel, Jean...7
Mantegna...83, n. 64
Margaret of York...118
Marmion, Simon...4; 7; 12
Mary of Burgundy...96
Mass at Bolsena...76
Mass for All Saints...186
Mass for All Souls...186
Mass for the Dead...186
Mass of the Virgin...186
Master of Berry...12
Master of Flémalle...30
Master of Jean Rolin II...4; 6; 12; 57 *et
    passim*; 115
Master of Margaret of York...4; 13
Master of Mary of Burgundy...118
Master of the *Coronation of Charles
    VI*...11
Master of the *Coronation of the Vir-
    gin*...4; 12
Master of the Duke of Bedford...see
    Bedford
Master of the Harley *Froissart*...4; 13
Master of the Munich *Golden Legend*
    ...4; 12
Mathematics...73
Matins...26; 80 and n. 44; 83
Maundy Thursday...204
Medallion Master...11
Medici...83
Medicine...73

GENERAL INDEX

217

Meeting of the Magi, The...130 *et passim*

Meeting of the Three Kings, The...131–133

Melchior...133

Mercy Seat (Trinity)...28

Michelangelo...73

Miroir historial...9

Miscellany...97, n. 16

Missal...77–79; 81–82; 91 *et passim*; 112, n. 9 and n, 11; 128 *et passim*

Missal-Hours...187

Missal of Montier-en-Mer...185

Missal of St. Denis, The...181, n. 15; 185, n. 28

monstrance...76; 80 *et passim*

Montleon...93, n. 8

Moses...25; 79; 81; 99

Moses with Aaron...97, n. 16

Mount of Olives...134

Mount Sinai...206

Mouth of Hell...97, n. 16

Mystère d'Adam...26, n. 2

Mystère de la passion...26

Mystical Body...74

Mystical Union...182

Nancy, Battle of...137, n. 24

Nassau, Counts of...13

Nativity...23, n. 8; 30, n. 16; 138, n. 28

Nativity, The...202, n. 4

Nativity of the Virgin...185

Nativity plays...26

Nebuchadnezzar...179

New Testament...25; 53; 97; 180 –181

Nicholas V...73

Nicodemus...100

Nocturns...28

None...46; 49

Northern Artist / Miniaturist...129 *et passim*

Nubia...133

O intermerata...11, and n. 1

Obsecro te...111, and n. 1; 113–114

Octave...30; 93; 101

Oettingen...13

Offertory...76; 79, n. 39; 183

Office of Advent...33

Office of the Dead...178; 182

Office of the Purification of the Virgin...17

Office of the Virgin...57, n. 1; 111

Office of Trinity Sunday...27, n.8; 32

Old Testament...25–26; 28, n. 9; 32–33; 48, n. 34; 61; 79; 97–98; 180 –181

Ordinary...79, n. 39; 184

Ordo Prophetarum...25–26: 48, n. 34

Orgemont Breviary...27, n. 8; 32

Orosius Master...11

Palm Sunday...28, n. 9; 30, n. 16; 187

Pandects...73

Pantheon...80

parable...100

Paradise...6; 76–77; 137; 180

Paradiso (Dante's)...83, n. 58

Parentucelli, Tommaso...73

Paris (or Manchester) Breviary...28, n. 11; 30, n. 18

Parnassus...74; 83, n. 64

Parthenay...93, n. 8

Partridge...152

Passion...27, n. 8; 50

Passion d'Arras...26; 33

Passion Sunday...187

Pater Noster...184

Pèlerinage de la Vie Humaine...7

Penitential Psalms...33; 57, n. 1; 178; 181–182

pennant...180

Pentecost...27 and n. 16; 92 *et passim*; 185–186

Pentecost...60 – 62

Pericope...100, n. 25

218   MEDIEVAL TEXTS AND IMAGES

Pesaro Library...73
Petites Heures...177 *et passim*
Philosophy...73–74
Philippe VI (de Valois)...180
Philippe le Bon, Duc de Bourgogne...4; 12–13; 31, n. 24
Philippe le Hardi...5; 177, n. 2
Phineas...179
Phoenix...158
Pièta...111, n. 2; 112, n. 6
Pilate...47, n. 27
Plato...73
Poetry...73–74
Post Communion...184
prayer-book...44 and n. 5; 46; 50; 51, n. 50; 132; 177 *et passim*; 201 *et passim*
Preface...77, n. 29
Presentation in the Temple...60
prie-dieu...60; 113; 115; 183; 188
Prime...33, n. 26
Procès du paradis...25–26; 33
Proper...79, n. 39; 184
Prophecy...98, n. 18
Provençal artist / miniaturist...128 *et passim*
Psalm...33, n. 26; 43; 96–97; 116, n. 22
Psalter...28; 96–97; 101; 112; 180; 184
Psalter of Yolande de Soissons...48, n. 34
Pseudo-Bede...80–82
Pseudo-Bonaventure...101, n. 28
Pseudo-Jacquemart...4; 6; 12; 184
Ptolemy...84
Pucelle, Jean...4; 11; 100; 181; 185; 187
Purification...138, n. 27; 185; 187
Purification of the Virgin, The...202, n. 4; 204

Raphael...71 *et passim*

relic...130; 133; 135
Repentant in his Cell...61
Requiem Mass...93; 95; 182
Response...80 and n. 44; 41; 202–203
Responsorial...96, n. 12
Responsory...27; 33
Resurrection...27; 29–30
Resurrection, The...202, n. 4
Resurrection of the Dead, The...77, n. 29
Resurrection of the Flesh, The...77
Rhetoric...74
Riddles: 19...158; *64*...158; *90*...158; *91*...159; *95*...152
Robert of Battle...99, n. 22
Rohan (workshop)...112, n. 6
Rolin Master...see Master of Jean Rolin II
Roman de la rose...9
Romans...180
Ruin...158

Saba...133–134; 136
Sainte-Chapelle...96, n. 12
Salisbury Breviary...25 *et passim*; 57–58; 77
Salvation History...180–181
Samaria...98
San Antonio (Piacenza)...2, n. 8
San Lorenzo (Florence)...83
Sanctoral...5; 82, n. 53; 92–93; 128–130; 136; 186–187; 206
Sanctus...184
Sapientia with Faith, Hope and Charity...62
Saul...59; 129
Saumur...93, n. 8
Savanorola...83, n. 57
School of Athens...72–74; 83, n. 57; 84
scroll...8; 25; 29–30; 33; 44 *et passim*; 78; 180
Second Coming...81
Secret...79, n. 39

GENERAL INDEX

Sedes Sapientiae...114
Seven Joys of the Virgin, The...117
Severus, Septimus...83
Sermon on the Mount...78, n. 34
Seven Heavenly Joys of the Virgin,
The...115, 117
Seven Last Words, The...50 and n. 44
Sext...33; 32
Simon Magus...186
Sion...98
Sistine Chapel...77, n. 28
Sixtus IV...83
Sobieski Hours...30, n. 20
Soissons...93, n. 8
Solomon, King...74, n. 14; 96
Song...74
Speculum...98, n. 21; 137
St. Agatha...5
St. Agnes...5; 202, n. 4
St. Amator...8
St. Ambrose...73; 202, n. 4
St. Andrew...6–7; 185; 187
St. Anselm...202 and n. 7 *et passim*
St. Anthony...6, n. 19; 202, n. 4
St. Antidius...128 *et passim*
St. Augustine...30; 76; 202, n. 4 and 6
St. Bernard...137
St. Bernardino of Siena...114
St. Bonaventure...73
St. Bridget...138, n. 27
St. Catherine...114; 202, n. 4; 205
St. Cecilia...8
St. Christopher...6
St. Denis...101
St. Dominic...114
St. Euphemia...8
St. Ferreolus...128 *et passim*
St. Ferrucius...128 *et passim*
St. Francis...92
St. Germain of Auxerre...8
St. Gregory I...73
St. Hilary...185
St. Jean, abbey of...92

St. Jerome...73; 77, n. 28
St. John...27; 50 –52; 81, n. 97–98;
100; 117
St. John, Gospel of...51
St. John of Patmos...59
St. John the Baptist...78–81; 99; 181;
184–186; 202, n. 4
St. Joseph...111, n. 2; 117
St. Juliana...5
St. Katherine...see St. Catherine
St. Lawrence...83, n. 51
St. Louis, King of France...9; 97
St. Lucy...202, n. 4
St. Luke...100; 202, n. 4
*St. Luke Drawing a Portrait of the Vir-
gin*...117, n. 26
St. Martin...202, n.4
St. Mary Magdalene...202, n. 4; 203
St. Michael...130, n. 8; 136, n. 20;
185; 187
St. Monica...202, n. 4 and 6; 203 and
n. 9
St. Nicholas...6, n. 19; 202 and n. 4
St. Paul (Saul)...81, n. 51; 97–98; 130;
180; 184; 186; 202, n. 4; 203 and
n. 9
St. Peter...81; 98; 100 –101; 184–186;
202, n. 4; 203 and n. 9
St. Peter's (Rome)...73; 80; 83
St. Philip...98
St. Stephen...81, n. 51; 129; 135
St. Thomas the Apostle...128; 131
St. Thomas Aquinas...73–74
St. Valentine...5
Stanza d'Eliodoro...81, n. 51
Stanza della Segnatura...71 *et passim*
Stoning of Stephen...129; 131
studioli...72
Sully...93, n. 8
Summa Theologia (Aquinas')...31,
n. 21; 74, n. 15
Susanna...59
Synagogue...180

220 MEDIEVAL TEXTS AND IMAGES

tabernacles...76 and n. 24
Tarsus...134
Temporal...26–28; 30, n. 16; 32;
   185–187
Theology...73–75
Thibaud, uncle of Charles de
   Neufchâtel...135
Thomas of Canterbury...51, n. 49; 112
Thouars...93, n. 8
Three Kings of Cologne, The...133
Three Maries at the Tomb...30
Throne of Grace...78
Tilliot Hours...133, n. 14
Timaeus...73
Topica (Cicero's)...74
Tours...93, n. 8
Transfiguration...81, n. 51
Transfiguration, The...129
Transport into the Third Heaven...81,
   n. 51
Tree of Life...61
Très Belles Heures...177 *et passim*
Très Belles Heures de Notre Dame
   ...31
Très Riches Heures...116, n. 22;
   132–133; 188, n. 36
Treviso...40; 79 and n. 40
Trinitas creator mundi...see *Creator*
   mundi
Trinity...26 *et passim*; 79 *et passim*
Trinity Sunday...185–186
Triumphus crucis...83, n. 57
Troilus...7, n. 23

Urania...72; 83
Urban...8
Urbino Library...73 *et passim*

Valenciennes...7, n. 24
Valerian...8
van der Weyden, Rogier...117 and
   n. 26
van Eyck...114, n. 16

Vasari...75 *et passim*
Vatican...72 *et passim*
Vatican II...184
Versicle...33; 80 and n. 44; 81;
   202–203
Vespers...27–29; 32; 78, n. 31; 80,
   n. 46
Vicomte of Thouars...93
Vigil...83; 93–93; 100
Vigils of the Dead...57, n. 1; 187
Virgil Master...4; 11
Virgin (of Humility)...111, n. 2; (of
   Mercy)...111, n. 2; (Queen of
   Heaven)...29; 114
Virgin and Child...29; 77, n. 29; 111
   and n. 2; 113 *et passim*; 181
Virgo lactans...111, n. 2; 116
Viri venerabiles sacerdotes Dei...137
Virtues...26–27; 72
Vision in the Wilderness, The...81,
   n. 51
Vision of the Three Angels, The...81,
   n. 51
Visitation, The...202, n. 4
Vitruvius...73
Votive Mass...93
Vrelant, Willem...4

Waldenses...2, n. 5
Wanderer, The...160, n. 24
Washing of the Feet, The...202, n. 4;
   204
Wharncliffe Hours...6; 26; 33
Whit Monday (Tues. etc.)...94–95
Widsith...159, n. 18
Wrapping a Corpse...60 – 62

Zodiac Signs...59

Index of Manuscripts Cited

Amiens
Bibliothèque Municipale
ms 114...29
Arras
Bibliothèque de la Ville
ms 630...12
Auckland
Auckland Public Library
Grey Collection Med. MSS
G 138–39...128, n. 3
Avignon
Musée Calvet
ms 121...96, n. 12
Baltimore
Walters Gallery
MS 34...97, n. 14
MS 62...96, n. 12
MS Walters 223...133, n. 14
MS Walters 251...60
Belvoir Castle
Library of the Duke of Rutland
Psalter...97, n. 14
Besançon
Bibliothèque Municipale
ms 140...112, n. 10
Brussels
Bibliothèque Royale
ms IV.111...57
ms 9008...77, n. 27; 78, n. 31;
81, n. 50
ms 9226...11
ms 9227...11
ms 9228...12
ms 9232...7
ms 9282–85...4, n. 14; 7; 12

ms 9961–62...97, n. 16
ms 25513–17...96, n. 12
Cambridge
Fitzwilliam Museum
MS 3–1954...6; 112, n. 10
MS 9–1951...112, n. 9
MS 22...13
MS 43–1950...99, n. 21
MS 338...112, n. 11
MS 369...97, n. 14
MS McLean 124...11
University Library
MS Ee 4.24...97, n. 14
Canberra
National Library of Australia
Clifford Coll. MS 1097/9...43
et passim
Chantilly
Musée Condé
ms 735...11
Châteauroux
Bibliothèque Municipale
ms 2...27, n. 8; 77, n. 29
Dijon
Bibliothèque Communale
ms 12–15...99, n. 21
Dunedin
Dunedin Public Library
Reed Fragment 45 (*olim* 44)...43
et passim
Exeter
Cathedral Library
MS 3501...149 *et passim*
Évreux
Bibliothèque Municipale

221

222 MEDIEVAL TEXTS AND IMAGES

ms 99...77, n. 29
Florence
Biblioteca Laurenziana
ms edili 115...77, n. 29; 81, n. 50
ms Plut. VII.23...100, n. 26
Museo Nationale
ms 68...77, n. 29
Geneva
Bibliothèque Pub. et Universitaire
ms fr. 2...99, n. 21 and 22
ms fr. 57...5; 12
Glasgow
University Library
MS General 1111...2, n. 8
Jena
Universitätbibliothek
ms Gall. 86...13
Lausanne
Lib. Cant. et Univ.
ms 964...97, n. 14
London
British Library
Additional MS 16907...12
Additional MS 17341...100, n. 25
Additional MS 18850...31,
n. 24; 58
Additional MS 19907...77, n. 29
Additional MS 25695...57
et passim
Additional MS 35311...27, n. 8;
30, n. 19
Additional MS 47692...100, n. 24
Burney MS 3...99, n. 23
Egerton MS 645...4, n. 15; 12
Egerton MS 2019...32, n. 25; 61
Harl. MS 1526–27...99, n.23; 101,
n. 29
Harl. MS 2897...27, n. 8; 28, n. 12
Phillips Loan MS 36 / 199...7
Royal MS 19.B.xvii...6; 12
Stowe MS 50–1...13
Collection of E.G. Millar
Le Somme de Roi...96, n. 12

Lambeth Palace
MS 149...160 and n. 25
Victoria and Albert Museum
MS A.M. 1346–1891...101, n. 31;
185, n. 22
Lyons
Bibliothèque de la Ville
ms 517...61
ms 5122...96, n. 12; 101, n. 31;
185, n. 22
Mâcon
Bibliothèque Municipale
ms 3...13; 77, n. 29
Manchester
John Rylands Library
MS 17...99, n. 21
Melbourne
National Gallery
Felton MS 1 (Wharncliffe
Hours)...6; 26; 33
Munich
Bayerische Staatsbibliothek
cod. clm. 15903...96, n. 12; 100,
n. 25
cod. gall. 3...12; 77, n. 29
NewYork
Pierpont Morgan Library
MS M. 672–75...13
MS M. 674...8
MS M. 675...8
MS M. 729...48, n. 34
MS M. 917...127, n. 2
MS M. 944...201 *et passim*
MS M. 1027...58
Heinemann Collection
MS H.8...133, n. 14
Spencer Library
MS 2...96, n. 12
MS Public 22...97, n. 16
Oxford
Bodleian Library
Bodl. 319...160 and n. 25
Douce 313...91 *et passim*

INDEX OF MANUSCRIPTS CITED

Paris
Bibliothèque Arsenal
  ms 660...77, n. 8
  ms 3682–83...7; 13
  ms 3705...11
Bibliothèque Mazarine
  ms 41...185, n. 22
  ms 1729...6; 11
Bibliothèque Nationale
  ms fr. 184...12
  ms fr. 241...11
  ms fr. 242...5; 12
  ms fr. 243...12; 77, n. 29
  ms fr. 244–45...4, n. 14 and n. 16;
  8; 11; 77, n. 29; 79, n. 40
  ms fr. 414...11
  ms fr. 415–16...12
  ms fr. 1535...11
  ms fr. 2813...9
  ms fr. 6448...5, n. 17; 7; 11;
  77, n. 29
  ms fr. 13342...95, n. 11
  ms fr. 17232...11
  ms fr. 23113...4, n. 15; 11
  ms gr. 54...101, n. 29
  ms ital. 115...101, n. 28–29
  ms lat. 757...101, n. 31; 112, n. 11;
  187 and n. 33
  ms lat. 919...6
  ms lat. 1024...28, n. 11; 30, n. 18
  ms lat. 1052...28, n. 9
  ms lat. 1161...113, n. 14
  ms lat. 10483–84...25; 29;
  30, n. 18; 96, n. 12
  ms lat. 10525...97, n. 16
  ms lat. 11534–35...97, n. 17
  ms lat. 11560...96, n. 12; 99, n. 21
  ms lat. 11935...97, n. 15, 99, n. 23
  ms lat. 16827...77, n. 29
  ms lat. 17294...25 *et passim*; 58;
  77, n. 29

  ms lat. 17323...77, n. 27
  ms lat. 17326...100, n. 25
  Donation Smith-Lesouëf, ms lat.
  759...112, n. 9
  Nouv. Acq. ms fr. 11198...3, n. 13
  Nouv. Acq. ms lat. 3107...113,
  n. 14
  Nouv. Acq. ms lat. 3180...185,
  n. 22
Perugia
Biblioteca communale Augusta
  ms 2781...29, n. 13
  ms 2783...29, n. 13
Rennes
Bibliothèque Municipale
  ms 266...12
Stockholm
National Museum
  ms B 1713...101, n. 28
Turin
Museo Civico
  *Très Belles Heures de Notre
  Dame*...31
Vatican City
Vatican Library
  ms Chigiani C IV 108...81, n. 50
  ms lat. 7235...76, n. 24
  ms lat. 4761...77, n. 29; 81, n. 50
  ms lat. 9217...77, n. 29
  ms Rossiani 85...81, n. 50
  ms Rossiani 125...79, n. 38; and
  n. 40
  ms Urb. lat. 112...78, n. 30; 80,
  n. 44
Vienna
Österreichische Nationalbibliothek
  cod. lat. 326...2, n. 8
  cod. 1840...132, n. 14
  cod. 1857...112, n. 12
  cod s.n. 13237...6; 58

Index of Biblical References

Acts 1: 11...81
Acts 2: 1–11...94
Acts 2: 14–21...94
Acts 5: 12–16...94
Acts 8: 5–9...95
Acts 8: 14–17...94
Acts 10: 34, 42–48...94
Acts 19: 1–8...94
Apocalypse 7: 2–12...79, n. 39
Daniel 3: 47–51...95; 99
Daniel 4: 24–26; 32–34...179, n. 9
Deuteronomy 26: 1–3, 7–11...95
Ephesians 2: 19–20...80
4 Esdras 2: 36–37...94; 97
Exodus 4: 13...25
Ezechiel 21: 7...25
Isaiah 1: 1...29
Isaiah 8: 17...25; 33
Isaiah 60: 1–2...134
Isaiah 60: 5–6...134
Jeremiah 23: 5...29
Joel 2: 23–24, 26–27...95; 98
Joel 2: 28–32...95
John 3: 16–21...94
John 6: 44...100
John 6: 44–52...94
John 10: 1–10...94
John 14: 15...100
John 14: 15–21...94
John 14: 23–31...94
John 14: 23...100
John 19: 26...50, n. 44; 51
John 19: 27...50, n. 44

John 19: 28...50, n. 44
John 19: 30...50, n. 44
Judges 6: 18...33
Leviticus 26: 3–12...95; 99
Leviticus 28: 9–11, 15–17, 21...95; 99
Luke 1: 35...25
Luke 4: 38–44...95
Luke 5: 17–26...95
Luke 9: 1–6...95
Luke 23: 43...50, n. 44
Luke 23: 46...50, n. 44
Malachi 3: 1...25, 33, 137
Mark 15: 34...50, n. 44
Matthew 2: 1–12...135
Matthew 3: 13...30, n. 19
Matthew 3: 4...179
Matthew 27: 46...50, n. 44
Matthew 27: 54...45–46
Matthew 28: 5...30
Psalm 24: 1...29
Psalm 39: 8...25
Psalm 50: 3...33
Psalm 67: 8–9...94; 97
Psalm 70: 8, 23...95; 97
Psalm 80:17...94; 96
Psalm 84: 8...26
Psalm 109...28; 78 and n. 31
Revelations 12:1...112, n. 5
Romans 5: 1–5...95
Romans 5: 5...95; 97
Romans 11: 33–36...80
Wisdom 1: 7...32; 94–95